China Trader

By the same author

SEA FEVER

"This book should grip anyone with a love of the sea, and of adventure, whether they are old or young; and should prove a real tonic to those who are sick and tired of the so-called psychological novel, churned out in their many thousands these days."

DAPHNE DU MAURIER

"Here is a fine story of the sea. It does not matter whether you are twelve, or a hundred and twelve, if you have salt in your veins—and which of us on this little sea-surrounded land has not?—you will love *Sea Fever*."

NOEL STREATFEILD

A. H. RASMUSSEN

CHINA TRADER

by the author of "Sea Fever"

CONSTABLE . LONDON

LONDON
PUBLISHED BY
Constable and Company Ltd
10 & 12 Orange Street, W.C.2

INDIA
Orient Longmans Ltd
BOMBAY CALCUTTA MADRAS

CANADA
Longmans, Green and Company
TORONTO

SOUTH *and* EAST AFRICA
Longmans, Green and Company Ltd
CAPETOWN NAIROBI

AUSTRALIA
Walter Standish and Sons
SYDNEY

First published May 1954
Reprinted May 1954

Made and printed in Great Britain by
William Clowes and Sons Ltd, London and Beccles

Illustrations

Foreword

WHEN I was wrecked in my ketch, the "Sari Marais," off Hartlepool in 1949,* I lost all my possessions including the manuscript of a book I had written about my experiences in China; in fact, this book. After my ship had been pounded to pieces I went down among the rocks at low water to see if anything of value had been washed ashore.

In particular I was looking for this manuscript, and no treasure-hunter could be more excited than I when I found a few pages here and a few there.

It was getting dark, but as long as I could see the gleam of white paper in the water I went on searching until I could find no more. In all, about half of the manuscript was recovered, but very few of the chapters were complete and some were missing altogether. What I recovered I dried and sorted out, for every page was of value to me because it was written while my impressions were clear, and bore, I believed, the tang of the Far East. I had written only about the most interesting experiences and of things that had stamped themselves clearly on my mind. It was not too difficult to fill in the many gaps afterwards from memory.

There have been more misleading books written about China than about any other country. Certain poor deluded souls think that Shanghai, Hongkong and Peking is China, and their rule appears to be the shorter the stay, the longer the book.

Mine goes to the other extreme, by covering a very long stay—thirty-two years—in the shortest possible space, without omitting anything of interest. Above all, it has no pretensions to being a book on China. It is my own story from the time I landed as a young sailor somewhat bewildered by this strange new life, bewitched by all I had heard and read and avid for new adventures. Many of the episodes may appear utterly incredible to readers who have never seen the real China but, believe me, they are true.

* Sea Fever.

In a country where human life was so terribly cheap and unimportant, where infanticide was practised unchecked during most of the period I stayed there, anything was possible. Nothing should surprise in a country where a dragon was the national emblem, and still is a national curse because there has never been a St. George to rescue a wonderful but oppressed people from their rulers, from the Ming dynasty to that of Mao and Moscow.

I doubt if any people have suffered more from misrule, tyranny and corruption than the Chinese. They have suffered for many centuries, living at the same time on the borderland of want and starvation, fighting ceaselessly for existence, dying by millions of famine and epidemics and as the result of rebellions, conquest and wars. Out of all this evil has emerged, and naturally so, a mentality so totally different from ours of the West that there is no contact, and no means of getting on even terms so long as we judge by our standards. This mentality will always remain the deciding factor in China, for it governs four hundred million people who feel, reason and act alike.

However, my primary interest is not the Chinese mind, but life in a small British Concession, one of the many scattered all over China, where foreigners were allowed to live and trade. China was a closed country to foreign trade, except at Canton, up to about 1840 when, as a result of wars with Britain and France, the so-called Treaty Ports, or Concessions, were opened to foreigners. Chinkiang was one such Concession, and when thirty-five people are jammed together in a confined space, where there are no diversions and nothing ever happens except sickness and death, and are left to sink or swim, strange things happen to their mental outlook.

That, coupled with my strange experiences while travelling in the interior, is the real stuff of my story.

A. H. R.

Skodjefjord, Sunmøre.
June, 1953.

Part One

The Yangtze

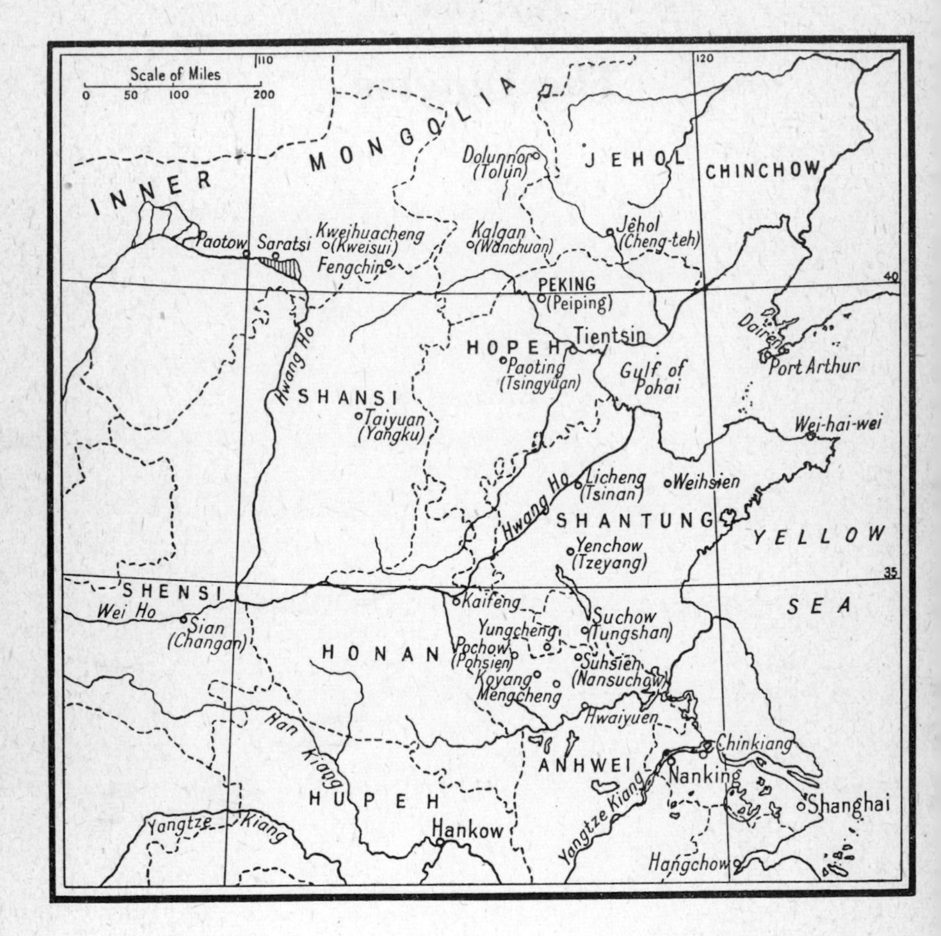
Scale of Miles
0 50 100 200
110
120
40
35
INNER MONGOLIA
JEHOL
CHINCHOW
Dolunnor
(Tolun)
Paotow
Saratsi
Kweihuacheng
(Kweisui)
Fengchin
Kalgan
(Wanchuan)
Jêhol
(Cheng-teh)
PEKING
(Peiping)
Dairen
Port Arthur
Tientsin
HOPEH
Paoting
(Tsingyuan)
Gulf of
Pohai
Hwang Ho
SHANSI
Taiyuan
(Yangku)
Wei-hai-wei
Licheng
(Tsinan)
Weihsien
SHANTUNG
YELLOW
SEA
Yenchow
(Tzeyang)
SHENSI
Wei Ho
Sian
(Changan)
Kaifeng
Suchow
(Tungshan)
Yungcheng
HONAN
Pochow
(Pohsien)
Suhsien
(Nansuchow)
Koyang
Mengcheng
Hwaiyuen
Han Kiang
Chinkiang
ANHWEI
Nanking
HUPEH
Shanghai
Yangtze Kiang
Hankow
Hangchow

CHINA TRADER

I

WHEN a sailor leaves the sea to start a new life ashore, his mates say that "he has swallowed the anchor." *I* did that after I had paid off from the steamer "Dagny" in Hongkong in the early spring of 1905, and, believe me, that anchor lay pretty heavily on my chest. No one is less fit for shore life than a sailor, especially one with sailing-ship training, because nothing of what he knows is of any use to him. He is a trusting chap as a rule, generous to a fault, and easily imposed upon; all a very great drawback ashore.

I did not think about these truths so much, as I left for Shanghai in the S.S. "Kamor", but pondered rather on the $5 (10*s.*) which was all the money I had, and my only hope of a job was with the Maritime Customs. I was told in Hongkong that I could get a Customs job at once, but I did not know if that was really so, or just talk to cheer me up. My two shipmates were much better off and did not seem to worry about themselves or me.

As we came steaming up the Whangpoo River towards Shanghai I was fascinated by the strange, teeming traffic. There were small launches staggering along under huge piles of chickens in crates ranged like haystacks on the decks; other craft perilously overloaded with passengers packed like sardines; junks from every part of the coast, some splendidly carved and decorated in bright colours, others with battered sails and a neglected look; scores of small sampans crossing from bank to bank, and steamers, large and small, under way, or tied up at the wharves or moored to buoys in mid-stream.

The S.S. "Kamor" tied up at Chang Ka Pang Wharf just ahead of the Russian cruiser "Askold" and the gunboat "Mandsjur", both of them having been badly smashed up in their escape from

Port Arthur, after the battle of Tsusjima, which had taken place recently. The owner's agent came on board and on inquiry recommended that we go to the Swedish Mission where Pastor Rydberg kept a small boarding-house for sailors. He took my two shipmates and me over to the Shanghai side of the river, told the rickshaw coolies where we were to go and left us. I was not quite carefree as we bowled along past the Public Gardens where most of the benches were occupied by wounded Russian soldiers, over the Garden Bridge and into Hongkew district, Shanghai's East End.

Pastor Rydberg gave us a kindly reception and a letter of introduction to the Chief Tide-surveyor in the Customs, Mr. C. P. Dawson. The Pastor also volunteered the comforting information that we should have no difficulty in joining the Customs Service as we had exceptional qualifications.

This was cheering news indeed for, although I had often landed in European ports with less than the few shillings and the tiny suitcase of clothes I now had, I knew the ropes there and could easily get a ship. But here I was twelve thousand miles from home and in an utterly strange environment. There were no ships to be had because they all carried Chinese crews, and there was no road back.

I had deliberately burnt my boats to take up a completely new life. It was not in my nature to be cautious or to take precautions, and at first I had taken this on lightheartedly as a new and very exciting adventure. Now common sense reared its head for the first time, and to quell a murmuring disquiet I went to see Mr. Dawson at once. The result was that the following day I became a probationary Tide Waiter in the Imperial Maritime Customs. The pay was Haikwan taels seventy-five per month (eleven pounds), out of which I should have to pay two pounds ten shillings for meals in the Customs Mess, but quarters were free.

I felt like a plutocrat when I went to a tailor to be measured for my uniform and was told that all I had to do by way of payment was to sign a chit and pay when it was convenient. It was then the golden age in China, when every white man's chit was accepted as readily as if it were a bank note. Things were incredibly cheap too, and all I paid for a hand-tailored serge uniform was two pounds.

My elation was not in the slightest damped by the fact that I had put my foot on the very lowest rung of the social ladder. Caste among the Europeans was a reality that no one could escape, and the outdoor staff in the Customs were almost like the untouchables in India, and nearly as low as the Eurasians. The indoor staff in the administrative offices were, on the other hand, very high in the social scale. Fortunately, an ex-sailor has few, if any, social aspirations, and I had none. Curiously enough there was no caste system whatever among the Chinese.

The strange new life I had entered, the fascination of the Orient, the colour and glamour of the teeming street and harbour life, satisfied me completely. All was new and fresh and wonderful. There was something else, too, which added spice to my enjoyment of these new experiences. Shanghai was only a recruiting centre for this vast Empire, and sooner or later I could expect to be transferred to one of the many widely scattered stations from Harbin near the Siberian border in the north, to Mengtze near the Burma frontier in the south. And all along the Yangtze River were stations, as far west as Tachienlu on the Tibetan border. This delightful uncertainty about where I might eventually go, ran like a strong undercurrent through my thoughts as I savoured the new life.

In my work I often came into personal contact with men of long service who told me tales of life in small distant stations, tales which stirred up new and strange longings in me. But they all said, "Sonny, Shanghai is not China! This is the Paris of the Far East. Enjoy it while you can, because there are many mighty lonely and tough spots in the Service, about half a dozen decent ones, and only one Shanghai. It is dead certain that you will not be kept here more than a few months to learn the ropes and the rest is on the lap of the gods. You may be transferred to a good spot or to some God-forsaken hole."

This, however, did not worry me in the slightest; on the contrary, the uncertainty rather fascinated me, and I thought only that they wanted to make my flesh creep because I was a griffin (the term for a newcomer) and, as such, fair game for the old hands. I must have been quick at learning my job, for in June, three months after joining the Service, I was transferred to Chinkiang on the Yangtze and only one hundred and fifty miles from Shanghai. The old hands assured me that it was one of the good spots. There was a very nice and clean Concession they said. A good club, excellent shooting and the railway to Shanghai would soon be completed. In fact, I was a very lucky chap.

Of my former two shipmates I had seen very little since we landed as we had different duties. We now had a little farewell party, and that was the last we saw of one another in China. The same night I boarded the China Merchants' Steam Navigation Company's new steamer "Kiang Hsin", and left for Chinkiang.

It is a wonderful thing to be young, adventurous, eager and impressionable. I can still remember my excitement and anticipation as I stood on the bridge deck of the "Kiang Hsin" and looked ahead early the next morning. I felt like an explorer probing the secrets of this mighty river and the wonderful and strange places it flowed past on its way from faraway Tibet to the China Sea.

Nanking, Wuhu, Kiukiang, Tatung, Hankow, Ichang and Chungking were just names to me, and I tried to imagine what they were like. It was June, the river was in spate and so broad near the mouth that the banks were barely visible in the flat countryside. The swirling waters were a dirty yellow.

I was the only European passenger on board, and Captain Blethen, an American, came up to me for a yarn. He was a fatherly sort and, of course, spotted at once that I was a griffin, for he said, "New on the coast, ain't you?"

"Yes, I have only been out here three months."

"Well, well, and this is your first outport?" I nodded. "Been told anything about the cholera epidemic in Chinkiang?"

"No."

"Been told anything about taking precautions?"

"No."

"They are dying like flies there, more than two hundred a day—that is, Chinks, of course. The place stinks like hell; the Magistrate's too mean to bury them quickly—costs too much, and he hopes the relatives will do it for him. Most of them ain't got no relatives, I reckon." He spoke in short, jerky sentences and appeared concerned about me. "Don't eat any fruit," he continued, "don't drink any water: the boy always says it's boiled, and boiled water is safe, but don't believe him—can't trust 'em—and don't leave any food uncovered. If you feel queer drink a beer-glass full of brandy and castor-oil, half and half, and hope for the best. Your doctor's no use—drunk half the time. There's no hospital—unhealthy hole altogether, Chinkiang is: city drain runs into the river in front of the Concession, just where you get your drinking water, after all the junkmen have crapped in it. Foreshore's full of junks and you can guess what that means. Now, don't forget—no water, no fruit!"

I thought at first he was pulling my leg. I was only a griffin and was used to that, and yet he looked sincere and really worried when he left me. It did not worry me much, for soon afterwards we came to one of the stopping-places and my attention was diverted by the swarms of lighters and sampans which came out for cargo and passengers. Beggar boats came too, manned by incredibly dirty and ragged families equipped with long bamboo poles with a small net bag at the end; this pole was thrust up among the passengers to the accompaniment of pitiful whines for coppers. All was hurry, scurry and excitement, and I soon forgot the dismal picture Captain Blethen had painted of Chinkiang.

Late in the evening we came through the Silver Island Pass where the river narrows and runs like a mill-race. It was full moon, and I could see clearly the temples on the little island and on the high perpendicular bluff on the south bank. In the near distance were the lights of Chinkiang, and beyond, the outline of a tall, graceful pagoda. Soon we were nearing the China Merchants' hulk, and the sailors made the heaving-lines ready. The hulk was packed with people, half-naked, for it was swelteringly hot. Most of them were hotel touts and baggage coolies; they were yelling like maniacs and the din was deafening.

While we were nearly ten feet from the hulk, they came hurtling through the air like pirates boarding a ship and swarmed over the railings. Each passenger for Chinkiang was fought over and almost carried off bodily, bag and baggage. It was bedlam. Then I saw the Customs Officer, a dapper little man with a small moustache, whose name was Hunter, coming over the gangway to get the ship's papers. He had a couple of boatmen with him to carry my baggage which by this time had grown from one very small suitcase to two fair-sized travel bags.

The boatmen cleared a way for us through the jostling crowd that poured into an incredibly narrow and stinking street. Shops, restaurants and tea-houses overflowed into the roadway on trestle tables; flares and enormous paper lanterns, gaudily decorated, threw a weird light over the maelstrom of traffic. One stream poured through this bottleneck from the ship and collided with another stream battling its way through from the opposite direction. There were sedan-chairs, wheelbarrows, donkeys, coolies carrying huge loads on bamboo poles, an occasional rick-shaw just to make things a little more awkward and, of course, people on foot. They all seemed to be shouting and fighting for room, and the noise was terrific.

Pariah dogs, most of them hairless from mange, slunk under the trestle tables to get out of the way of trampling feet, and to the right and left shopkeepers, crying their wares, added their shouts to the noise. The smells were nauseating, and the street seemed endless. At long last we came to a broad canal, crossed a bridge and, suddenly, all was quiet. Ahead lay the deserted, broad "bund" of the Chinkiang Concession with its three rows of tall shade trees and a wide pavement with one occupant, a man in a white uniform, sleeping in a long-chair. It came almost like a shock, this stillness, and the long, tidy twin avenues bathed in moonlight. The only sounds were the queer buzz-saw noises of a few cicadas and the gentle snores from the sleeping officer.

Hunter woke him up to sign the ship's papers, and I was intro-duced. Thatcher was his name, first-class tide waiter in charge of night duty. We went into the swelteringly hot office, lit by a big paraffin-lamp, and Thatcher shouted to the punkah coolie to bestir himself. A wizened old man, naked to the waist and glisten-ing with sweat, pulled away at the rope, the punkah started to swing back and forth over our heads, and the pleasant little air current it stirred up cooled and refreshed me wonderfully.

Thatcher was soon through with his work. He turned to me and said: "Your room in the quarters is not ready yet. Millar, your predecessor, was only buried yesterday and his furniture has to be auctioned first. I suppose you know that the staff only get unfurnished rooms, and you have to buy furniture and kitchen gear yourself. There'll be an auction tomorrow, and things go very cheaply here. By the way, you needn't be afraid of buying some of Millar's stuff: he died of typhoid, so there is no fear of contagion. Don't buy his ice-box though, for that is probably where he got his germs from. We can get only native ice here, filthy stuff from the ponds. I'll fix you up with a long-chair tonight; it's cool out on the pavement and the rooms are hot as hell. Hunter will show you the ropes tomorrow."

One of the boatmen brought a long-chair and placed it alongside Thatcher's out on the pavement. We talked for a while, slapping mosquitos from time to time: there were swarms of them.

The river was packed with junks near the Customs jetty, only twenty yards or so off, all of them, except one, silent and deserted. On this people were moving about and I could hear an occasional low moan from someone in pain. It was difficult to sleep, but I dozed off at last only to wake with a start. Someone over on the junk was screaming as if in mortal agony.

"What's that?" I called out, startled out of my wits. Thatcher stirred and said sleepily, "Only a Chink dying from cholera. He's got the cramp now, and it will soon be over. Dying like flies in the city!" His voice trailed off and ended in a snore.

I was wide awake and could not rest. The screams continued and ended in a strangled sob. I jumped up and ran over to the junk. A man was writhing on the foredeck, bent double and moaning feebly. A woman and some other silent, helpless people squatted at his side. There was nothing I could do and I could not bear to watch the man's death agony, so I went back to my chair. I looked at Thatcher, fast asleep, and muttered, "Callous swine!"

Then all was silent for a few moments, but not for long. A long piercing wail of uncontrolled grief, followed by heartbreaking sobs, made me jump up once more and go down to the junk again. The dead man's huddled form lay still and lifeless in the moonlight. His staring, terror-stricken eyes were bulging from their sockets, and his skin was nearly black. The woman, weeping and wailing, had flung herself over him.

Round them was a ring of curious junkmen, jabbering away, completely unmoved. Some laughed at the woman's noisy grief. I turned away, sick at heart. This was my first experience of the real China, and I was not yet hardened to its grim realities.

I was soon to learn that the callousness of Thatcher and the boatmen was only the result of daily contact with life as it was in a country where human life had lost all its value, because the earth was overburdened with unwanted millions.

II

My recollections of the first days in Chinkiang are rather confused.

I reported to the Harbour Master, Mr. Byworth, first thing in the morning and was put on the duty roster. Being an ex-sailor I was given harbour duties afloat and a sailing sampan, a nice clean craft with a small, but comfortable, cabin, was placed at my disposal. I was given a couple of days off duty to buy furniture and get my room organised.

I attended the auction of Millar's stuff and bought all the essentials and, again, I had only to sign a chit and pay when convenient. I took over Millar's boy-cook, a tall, smiling and willing lad named Ah Ping. I was lucky in getting a corner room, or rather two rooms separated by pillars supporting two arches. That gave me a large living-room and a small bedroom with two big windows. From the living-room two french windows led out to a wide veranda. It was one of the best rooms in the building and could have been taken by one of the senior members of the staff, but none of them claimed it: probably because they were friends of Millar's and he had died there.

Hunter, who was free in the daytime, took me round to the Customs Club and put me up as a member. There was a big billiard-room, in almost constant use, and a small card-room. One wing of a stage, reached by two steps from the billiard-room, was taken up by a well-stocked bar. There, the first thing I noticed, was a sepia-coloured picture of a desert and a dejected-looking camel trudging over the burning sands. Under it was this inscription: "They say that a camel can go fourteen days without a drink, but who the hell wants to be a camel!"

The port doctor, a thickset man with curious pale-blue,

bulging eyes and a bulbous nose of a slightly deeper shade of blue was the only customer. His hair was close-cropped on a bullet head and stood straight up, German fashion. He was very tight and spoke with a strong accent. We left him, after having a glass of beer, and Hunter took me into the big library in the adjoining building.

Here indeed was a pleasant surprise. Hundreds of books, and all my favourite authors: Kingsley, Kipling, Dickens, R.L.S., Conan Doyle, Charles Reade and Marie Corelli, who was then all the rage. I had been rather depressed by the sight of the doctor, although Hunter assured me that he was a wonderful surgeon unless he was sober when his hands shook too much. But as he was nearly always tight, that was all right. I took new heart when I saw this collection of good books, as I had a passion for reading and previously I had not been able to get hold of many books, at any rate not half enough to satisfy me. I was already appalled by the feeling of being shut up as in a prison in this tiny Concession, three hundred yards long and two hundred wide. I had seen all there was to be seen of it in less than a quarter of an hour.

It had three streets and two clubs, one for the outdoor staff and one for the Consul, the indoor staff and the merchants. There was a recreation ground two miles outside the Concession, called the Victoria Park, with tennis courts and a football and cricket field, but to get out there you had to fight your way through a crowded and filthy street before getting into open country. Hunter told me that there were a lot of corpses lying about stinking to high heaven, and no one was attempting to go outside the Concession until the cholera epidemic was over. He left me reading in the library, as he had shortly to go on night duty.

After a while I heard the Club filling up, and when I came in it was packed, hot and stuffy. All present had sorted themselves into three groups—billiards, cards and bar. At the bar there was a German engineer, with a voice like the roaring bull of Bashan, having an argument which nearly ended in a fight. His face was bloated with drink and purple with passion, and I thought he would have an apoplectic fit at any moment. No one paid any attention to him.

The seats round the billiard-room were filled with silent onlookers, their eyes following every movement of the balls and sweat oozing through their white coats. The card-players went on playing without turning a hair. The only sounds came from the roaring German, punctuated by sharp clicks from the billiard-balls. Then I went into the silent street for a breath of fresh air and walked up and down the bund, three hundred paces one way and three hundred paces back. To get a little change I walked up and down the only cross street to the south gate of the Concession, two hundred paces one way and two hundred paces back. It was deathly still save for an occasional buzz from a cicada and the clicking of billiard-balls, either from one club or the other. Click, click, buzz, buzz, click, click, buzz, buzz.

The monotony drove me back to my room. I had dinner, and afterwards slept fitfully in a long-chair on the pavement as I found Millar's bed had a very lumpy mattress. It was much too hot in my room to make sleep possible, a terribly depressing damp heat, hovering between eighty-five and ninety degrees. It would be like that until September, I was told, the hottest month being August when temperatures ranged between ninety and a hundred degrees at midnight.

Well, I should have to make the best of it, I thought, as I lay and listened to Thatcher's gentle snores and the new, weird night noises. The pavement outside the Customs House gate was the coolest place for sleeping, but Thatcher was "salted" and I was not and whereas he could sleep contentedly and without apparent discomfort, I woke with a start every time a cicada buzzed or a night-watchman on his rounds beat his gong to warn thieves that he was there and on the job. Occasionally a fiddler played a strange, lilting tune to while away the sleepless hours, and a high falsetto voice sang a weird melody. Up in the trees fireflies glittered in the darkness and mosquitos hummed their own maddening tune or drank deeply of the griffin's blood.

I thought of the old hands in Shanghai extolling the charms of Chinkiang and of him who slapped me on the back and said, "Lucky chap!" But then came a breeze, and I fell asleep under its magic touch.

These were my first impressions, and a cold fear gripped me at the prospects of a long stay. But at the same time I felt that this was a challenge. Other people had done it, so why should I funk it? As time went on I found my bearings and discovered ways and means of getting the utmost out of life.

Being thrown entirely on our own resources was a problem that each one of us had to meet in his own way. There were thirty-five people altogether in the Concession, mostly bachelors, and, as there was no social life for the outdoor staff, we had to make the most out of the Club and find other interests. Each one of us had his own particular hobby, which he rode hard. Some took to billiards, some to poker and whist, some to drink, others to riding and shooting, and some just disappeared. Many died. The doctor was a very good surgeon, but surgery was not the great need when it was mostly virulent diseases such as cholera, typhus, smallpox and typhoid fever which caused death. These infections required hospital treatment and skilled nursing. We had no hospital and no nurses; in any case there were no facilities for operations except on our own dining-tables. The reason for this was that the Concession had to pay its own way, and rates and taxes from thirty-five people were insufficient for the least luxury.

When anyone was seriously ill the men did the nursing. The doctor sent out a round-robin, and we marked down the time we were able to nurse; then a rota was made out. We also helped with operations when chloroform had to be given, so we acquired a good deal of useful knowledge, but not always, however, enough.

Kelly, the Chief of Police, was once tempted to make his own diagnosis and had acted on it, with rather startling results. A Chinese was carried to the police station in a comatose state, his face the typical blue of cholera in its last stage. Kelly did not want to trouble the doctor with a straightforward case of cholera so he had the Chinese put to bed with hot bricks at his feet, forced a tumbler of castor-oil and brandy down his throat, and covered him with a blanket wrung out in boiling water. When all was done he wandered round to the Club where he knew he could always find the doctor and told him with pride what he had done, all by himself.

The doctor asked a few questions, became suspicious and insisted on going round to see the patient. Kelly went with him, fully expecting a bouquet, but no sooner had the doctor seen the man than he tore off the hot blankets, hurled out the hot bricks and wailed in his broken English: "Mein Gott, vat haf you done! He has no cholera, he has heat apoplexy—quick, get ice-packs!" Wonderful to relate, the man recovered, but that was the only diagnosis Kelly ever made.

The chief source of the trouble was the main drain from the native city, which emptied itself on the foreshore in front of the Concession, where we got our water supply. This fact may have been the reason why the Chinese government gave us the place to live in, or rather die in, for it was the only place on the waterfront where nothing but contaminated water could be had. Our waterworks system was certainly rather primitive. Coolies with large wooden buckets waded out in the river up to their knees, filled the buckets and brought them to the houses where they were emptied into big earthenware jars. The water looked like thin pea-soup, but the cook doctored it with a handful of alum, stirred it round with a mop handle and, hey presto! the sediment dropped to the bottom and in no time the water became clear. It would have been quite harmless had it been boiled, but when we were on duty we had no means of ensuring this.

The city's drains were not alone to blame, for there were constantly fifty or sixty junks lying off the foreshore, and their only conveniences were over the side. In addition, the foreshore was the favourite place of Chinese women for washing clothes. I very soon got used to this and took it for granted. It's strange what one learns to take for granted.

When the first summer was over there were splendid days with dogs and gun in the foothills or in the tall reeds on the river bank, for the country swarmed with game, especially pheasant and duck. Those wonderful beats in the tall reeds alone were enough to make one forget all the other drawbacks. We went in parties of three or four, and I shall never forget those tense moments when the beaters approached, broken by the sudden startling shout: "Mark over!"—the whirr of wings, the mocking challenge of a cock pheasant breaking cover, and the fireworks when they sky-rocketed out of the reeds.

Even a small bag under such difficult conditions is something to remember, and there was the added pleasure of seeing so many of these splendid birds in glittering green, bronze and gold hurtling through the air untouched and triumphant.

III

My colleagues were a mixed lot from all walks of life. There was an ex-banker from 'Frisco, always immaculately dressed, two ex-sailors from the U.S. Navy and a stoker from the Royal Navy.

Delahunty, an Australian, had served as a trooper in the Boer War; Smith, an American, had been through the Boxer campaign; Mahoney never volunteered any information, but you could cut his Irish brogue with a knife, and he wrote a beautiful copper-plate hand. Hunter was born on the China coast and was, perhaps, the only good, steady lad of the lot. There was also a curious Norwegian with a milk-and-roses complexion, as if he used cosmetics, effeminate ways, a small moustache and a big thirst. To have a countryman like that thrust upon me was one of my biggest trials.

Two Australian ex-horsebreakers, Doolie, a Liverpool Irishman straight from the British Army, and Hicks, a young Welshman, completed the junior staff living in the bachelors' quarters. Other members of the staff, who had native housekeepers, lived in flats in the Concession in open sin. Only two of the senior staff were married.

The Customs Service at that time was the Foreign Legion of the Far East. There were men from every imaginable stratum of society: remittance men, drunks and sober men, gentlemen and rascals, ignorant and highly educated men. Love of adventure had attracted some of them to the Service; others were probably fugitives from justice, hiding under assumed names, and some like me had joined from necessity. They were a good and very interesting company, men who had seen and experienced a great deal.

Smith and Mahoney were salt-watchers, and were partly

responsible for my first adventure. Their only job was to search for smuggled salt. Salt was a government monopoly and, perhaps, the biggest and surest revenue producer because it was used in every family and was heavily taxed. For this reason salt smuggling was a highly profitable business, organised by powerful and ruthless gangs with wide ramifications throughout the country. They would tolerate small seizures, but if anything big was attempted they would stop at nothing to prevent it.

Mahoney told me that there was a Japanese steamer doing salt smuggling on a very large scale, and that I could help them to make a really big coup. This ship would anchor just outside the harbour limits in the dead of night: a big junk would come out and take on a full load. As I was on harbour duty Mahoney said I could probably catch them red-handed. It never struck me to ask why he did not do it either by himself or with Smith, for it was their job and they had boats at their disposal.

It sounded exciting and that was enough, for the monotony was wearing me down. As soon as I began night duty, I started my prowling, either in my sailing sampan when there was a strong breeze, or in the six-oared gig in calm weather.

I was very keen, and my colleagues predicted an early and sticky end to my career, for they had learned from experience to leave salt smugglers alone. This is not to be wondered at, as we were not allowed to carry arms and the smugglers were always armed. Officers on night patrol generally had "Nelson's eye" where salt smuggling was concerned. They had no intention of "dying nobly in the execution of their duty" as the epitaph ran on a Customs official's tombstone in the little crowded cemetery.

But to me this work had a strange fascination in which the ideal of dying nobly in the execution of my duty played no part. I wasn't cut out for heroics or playing that kind of role, but the probability of playing it willy-nilly was ever present.

Mahtzu, my pockmarked coxswain, was, at first, very disgruntled. He had a wife and family ashore and could not understand why in the name of all his gods I should prowl about the river at night, risking being carved about by a lot of cut-throats instead of sleeping peacefully ashore like other sane men. Then it so happened that one night we caught a small junk full of salt. There were only four men on board and we had little trouble with them after laying the skipper out with a boat-hook. Mahtzu's share of the seizure money was twenty-five dollars, a whole fortune to him.

I have seldom seen a man so overjoyed as when I handed him the money. He counted and chinked each dollar against another to make sure there was not a single doubtful one, and counted them over and over. It was untold riches to him and the other boatmen, for I had given them half my share as an encouragement. Now the night patrol made sense to them at last, because, being hard-headed and practical, they thought it was money I was after. If they had known I was doing it for the excitement and fun of it, they would have thought me crazy. But for me these night patrols were fascinating beyond words.

I would often tie up by one of the reed islands near the Golden Island Pagoda where the junks lay anchored. Most of them were big sea-going craft with huge staring eyes painted in their bows. Mahtzu explained in pidgin-English: "He go long way. Suppose he no have gottee eyes he no can see. Supposee he no can see, he no can savvy what place he belong, what place he go."

By night they looked like huge sea-monsters from another world resting on the swirling waters, their eyes open and watchful. It always gave me a thrill to approach one of them silently at night, clap alongside and jump on board. They were mostly trading junks with their papers in order, and if they did carry a moderate amount of smuggled stuff occasionally I let them keep it. The sailor in me was still very much alive, and I had a sneaking regard for people who had the good sense and decency to give their ships eyes to see with. It was for this reason I often closed my own to many irregularities.

And then came the night when I spotted a steamer coming up through the Silver Island Pass and anchoring below the harbour limits. "Give way!" I shouted to Mahtzu, and the gig went streaking downstream with the strong current. We came along at great speed. Well above the ship I turned the gig to stem the current, but even with six men straining at the oars we were drifting fast as the river was pouring into a bottleneck and running like a mill-race.

I steered close enough with the bow to give the bowman a chance to get his boat-hook fast in anything he could hold on to, but there was nothing to grab at, not even a Jacob's ladder, until we reached the rudder, which was fitted with rudder chains. The bowman got his hook into these and made the painter fast. It was a nasty spot to be in, for the current was swirling round in huge whirlpools and the gig was bouncing and shipping water while snubbed to the rudder chains.

How to get aboard was the puzzle. The ship was light and very high in the water, and it was pitch dark. I had received no reply to my hail when I was looking for a ladder, and the ship appeared quite deserted, but I was perfectly certain that we had been seen.

I climbed over the thwarts towards the bow to see what could be done when I saw a rope hanging down, undoubtedly meant for the junks. I put my weight on it and found that it was fast on deck, and being mad at our predicament I started to climb. I was only a couple of feet from the guard rail when I saw a naked arm against the night sky, and a fist gripping a cleaver, poised over my head. In an instant I slid down the rope a couple of feet to avoid the blow. I heard a dull thud, the rope was severed above me and I sailed through space to crash into Mahtzu in the bow of the gig. Had I fallen into the water nothing could have saved me, for the whirlpools would have sucked me down. I cannoned from Mahtzu into another boatman and laid both of them out. Two oars were lost and Mahtzu let go the painter, so we went spinning down through the whirlpools with four frightened oarsmen trying to get the gig under control. I was stunned and hurt when I crawled aft to the yoke-lines.

I headed the gig towards the bank to get her into the eddy and made it just in time, or we should have crashed into a rocky promontory only a few yards away. As soon as we were in safer water a little higher up, I grounded the gig to take stock.

Mahtzu and the other boatmen didn't seem to be badly hurt, and I decided to make one more attempt by pulling up the eddy and then rowing like blazes when well above the steamer. I was so furious that I did not stop to think how crazy the idea was.

However, the Jap steamer decided the issue. Before we had got far enough I could hear the anchor chains clanging, and shortly after she steamed up river and disappeared. I got my battered crew back to the Customs House, and from the way they were chattering one would have thought that all of them had hurtled through the air at the end of a severed rope. There was a subsequent inquiry based on my report, but the Jap captain was like the three famous Japanese monkeys: he had seen no evil, heard no evil and spoken no evil! The ship was fined for anchoring outside the harbour limits, but that was all.

I had one more narrow escape before I decided to turn my attention to more healthy pastimes. One night, during a gale, I made a surprise call on the China Merchants' paddle-steamer "Kiang Kwan" as she lay discharging alongside the hulk. Smugglers generally use a dirty night for their big jobs.

These paddle-steamers had a superstructure outside the hull like a long, narrow veranda running fore and aft from the paddle box. There would be a good hiding-place for the gig underneath this superstructure, and we slipped in quietly from the stern and lay waiting, not far from the paddles, after unshipping the oars. We were too well hidden to be seen from any junk coming alongside to take off smuggled goods and if one came near we should be boxed in and completely concealed.

That was my theory, but it did not work out quite that way in practice. It is true that a junk did approach, but at the same time the paddles started turning full speed astern, and in a few seconds we were fighting for our lives as the gig was being sucked into the paddles. There was nothing to hold on to, and the ship's side was as smooth as glass. The bowman pushed off with his bare hands, the oars were slipped like lightning but, before they could start pulling, the stern where I was sitting got sucked in towards the paddles. There was a crash of splintering oars, the splash of two men flung into the water, and the next moment I found myself fighting off the paddles for dear life, with my hands gripping the edges as they came smashing down and pushing off while they were moving. It was a terrifying experience, as each push had to be timed to a split second and one miss would have meant death to all of us. Suddenly the oars took effect and we got clear. There were only two oars left, four were splintered, and two terrified boatmen were in the water, clinging to the gig. The paddles stopped just as I scrambled on board the ship and dashed down into the engine-room, which I found empty. I had had the fright of my life and I was as mad as a hatter when I went into the chief engineer's cabin.

He was in bed reading, and looked at me in great surprise when I shouted: "Who the hell turned the paddles on me?"

"Turned the paddles?" he replied. "You must be dreaming. We won't be going for another hour, and we don't try out the paddles until just before we leave. Better ask the second engineer, he's on watch."

I went to the second engineer's cabin and also found him reading and equally ignorant, or pretending to be. I could not imagine a more determined and devilishly clever attempt at murder and I reported the matter at once to the Harbour Master. He detained the ship for several hours and authorised me to have her thoroughly searched.

We made a huge haul of salt, hidden in the coal bunkers with other smuggled goods, and a whole chest of opium worth thousands of taels.

Mahtzu was so overcome by the thought of seizure money that he could hardly speak. He had often told me that his great dream was to buy a little shop ashore and retire from chasing smugglers, which he regarded only as a means to an end. For my own part, I kept away from paddles and ropes dangling invitingly over ships' sterns from that day. I took it as a gentle hint from the salt-smuggling fraternity that my attentions were unwelcome. I *can* take a hint.

I was eventually removed from further temptation by being transferred to examination duty, which was a shore job. By this time Mahtzu had received his seizure money and had resigned. He came up to my rooms to say good-bye, his ugly pockmarked face wreathed in smiles. "My too muchee happy, master, my have gottee one velly goodee shop. My by am by makee plenty money. This Customs pidgin no bloody good! Too muchee pullee pullee night-time—no can catchee sleep—no can go homeside. My wifee—he allee time bobbely (scold) my—he tinkee so my go singsong girlee night-time. He no tinkee my belong dam fool pullee pullee boat evely night—he no tinkee so my belong dam fool fightee fightee smuggle man. Just now my wifee no bobbely my. Have gottee shop—stop shoreside, sleep homeside, makee money. Bloody, number one goodee!"

All this came in pure, voluble pidgin, all but the "bloody", which he must have learnt from me.

IV

THE Concession in Chinkiang dated back to 1858, when it lay in lonely grandeur on the river bank. The walled city was a good deal farther back and had for many centuries been of great importance because of the Grand Canal traffic and, strategically, because here the ascent of the river by enemies could best be prevented. The name Chinkiang means "Guard the River", but the walled city was almost destroyed in the Taiping rebellion in 1851, when the defenders and inhabitants were wiped out, and no attempts were made to rebuild the haunted ruins.

The tremendous growth of trade in the British Concession made the Canal trade quite insignificant by comparison and sounded the death-knell of what was left of the walled city. But the intervening ground became the site of a new native city, outside the walls, which eventually clamped itself tight round the Concession boundaries, as if it could not get too close to the life-giving business centre of the whole of that part of the country.

Our main exit to the country or to the recreation ground went through part of this new city and a street with the grand name of "The Maloo"—the horse road—which in Chinese denotes a very fine wide road indeed. It is true that it was wider than the incredibly narrow lanes which the Chinese called streets, but it also carried twice the traffic. The Chinese authorities were very proud of that road because of the wide concrete surface drains, at least a hundred yards long, which ran along either side and represented the sole attempt ever made to introduce modern sanitation. That was the street through which we had to battle our way every time we wanted to leave the Concession. Beggars, lepers among them, in indescribably filthy rags would thrust scaly hands into our faces, and the more revolting-looking they were, the more importunate they became and the more eager to show maimed limbs and filthy sores. Altogether a nauseating experience before we got hardened and callous.

On one side shops were packed tight together, pushing their wares, mostly food, into the street on trestle tables which straddled the open drain. This monument to up-to-date sanitation was used as a dust-bin by all and sundry, and stank loudly and lustily. On the other side of the street, just outside the Concession gate was the small Methodist chapel. There had recently been quite a scandal about the Methodist chapel. During an evening service the whole congregation had started to wriggle and scratch themselves, and many left hurriedly; the preacher being almost alone when the service ended. It was found on investigation that the Chinese caretaker had turned the chapel into a paying dosshouse for coolies and beggars, and every pew was crawling with bed-bugs and lice.

Beyond the chapel a few isolated shops had been built, with open spaces between them. The open spaces were used as public conveniences, constantly patronised by squatting men and the ubiquitous and enterprising mangy pariah dogs sitting patiently waiting to perform their sanitary duties after their "patrons" got up. The edge of the drain on that side, and the margins of the open spaces, were favourite de-lousing places for idlers. They would sit there patiently with their feet in the drain, going carefully through the seams of their coats and trousers, cracking lice if there were only a few, eating them if there were many, and doing it with great gusto.

Perhaps I should not have gone into these disgusting details, and I will do it only once. I had to endure it every day for more years than I care to remember, but fortunately the shock soon wears off.

Once the Maloo had been passed, the road forked and went uphill into open country. On the left-hand side was a small fort with mud walls and a few ancient muzzle-loading guns. One of them fired a shot at noon every day, until a gunner was killed. He had been sitting on an open powder-keg smoking a cigarette and had dropped the end into the keg. He was brought to the doctor, and

I helped to smear carron-oil over him; but he was too badly burnt to respond to treatment and died. After this accident the fort stopped firing the noon gun for quite a while, until the evil spirits had been exorcised.

The country all around the fort, as far as the recreation ground a mile farther out, was covered with graves so tightly packed together that there was hardly walking room between them. This was Taiping country, and Chinkiang and Nanking were two of the cities where all the defenders were slain by the Taiping rebels. This scourge, which cost twenty million lives, was brought to an end by General Gordon after the Chinese Army had failed dismally. Gordon's trenches were still to be seen in outline on the surrounding hills, and some of his guns were found sunk deep into the soil of the old embrasures. The only reminder now of the Taiping rebellion was thousands of graves covering the countryside, and the ghost-ridden walled city where the whole population had been put to the sword.

But it was very peaceful up among the graves after the deafening noise of the Maloo only a few hundred yards away, and the top of the first hill was a favourite place for the Chinese out for a walk with their cage-birds. There were a few trees standing there, and cages were hung on the low branches. The favourite birds were the Peiling lark and the Huamei, a thrush with a wonderfully joyous song. The cages were very fine, many of them works of art, always spotlessly clean and about the only thing the Chinese *would* keep sweet and clean. They are not animal lovers, and very few of them would dream of keeping a dog as a pet, but it was strange to see the affection they showed for their birds and the way they took them for long walks and cleaned and changed the red sand in the bottom of the cage every day.

It was not only the Chinese who found this first hill-top such a pleasant spot for lingering in the early evening. I always stopped there to fill my lungs with fresh clean air and to admire the wonderful view. To the north a wide sweep of the Yangtze was dominated by the Golden Island Pagoda on one side, and Silver Island and Consular Bluff on the other, with the temple buildings glowing in the sunset. To the westward lay a range of hills deep blue on the shady side and a warm pink where the setting sun touched the slopes. In the foreground were rolling hills, and

ATE I

Top: Scene from the Grand Canal
Bottom: Chinkiang City Wall with the Grand Canal in the foreground

PLATE 2

Top: Some junior members of the outdoor staff. Author third from left
Bottom left: The Golden Island Pagoda
Bottom right: Mahtzu, my boatman (with round cap)

between them rice fields and irrigation canals. To the south were two treeless, solitary hills, and to the left, only a few hundred yards off, were the American Presbyterian and Methodist Mission buildings, with a hospital for Chinese. From here a winding road led southwards to the Victoria Park and its clean little club house, tennis courts and cricket field. It always struck me as strange that the Chinese converts had hospital facilities provided by money subscribed from abroad whilst the whites in the Concession had none, and were never offered a bed there, nor received help from the nurses. However, let that pass.

Curiously enough, the thousands of graves lining the road never had a depressing effect on me. They were just grass-covered mounds five feet or so in height, with a cone-shaped piece of turf on top. But one sight I never could ignore and one that always made me shudder was the corpses of girl babies, strangled just after birth because the mothers could not afford to feed them, and left there, rolled up in a dirty piece of matting, for the dogs to devour. However, even the most ravenous mangy cur would slink away in shame when caught in the act.

Victoria Park was a godsend to us, and it was generally packed, especially in the summer evenings. When the autumn came, most of us went shooting; wonderful snipe-shooting in the paddy fields in September when the birds moved southwards from Siberia, and again in May when they came back.

Pheasant-shooting started, of course, on October 1st, and wild boar- and deer-shooting about a month later. Most of us possessed a gun of sorts and a dog, for without the company of a dog life would have been almost impossible. In a small place like Chinkiang, where nothing ever happened and boredom laid its heavy hand on the little community thrown together in a confined space with few amusements or diversions, strange things happen to the individual.

In a few months one exhausted all one had to say, each knowing the extent of the other's conversation and their reactions under all circumstances. Then came the strange sensation of knowing word for word what each man was going to say before he opened his lips, so why the hell did he insist on *saying* it? Eventually all conversation became quite meaningless and often very irritating. It was like the clicking of the billiard-balls, the buzzing of cicadas and the roars of the drunken German engineer—just an irritating noise.

The card- and billiard-players had a comparatively easy time, as they could go on for hours in silence; they were not supposed to speak anyway. You longed madly for something to happen to give you something new to talk about. Above all, you longed for new faces and new impressions, a wish granted only when people died and were replaced.

Six died in my second year, and we all followed the funeral processions out through the Maloo and then bore right along the so-called Nanking Road towards the site for the railway station. A mob of yelling Chinese followed us and surrounded the little cemetery on the slope of a low hill overlooking Golden Island Pagoda. It was nearly impossible to hear the funeral service because of the yelling from the noisy mob, but the words: "Oh, death, where is thy sting?" took on a new significance. There *was* no sting over a departed colleague, no sorrow, only a macabre feeling of relief and speculation over what the new fellow would be like. Friendship and close attachments were almost impossible under such conditions, so there could be no real grief or sense of loss over those who died.

This was the dark side of the picture, the side that led to two suicides, to drunkenness and to dope. But for me it only put the good things into bolder relief. There were matchless spring days out in the hills, when the wild azaleas dappled the slopes with yellow and mauve and the Huamei filled the silent gullies with his song. Later, spring snipe, fat as butter, would be swarming in the paddy fields, lazy and not too difficult to shoot for a tyro like myself out with a few kindred spirits. The only trouble with snipe-shooting was that the fields swarmed with Chinese who had a disconcerting habit of being in the line of fire when the birds flew low. It was inevitable that they should be hit occasionally, and some brilliant diplomatist in years gone by had introduced a tariff of ten cents per pellet, which was accepted as full and adequate compensation by every farmer in the district.

If anything, the scale of payment erred on the generous side, for No. 9 shot at forty yards or so does not hurt much, and it would be a very unlucky Chinaman who did not collect twenty pellets and two dollars at that range. A tremendous hullabaloo was always raised when a man was hit. Fellow workers were called and negotiations began. The lucky man, if hit in the seat, was naturally unable to assess the damage, and, as he was anxious to have every pellet accounted for, a minute inspection followed after he had removed his trousers. Every pellet was then counted by a Chinese "inspector" and checked by the sportsman. Accounts were then made out and settled, the "inspector" generally receiving twenty cents for his trouble. Then up came the trousers, there were friendly exchanges of courtesies and the incident was closed.

Negotiations were not so easy when a woman was hit, as she would never consent to pull down her trousers and expose the seat of the trouble. Hunter, who often came out with me, had a wonderful way of dealing with these awkward situations. He spoke the language fluently and knew the mentality of the Chinese. He would say to the woman: "I am sure you have only got ten pellets in you and I will pay you one dollar. But, of course, if you think you have more you must prove it. You can't expect me to pay for pellets that are not there." A general murmur of approval and assent came from the Chinese. This was just, and no one could expect payment for damage not done. The onus of proof was on the woman, the only one to disagree to the proposal. "Take down her trousers—no fear, not for ten dollars!"

She would assert loudly that she had at least thirty pellets in her bottom, if not more, but she was willing to accept two dollars. A spirited bargaining would follow, and Hunter would finally agree to pay one dollar and fifty cents, the limit he had decided on at first. Custom in China demanded that, when bargaining, one party begins too low and works upwards by slow degrees, the other starts too high and works downwards until both agree. Custom was satisfied, all the rules of the game had been observed and everyone was happy.

But one may rest assured that the woman's husband counted the pellets at the first opportunity to ascertain that they had not been cheated out of anything and that his hope of a favourable profit-and-loss account was realised. A ten-cent piece more or less meant a great deal to a poor Chinese farmer in those days, when ten cents was all a farm labourer earned in a twelve-hour day. The gamble in this guessing game when a woman was hit added spice to the affair, for every Chinaman loves a gamble.

V

I HAD not been long in Chinkiang before I bought Nellie, a brown pointer bitch, and a gun.

Nellie was two years old, had never been trained in the field and, as far as I knew, had never been out shooting. Everybody told me she was too old to train, but Nellie put them all to shame by turning out a perfect gun-dog with a wonderful nose. During my first two years, her companionship meant more to me than I can tell: there was no mistaking her welcome when I came home from duty.

Apart from her I had only one real friend in the port, and he died in my third year. He was a countryman of mine, Frost by name, who worked in the postal service. We met over books in the library and had long discussions about the writings of R.L.S. and Chesterton, whom we both admired. Later I often dropped in at his flat of an evening, or he came to me for dinner and a quiet talk. He was a highly sensitive man who suffered acutely from the deadly monotony of the place, and this made him more or less a recluse. He was not physically strong and therefore could not fall back on sports and shooting.

One evening his boy came to my rooms in an excited state and asked me to come as his master was ill. I went immediately and found my friend in great pain. The doctor had diagnosed appendicitis and had gone for his instruments, and Frost had asked if I could be present at the operation.

I went into the dining-room to get the table ready, told the boy to bring a tea-table for the instrument trays and to boil plenty of water. Then I placed a couple of oil-lamps, so that they gave the doctor a better light than that provided by the hanging lamp over the dining-table. I had assisted at many operations before and knew what to do and how the doctor liked things arranged. He came just after I was ready and started to boil the instruments while I went in to try to cheer my friend.

He was in a bad way, deathly pale and in great pain, but a flicker of a smile came over his face when I sat down on the edge of his bed and held his hand. "Cheer up, old man, it'll soon be over," I whispered to him. "It is the waiting that's the worst part. I'll stay with you after the operation is over, so you won't be alone." This seemed to comfort him a lot and he smiled again, a pitiful, wan smile.

The doctor came in and together we carried the patient into the next room and placed him carefully on the dining-table. The doctor reeked of brandy, but his hands were steady and deft. I gave the chloroform, watching the colour of Frost's face carefully and so intently that I did not notice that the doctor was well under way with the operation. Suddenly I heard him mutter: "Oh, mine Gott, vat a bloody mess! Poor bastard, no bloody hope—peritonitis, bad peritonitis."

He was suddenly quite sober, and there was a new light in his bloodshot eyes, a light of infinite compassion that I had never seen before. Then he spat out : "Vat a bloody hole! No hospital, no facilities, no nurses! Fife years I haf been here and peoples only die—all the time die. Dey say I drink too mooch. Vy I drink too mooch? I am doctor—I like see people get vell, I don't like see people die. Ven I am droonk I don't care so mooch. This man perhaps I could not save, but many, many men I know I could save if I haff hospital and nurses."

He went over to the sideboard and poured out half a tumbler of brandy, which he tossed off: then he came back and completed his work.

We carried Frost back to bed, and the doctor dozed in a chair until the patient came to. No one could have fought more fiercely for a man's life than the old Austrian, but saline injections and every other means failed to save the patient. He himself knew he was dying and asked me to sit and hold his hand, he whispered that it comforted him and gave him courage. He died almost without a sound or a movement, and I only realised he had passed on when I felt his hand icy cold in mine. I may have dozed off when it happened, for I had been sitting there for hours.

Life would have been pretty grim after that but for Nellie. She seemed to sense that I needed all the comfort she could give me, and tried by joyous welcomes and her adoring look, with its silent message of love, devotion and faithfulness, to cheer and console me when everything else failed.

As I was on examination duty on the hulk "Bremen", a receiving ship for cargo arriving in the German river-boats, I could take her with me to work every day. There was a comfortable office on board and also a friendly and hospitable hulk-keeper, Captain Lange, an old German sea-dog. He had a good cook who could make his favourite cake called *Hamburger Kloeben*, and every afternoon Nellie and I were invited to his comfortable cabin to coffee and *Kloeben*, which also was Nellie's favourite cake.

I seemed to be fated to meet with adventures even when I least expected them, and certainly that old hulk "Bremen", securely anchored close to the foreshore, with four anchors ahead and four astern, was the last place to expect anything untoward. And yet it came one day.

It was blowing a gale and the hulk was straining at her moorings when I suddenly heard loud yells and the trampling of feet on deck, where the cargo-coolies were stampeding. I ran out and saw a big steamer coming straight for us, apparently out of control. She was the Hamburg-Amerika Line steamer "Ascania" and she had no business to be there. She seemed unable to turn, and I wondered why she did not drop her anchor and turn on that, for the mate was on the fo'c'sle head and the anchor was ready to be dropped, but no order came from the captain.

I stood there, feeling quite sure that the obvious order would come at any moment. All the coolies on board had rushed ashore; the "Ascania" was only a few feet off now, and nothing could save the "Bremen". Then the crash came, and I was flung nearly off my feet. Mooring chains snapped, a big bollard near me was torn clean out of the deck plates at the same moment that the captain of the "Ascania" yelled "Let go!"

The mate, being a dutiful—or dutifool—German, let go the anchor on the deck of the "Bremen", which was pushed hard against the river bank, and smashed the connecting bridge. Captain Lange came rushing out from his cabin half-demented, followed by his two servants. Still I did not think there was much danger as I felt sure the "Ascania" would keep her bow into the huge hole she had made in the "Bremen's" side and press her against the bank. Any fool would have done that, but not that captain. He continued the series of appalling blunders by going full speed astern.

The "Bremen", with the "Ascania's" anchor buried in her deck, tilted over, and I heard the roar of water pouring into the hold. Captain Lange let out a terrified howl and ran over to the other side, with me after him. There were two cargo-boats alongside and Captain Lange and his two servants disappeared over the side.

I called for Nellie, who was bolting in panic, but she would not come. I ran after her, knowing that seconds counted, but she was mad with fright and dodged under the fo'c'sle head, where I eventually cornered her. Grabbing her by the collar I ran towards the midship section where the cargo-boats had been. One was already ashore with Captain Lange; the second had fortunately got her mooring-rope snarled and the junkman was trying to clear it, not realising that the "Bremen" would sink at any moment. We were well out and in deep water by now.

Holding Nellie by the collar I jumped and landed with a crash on the foredeck of the junk. By that time the boatman's wife, who had a good deal more sense than her husband, had brought a cleaver and cut the rope. Then they pulled like fury away from the sinking hulk.

The next moment the "Bremen's" bow rose high in the air, a terrified sailor who must have been asleep in the fo'c'sle stood paralysed, gripping the railings, and then the hulk went down like a plummet.

I watched the whirlpools for a while, then told the boatman to pull out and look for the sailor, although there did not appear to be any chance of seeing him again. Then he suddenly came popping out of the water like a cork and floundered about in a panic, and it was clear he could not swim. The boatman stood in the bow with a long boat-hook poised and ready to strike.

It was nice and sharp, and with unerring aim it struck the floundering man in the seat. A fearful yell followed as we dragged him on board, where he used some shocking language. The stupid fool did not understand that if the hook had been blunt he would have drowned.

Nellie was frightened for days afterwards and would not leave my side. I therefore took her with me when boarding ships to get the papers. One day I lost her on board a crowded river steamer which stopped only long enough to land and take passengers, as she had no cargo. The decks and passages were packed with people. I called and called, but Nellie never turned up.

Finally I thought she must have run ashore, as she was given to panic when separated from me. I went ashore just as the steamer was leaving and returned to the Customs House. There was no sign of Nellie anywhere, and I spent the rest of the night looking for her and calling her in the native city on the route I had taken. I was sick at heart in the morning and very weary.

The ship's next port of call was Nanking, forty miles away, and there seemed no hope of getting her back. This was no ordinary loss—the dog was my best friend and constant companion, and the uncertainty of what had happened to her was almost unbearable.

Six days later I was sitting reading late in the evening, when I heard a faint scratching at the door. I ran across the room, opened the door and Nellie came staggering in, feebly wagging her tail. Her coat was muddy, flat and staring, every bone was sticking out and she was completely exhausted.

It did not take me long to raid the ice-box and find some raw beef: I cut this fine and gave her a little at a time. She ate ravenously and finished everything I gave her. Then I routed Ah Ping out of bed and ordered soup. It seemed too good to be true to have her back again, and I spent half the night fussing over her. Ah Ping was nearly as excited as I, and between us we gave Nellie the welcome of her life.

How on earth she had managed to find her way back I don't know. I heard afterwards that a Customs officer in Nanking had seen a brown dog streak ashore when the ship arrived: he called and whistled, but she paid no attention. I had sent a wire to Nanking in the hope of tracing her. Somewhere on the way back she must have been caught, for there was a piece of grass rope round her neck. It was more than two weeks before Nellie was her old plump self again.

VI

CHINKIANG was growing apace during the first few years I was there. The whole native population of some one hundred and forty thousand were directly or indirectly earning their living from the foreign trade which came through the Concession, as there were no factories or industries.

Various shipping companies, two British, two Japanese, one German and one Chinese, ran lines of river steamers—in all some twenty ships—between Shanghai and Hankow, all of them calling at Chinkiang. In addition, coasting steamers came and went daily, the great majority of them British, Norwegian and Japanese, with occasionally a German or Chinese boat.

Most of the ships anchored in the river, loading and discharging by means of large sailing cargo-boats. The whole foreshore was a seething hive of activity, providing work for thousands of boatmen and coolies. All this had been practically non-existent before the port was opened to foreign trade, and now the Chinese were almost entirely dependent on it. Chinkiang had become the main trading centre for the whole of Kiangsu province, with a population of over thirty millions. Under these circumstances the anti-foreign feeling was hard to understand. I must admit I did not try to understand it in the beginning; I was too busy finding my own feet and too devil-may-care to worry about it.

However, when you had "Yang Kweitzu!" (Foreign devil!) hurled at you every time you went in and out of the Concession one became more and more conscious of this hostility. It is true that the shouting came mostly from street-urchins, but they must have learnt it from the grown-ups. At first I put it down to ignorance, and it was only after I started studying Chinese that I began to realise that it sprang from hate, carefully fostered and fanned by the officials. The Chinese are the most peace-loving, law-abiding people in the world, until stirred up by agitators.

Nevertheless, there is a latent streak of the opposite characteristic in nearly every Chinaman. When stirred up to mob violence the same quiet, peace-loving man becomes a demon, a yelling, crazy brute bent on rapine, arson and murder. In 1889 such a mob had overrun the Chinkiang Concession and burned and looted the foreign houses. The riot gates, since erected at either end of the Bund, were a daily reminder. They were very strong double gates of stout iron bars each with a span of some twenty feet, so that the whole width of the Bund, some forty feet, would be barred when they were banged to. The Concession police force consisted of about sixteen Shantung men from the famous disbanded Wei Hai Wei regiment, trained by British officers and loyal to the core should trouble come.

In 1891 there had been an epidemic of anti-foreign riots in nearly every Concession on the Yangtze, at Wuhu, Nanking, Ichang, Shasi, Haimen, Tungchow and Hochow. At Ichang all the foreign houses were looted and burned, and it was significant that the riots took place in the months of May and June, as if part and parcel of a general plan. The abysmal ignorance of the average Chinese, and the fact that nearly fifty per cent of them were illiterate, precluded the idea of popular indignation over some wrong, or of some national patriotic movement.

The vast majority of the Chinese did not know the first meaning of the word patriotism, neither had they any personal dealings with Europeans. At that time there were scarcely one thousand Europeans altogether in the Yangtze valley, and they were scattered in small isolated communities from Chinkiang to far-away Chungking and surrounded by at least one hundred and fifty million Chinese. Out of this great multitude, probably only ten thousand had ever had any dealings with the Europeans and such dealings had been of benefit to them: the Chinese were the last people in the world to bite the hand that fed them. Coupled with their ignorance was a deep-rooted superstition and credulity: they were a people who lived in constant dread of the feng shui, the spirits of wind and water, and of demons and evil spirits.

These riots were obviously the result of fear; it was not so much the people who took part who were afraid but the literati and officials, who feared that the impact of European civilisation and science would put an end to their corrupt system of government and to their profits. There may also have been the dread that we might eventually wrest the country from them. So they stirred up the mobs and "sicked" them on to us, keeping carefully in the background themselves.

They came out into the open only during the Boxer trouble, which took place five years before my arrival. That rising had the blessing not only of the officials but of the Empress Dowager and of the whole Imperial government. They really thought they would smash the Europeans in one glorious massacre. The terrible fact remains that most of the victims were missionaries who had devoted their lives to serving the Chinese people. Of the Protestants alone, one hundred and thirty-five missionaries and fifty-three of their children were murdered.

With all this as background, and the fact that we never got the slightest protection from the officials, life in the Concessions would have been very precarious, even intolerable, but for the Royal Navy, bless them. Let those who have never had to put up with the appalling living conditions and risks of the "out-porters", talk sneeringly of what they called Britain's provocative gunboat policy. We, out there, blessed those little ships flitting from port to port like migratory birds. And birds they were, too: the "Nightingale", "Snipe", "Teal", "Sandpiper", "Wood-cock" and "Widgeon". It was a joy to see them every time they came steaming in, white and spotless, all aglitter with shining brasswork. We did not live in fear and trembling, far from it, but their presence was always a reminder that we had not been forgotten and left to the tender mercies of our Chinese "protectors". Never were smaller ships entrusted with a bigger job nor more successful in preventing bloodshed by a mere show of arms and not by their use. That White Ensign meant more to us than I can say. It stood for so much, as did the officers and men on board—something good, clean, strong and dependable. Even the presence of a gunboat in the harbour had an extraordinarily sobering effect on the Chinese. If agitators had been busy, a small landing-party of business-like bluejackets drilling on the Bund was enough to quell an incipient riot.

We also had occasional visits from ships on the coastal patrol: H.M.S. "Thistle" and "Britomart" and the sloops "Clio" and "Cadmus". Then the whole port was *en fête*, and both clubs were crowded with new faces and new voices, men to whom we could talk without irritation, and revel in it. At such times we had a chance of meeting that great character Pote Hunt, the Admiralty pilot, or Pote'unt, as he called himself. He was full of priceless tales of his adventures with the admiral, which always started with: "Me and the admiral . . .".

Another well-known character who often visited us was Captain Paddy Bright of the B. & S. steamer "Tamsui". He was known for his practical jokes, his hospitality and his generosity. He was a wild Irishman who could hold down an incredible lot of liquor without wilting. One evening he invited Kelly of the police, Tonkin of the post office and myself on board for dinner. We had just finished the meal when I heard the anchor chains rattling. He was leaving that evening and I thought they were just shortening in on the anchors, until the mate came in and said: "We are under way, sir." Paddy beamed seraphically on us and said, "Sure, and it's a pleasure to have you gintlemen's company to Hongkong, unless ye prefer to swim ashore!"

We first thought he was joking, but divil a bit. It was a long swim but we made it; it was summer, the water was nice and cool, and the whole adventure rather a lark. Anything to break the monotony.

That same autumn there was a good deal of excitement over a young railway engineer who died of internal bleeding after dining at the Consulate. Ground glass was found in his soup, and the whole affair was rather a mystery. My Chinese teacher told me it was common gossip that he was poisoned by a Chinese contractor who had failed to "square" him over a big delivery of ballast and sleepers, but it was very puzzling how the contractor could have arranged for the glass to be put in his soup at the Consulate. The young engineer was a very popular man, honest and apparently without an enemy, so the murder caused rather a stir and much speculation.

I had started studying Chinese the year before, and my teacher, Mr. Wang, was, like most Chinese, an inveterate gossip, and he knew the inside story of most happenings.

It was he who told me about the contractor and also many other queer stories. Mr. Wang was flabby and, like most opium smokers, his complexion was almost without colour and his eyes without any kind of life unless he had smoked a few pipes. Apart from "yes" and "no" he knew no English, so I had to speak Chinese with him willy-nilly.

How I swotted over that frightful language and twisted my tongue until it ached! But I was determined to learn it so that I could speak to people and not be dependent upon interpreters. Like all beginners I was very ambitious; I wanted to learn to write it, which is just asking for trouble.

To write Chinese you first have to learn by heart the two hundred and fourteen radicals, what they look like, their rotation and sound. The radicals are the different strokes of which the characters consist. They begin with six easy ones of a single stroke, then come twenty-three of two strokes, thirty of three strokes, thirty-nine of four strokes and twenty-four of five strokes. After that the real difficulties increase at a frightening rate, culminating in a radical of *seventeen* strokes!

If the sounds of these seventeen different strokes were written down it would make a word of about sixty letters, but their sounds have no bearing on the final character they form, which is a miserable little sound—*yo,* meaning a flute. Fortunately I discovered this in time by reading through a thirty-page introduction to a grammar.

I then discovered that after learning all the radicals by heart I would also have to learn an "Ode to the Radicals" written by a famous Sinologue, the Rev. J. S. Silsby. I will give only the first verse and the last as the whole occupies four large pages :

Ode to the first strokes

Beginning with unity, just as you ought,
You next make an upright and then make a dot,
Make a stroke to the left, then a curve and a crook
And you've summed up the use of one stroke in a book.

Ode to sixteen and seventeen strokes

Sixteen dragons sat on a tortoise last June
Playing seventeen flutes
And that winds up my tune.

This is not a joke but a fact. It is there in black and white in Mateer's *Mandarin Lessons*.

When I found that I had to learn seventeen different strokes to write one character with a little bleating sound like *yo*, which meant only a flute, I lost my ambition to write Chinese. After all, R.L.S. wrote "Yo ho ho, and a bottle of rum" with only twenty-one letters, and that made sense.

However, I persevered with my studies, being determined to learn to speak the language. This may sound comparatively easy, but nothing is made easy in the Chinese language. The book language one learns through a teacher is almost unintelligible to the average man in the street, who speaks colloquial Chinese, and one must pick up that separately. To make confusion more confounded, each word has five different tones or intonations. The word *tang*, for instance, may mean a hall, sugar, soup, warm or to iron, according to the tone you give it. As it is a monosyllabic language such tricks are inevitable, and if it were not, you would find them there just the same, to confuse you as much as possible. No wonder China's greatest sage was named Confucius!

Throughout the ages, Chinese literati have bent all their devilish cleverness and ingenuity to the task of evolving a language so intricate and full of pitfalls that ordinary people can never learn it. Thus the great masses may be kept in ignorance and docility, illiterate and easily duped. They have succeeded admirably.

As for me, by dint of hard swotting and putting my memory to its greatest test, I learnt two thousand characters by heart. Then I began to see characters on the walls and ceilings and sometimes dancing ring-a-ring-o'-roses round me when I was out walking. I saw the red light and stopped my studies. Too much drinking makes you see pink elephants : too much studying Chinese makes you see characters—equally frightening, because you are cold sober.

I was never a studious man and was much more inclined to an active outdoor life than to staying cooped up in my room with a wooden-faced teacher. To me study was a means to an end, and it was only my stubbornness which made me persevere. I wanted to get into closer contact with this strange people and to understand more about the country where I intended to stay and make a future for myself.

In spite of the awful living conditions there was a strange fascination in it all. Beyond the filth, the smell, the disease and the hostility there was an undoubted glamour and irresistible lure, especially after I learnt to speak a little and so was able to crack an occasional joke and get an immediate response. The Chinese are great lovers of a joke, and I began eventually to feel a contact that was never there before. The average coolie, boatman and countryman was a friendly fellow. They were clean-living and healthy, and it was a pleasure to look at them when they sat on the barber's stools on the foreshore having their heads shaved round their queues. Their pigtails grew from the top of the skull, the rest of the head being shaved daily unless they were in mourning, when they were not allowed to be shaved for a certain period. This daily rite of a rest and a shave, a little massage and having their ears cleaned, gave them a great sense of well-being and contentment. It was also a sign that they were in regular work and could afford this luxury, which was incredibly cheap. The rest of their bodies rarely saw soap and water, but they looked fine when they got up and strode away with a swagger, each queue oiled and shining after the plaiting, and with a long black silk tassel at the end. Their baggy trousers were neatly fastened round their ankles with broad black silk ribands. It was curious that they should take such pride in their queues and ankle ribands, both of which being signs of bondage imposed by their Manchu conqueror. Perhaps it was their way of turning defeat into victory, and emblems of bondage into a sign of well-being, pride and freedom from want. But then they had all they ever asked of their rulers : peace, and food, and work.

Food was then very cheap, rice costing ten shillings a picul (133⅓ lb.), pork and beef a little over one penny a pound; a small chicken cost threepence and eggs were two shillings for a hundred. Don't think that rice and vegetables were the only food of the Chinese. Even on the cargo-boats, where the crew did not earn much, I often saw pork or beef being served at the main meal, fish too, and nearly always bean-sprouts, cabbage and bean-curd.

There was general contentment among the lower classes, but higher up there was growing discontent, because they felt more and more the squeeze applied by officials well versed in the gentle art. Officials had to squeeze or starve, as this was part and parcel of the system, a system going back many centuries. They all had to buy their jobs, the highest officials from the Court at Peking, those of the lower scale from their immediate superiors. The highest job in the land, that of a Viceroy, carried an official salary of only a hundred pounds per annum and an allowance for expenses ranging from nine hundred to twelve hundred pounds per annum. From this all office expenses, staff, bodyguard, retinue, entertainments on a royal scale which must have amounted to at least ten times the sum received, had to be defrayed. Above all, tribute must be sent to the court officials in Peking to retain favour.

A couple of grades downwards there was no salary at all. The whole of this horde of officials had to live off the people, and naturally the well-to-do were milked the hardest. The system, of course, led to abuses on a very big scale, the worst feature being that nothing was done in the way of civic improvements—road-making, sanitation or welfare. With all the taxation and other exactions it would have been natural for people to expect something done, but money from taxation had an amazing knack of sticking to the official palms.

There was a story going the round of the China coast when I first came out which was a good illustration of this. The Emperor went out one evening with his retinue, and in the unlit street one of his chairbearers stumbled and the Emperor nearly fell out of his sedan-chair. He was very angry when he returned, and summoned the Minister of Finance. "The darkness in my capital is a disgrace!" he thundered. "Let lamps be lit in every street. Make an appropriation of a hundred thousand taels." The Minister of Finance went to the Minister of Public Works. "The Emperor decrees that there be light in every street. Here is an order for fifty thousand taels." The Minister of Public Works sent for the Chief of Police and said: "The Emperor has decreed that there be light in every street, and has ordered me to devote twenty-five thousand taels towards the cost. Send for contractors and have it done." The Chief of Police sent a proclamation to all householders: "The Emperor has decreed that there be light. Every householder must provide a lamp outside his house and see that it is lit and kept burning every night. Disobedience will be seriously punished." And there was light!

I often wondered whether the well-ordered, safe Concessions and settlements, where those evils did not exist and where all taxes went into improvements, were not a daily reminder to the Chinese living outside of what they were entitled to and never received. I also wondered whether this was not at the back of the anti-foreign feeling fostered by the officials. The example of these Concessions was a danger to their own livelihood, and hate thrives on envy, fear and a bad conscience.

However, there was once an honest Chinese official, Chu Yuan, who lived about 300 B.C. He drowned himself in the Mi Lo river and became the nearest equivalent to a saint in China. On the fifth day of the fifth moon, every year, the Dragon Boat Festival was held in his honour. Huge canoes shaped like dragons, with as many as eighty paddlers, searched for his body, and rice was scattered on the water to appease his spirit.

It is passing strange that *one* honest official should be so well remembered and deeply mourned. Two thousand years is a long time to wait for his reappearance or for another to take his place, but the Chinese are a very patient people.

VII

As far as I remember, it was in my third year in Chinkiang that Jock Sellars, his wife Jean and their baby daughter came to the port. Jock came from Glasgow to erect the machinery of a Chinese paper-mill on a site below Consular Bluff.

It was a desolate and lonely spot three miles or so from the Concession, right in among the reed marshes, as reeds were to be the raw material of the mill. A house of sorts had been built for Jock and his family by the Chinese mill-owner, but no furniture had been provided, and someone in the Concession put them up while they got a few odds and ends together. They expected to stay only six months or so, until the machinery was installed, and then they were going back to Scotland. The mill was a purely Chinese concern and the owners rather mean, so Jock, either because he had little money or on account of native thrift, did not buy much furniture and they were more or less camping out down there.

Neither of them had ever been out of Scotland before, and it must have been a strange and rather terrifying adventure for a woman to find herself in that little, bare brick house, completely isolated in reed swamps swarming with mosquitos. They had not even got a net and had no idea of how to take precautions against the prevalent diseases.

One afternoon we took them out to the Victoria Park and had got as far as the end of the Maloo when Jean pointed to some children playing. "Oh, look at those bonny bairns with the red turrbans!" I only just managed to stop her going over to them with her baby. Those "bonny bairns" had smallpox. The Chinese form of inoculation is to put a scab from a smallpox patient up the nostrils of the children. This gives them a mild form of smallpox, and the red turban is a sign that they have got it. I asked Jean if her baby had been vaccinated, and she shook her head. I took them straight back to the doctor and had them all done.

They were a dear couple, sincere, honest and kindly, with a burr that went straight to my heart. I had reason to be grateful to them for many happy hours spent in their bare, pathetic little home, lacking even the most elementary comforts, and yet so full of cheer and friendliness that frills and trappings did not count. What does it matter if you sit on a soap-box drinking tea out of an enamel mug, when it is three years since you have seen a woman pour out the tea or tasted scones that melt in the mouth? And then the strange wonder of seeing a real, live, white baby with fair curly hair, pink, plump and gurgling with happiness.

Hunter and I had built a boat together and often rowed down to their dwelling of an afternoon. Then we brought them back for week-ends so that they should not feel the isolation too much. Jean was plump, with a fine complexion and happy, sparkling eyes: Jock, sandy-haired, freckled. He was short and spare, all whip-cord and inclined to be serious unless he was romping around with the baby.

One Saturday we came to fetch them and found Jock in bed. He had been poorly for a few days, Jean said, listless and feverish, but had been working every day. We took them back to the Concession, and I sent for the doctor. We had just got a new one, as the old Austrian had suddenly left. The new man was quite a different type: married, very sober and highly qualified, a rare combination in an out-port doctor in those days. His name was Balean.

He diagnosed typhoid fever, and Jock and Jean were offered two adjoining rooms by an elderly German couple who lived in the Customs married quarters in the Concession. Jock was put to bed in one of them, and the long fight for his life started. With typhoid it is nursing that counts, and Jock did not have much of a chance. Jean did her best and nursed him all day, but she knew little or nothing about nursing. The volunteer men nurses took over at night, in four-hourly spells, but, although we had been doing it before and had some experience, we were far removed from the standard of professional nurses.

Jock got worse and became more and more violent when we prevented him from getting out of bed. He was still amazingly strong, and we had at last to tie him up in the customary way. A large sheet was passed under the bed and two corners tied to his wrists, after his arms had been crossed. The other two corners were tied to his ankles. He could still move, but could not get out of bed.

Jean was quite exhausted by now. Something had gone wrong with her milk on account of the anxiety, and the baby could not keep it down. The poor little thing was crying so much that Jean got practically no sleep, and hearing his baby cry may have been the cause of Jock's struggle to get out of bed.

I came on duty at ten one night, and the man I relieved told me the patient had been very violent the whole evening. Now he lay panting and exhausted, emaciated almost to a skeleton and with sunken, lifeless eyes. The end could not be far off. He kept on whispering something I could not hear until I bent down over him: he was repeating "Jean—Jean—Jean!" I untied his hands and feet and called her.

He remained motionless except that he turned his head expectantly towards the door. Then, when Jean came, he opened his wasted arms for her. I went outside into the passage and closed the door.

A few minutes later I heard the sobbing of a heart-broken woman, and knew that Jock had passed on. When silence came, I tiptoed in to see if I could help. Jean was still sitting on the bed with Jock in her arms, rocking him gently to and fro like a tired child. I tiptoed out again and closed the door.

After that Hunter and I did not care much for our boat and we soon swopped it for a pony with a Customs officer in Wuhu. I had bought a small mare the year before and had taken to riding like a duck to water.

Why a sailor on horseback should be a term of derision I have never been able to make out. On the contrary, a sailor has all the makings of a good horseman, except, perhaps, in the matter of good hands. He has perfect balance, a cool head and a strong sense of rhythm learned from walking in tune with a heaving ship. I felt at home the moment I mounted my mare for the first time, and all went well, until I turned her round for home. She had a young foal in the stable and was off like a rocket. A bolting horse on your first ride is not easy to cope with, but I somehow managed to stick on.

I loved riding in the early mornings, before the ordure cavalcade polluted the air. This daily operation took place between seven and eight, when long strings of donkeys were led in from the country with wooden containers slung from the pack-saddles, to fetch human manure, that indispensable article to the farmer and market gardener. Every householder sold it to contractors, who collected and sold it to the farmers. The stench in the Maloo when the cavalcade moved out was indescribable.

I generally rode out at six, when I went off night duty, and came back at nine. Riding was a very inexpensive hobby, the mafoo (groom) receiving sixteen shillings a month, on which he kept the pony and himself.

But the mare was constantly going shoulder lame, an old trouble I had not discovered until after I bought her, and finally I sold her again. Now I was looking forward to the arrival of the new pony which, I was told, was a very fine animal from Lord Li's famous stables in Wuhu.

Lord Li was Li Hung Chang's adopted son, and horse-breeding was one of his hobbies. The pony I was getting, a stallion, was a gift to a missionary who had done Lord Li some great service, and he, in turn, had sold him to Mr. Lelas in the Customs. Lelas wrote and told me that he found the stallion a bit too mettlesome for a beginner, and as he was keener on boating than riding he would gladly swop.

One day I got a wire saying that the pony was coming down in the steamer "Nanking", and Hunter and I went to receive him. There was almost a riot at the landing-stage when we arrived, with people shouting and scattering in all directions.

In the middle of the crowd came something like a huge black panther, dancing on his hind legs, the two front feet pawing the air. It seemed to be all flashing teeth and eyes, and a mafoo was dangling at the end of the halter, his feet kicking the empty air.

Then the animal screamed, swapped ends, and a stout Chinese woman hurtled backwards.

This apparently was Lelas's "mettlesome" steed, now ours. The Chinese woman was badly hurt and the first thing we had to do was to pay her five dollars compensation. Hunter suddenly decided that he did not want anything to do with the pony and offered me his share for twenty dollars. The stallion was all mine before we got him off the landing-stage. The mafoo was hanging on for dear life, and the pony's hooves exploded in all directions until he had a wide clear space around him.

He was the most beautiful animal I had ever seen, nearly black, with a coat like satin, a long mane flowing from a proudly arched neck, a tail that almost touched the ground, and a handsome head with flashing eyes. The mafoo called him "Kweitzu" (devil), and I named him Satan. I never had a dull moment as long as I owned him, and, for the Concession, the Wild West had arrived.

I gave Satan bran mash the first night, to soothe him and steady his frayed nerves. Then I offered him a lump of sugar. This was apparently a deadly insult, for with a vicious snap he tore the sleeve clean off my coat, a good deal of shirt went with it and a slice out of my bicep. I gathered from this that he wanted to be alone.

I soon found out that his antics on arrival were not caused by an upsetting journey, the noisy crowd or the excitement. He was like that as long as I had him, except when I rode him. Then he was a real gentleman, with a wonderful turn of speed, and he was a joy to ride. The trouble was in putting on the saddle and then mounting him. These necessary preliminaries could be very dangerous and the only solution was to hogtie him first, then lash his neck to a tree and then saddle him. After I had then mounted, the mafoo undid the ropes and away we went at great speed, but he never tried to unseat me once I was in the saddle. I suppose he had had all his fun in resisting being saddled and giving us endless trouble. After that, like a good sport, he gave me a wonderful ride, a ride that never seemed to tire him or dampen his spirits. On the return trip through the Concession I was always hailed with what became a stock greeting: "Still alive?"

It was certainly a good way of working off steam after Jock's death, but it was becoming increasingly dangerous, and very expensive, as I had to pay a good deal of compensation to people Satan had hurt. Two mafoos gave notice in one month, and I began to wonder why my pony seemed to be getting worse tempered until I discovered one day that my own boy, Ah Ping, was tormenting him with a long bamboo stick while the animal was tied up, much to the entertainment of the other boys. However, Satan dealt with him before I had time to run down and do it myself. He gave a savage pull and broke the halter, wheeled on the boy like a tiger, and before the terrified Ah Ping could reach the safety of the kitchen he bit him in the face and tore half his cheek out, and then raced madly round the backyard. It took us half an hour to secure him.

Of course all the wise men in the Club gave me good advice as to how to manage him, and told me all the wrong things I was doing. I had never pretended to know anything about horse management, but their counsel rather riled me. So, one day, when Rosser, one of the horse-breakers, told me that Satan had never been properly broken in and that he never would be much good until disciplined, I said, "Well, why don't you offer to do it? You are a horse-breaker!"

So Rosser offered to start the next day. Nearly all the fellows in the Customs were on the back veranda to watch the show that afternoon, and few of them will ever forget it. Rosser was too confident, and I think he wanted to show off a bit. He never even got into the saddle after undoing the halter, for in the next second Satan was on him like a tiger, nearly tearing him to pieces with his teeth. The mafoo and I were the only two with him, and we had to stun Satan with bamboo poles to save Rosser's life. While the mafoo secured Satan, I dragged Rosser to safety.

He spent three weeks in hospital in Shanghai, and that was the end of Satan's career so far as I was concerned. I received a letter from the Consul demanding his destruction or removal from the Concession, as he was considered to be a public danger. I sold him to a Chinese horsebreeder and saw him off in a cloud of dust and whirling hooves, with the new owner and a mafoo frantically holding on to him for dear life: unbroken to the end. He left a memory of something really proud and untamable, a vision of flashing eyes and teeth, flowing mane and shining satin coat. A creature not meant for cities and crowds or for men to paw, saddle and ride.

And I am sure Satan felt that too, sure that he felt the degradation of streets and crowds, of restraining hands and halters, and that his whole fine spirit rebelled. He belonged to the vast rolling grasslands and unbroken horizons of the Mongolian steppes. I could only regret that I was unable to take him there and set him free.

VIII

When the Concession really got me down I "lifted up mine eyes unto the hills" and got new strength from them. A ride of about eight miles took me to a hill called Wu Chow where for many years there had been a community shooting bungalow for those who were keen on wild boar-shooting.

It was rather an expensive sport as it required about fifteen beaters at fifty cents (or one shilling) each a day. Satan had been a far from cheap hobby, and I was pretty near broke. However, a rifle had to be bought and fortunately I came across an ancient Lee-Metford single-shot carbine used in the Boer War. I bought it for fifteen dollars.

In view of the daily cost it was important to get shooting companions to share in the beating expenses. No serious shooting had been done out there for several years, and no one in the port seemed to know the ropes. I went out one week-end to investigate and to get away from everybody, most of all from my old bored self.

I had been through a long spell of shunning people, a phase which we generally experienced in turn. One of my troubles was that I did not like spirits, which were the cheapest form of relaxation, for "Black & White" or any good proprietary kind of whisky cost only two dollars a bottle, and gin one-fifty, so one could go on a glorious spree for next to nothing and forget your troubles for a while.

However, I drank only when I was thirsty, and then one whisky and soda was enough, and I had an absurd objection to seeing people so drunk that they had to be carried home from the Club. In fact, I was turning into a frightful prig. I allowed the brawls in the Club to get on my nerves, too, instead of taking it as a healthy sign that people *could* brawl rather than become high-minded and morose like some of us. In fact, I was a sick man, soul sick, when I sought the hills.

It was beautiful out there, amid real pine-woods. Near the bungalow was a small monastery and the monks in their wisdom did not allow any wood-cutting on their property. The bungalow was clean and well kept by the caretaker. Chun was his name so far as I remember, a sinister-looking rogue with a squint, who rarely smiled. Perhaps it was the loneliness which made him morose and surly. He had no wife, at least, not officially, and the pay was so small that he could barely live on it, for it was expected that he would make a good deal of extra money from visitors. He brightened up when I ordered supper and told him I was staying for the night.

There were two big rooms, plainly but comfortably furnished, and the kitchen and scullery were outside. A number of good books were on the shelves and I found a lot of old visitors' books, some dating back to the early 'eighties. I had no idea the bungalow was so old, and I became so immersed in the books that I forgot everything else, until Chun came in with the supper. It was October and getting chilly at night, so I told him to get a fire going in the big round stove, as I wanted to have a long, cosy browse afterwards.

Chun was becoming quite amiable, and started a long story in pidgin about a bewitched boar, a big fearsome brute, which no one could kill. I knew how superstitious the Chinese were and took the whole story with a pinch of salt, until he took out one of the visitors' books and showed me an account of a shoot written by a Mr. Currie, an old-timer no longer in the port. Chun must have memorised the place for he knew no written English, and it was clear that Mr. Currie—or "Cullee", as he called him—was Chun's great hero, and when Currie roamed the hills after pig that was the Golden Age for Chun. He got more and more excited: "That time, Master, plenty man come shootee shootee pig. Evely week four five piecee man come. My catchee plenty cumsha (tips). My velly solly Mista Cullee have go homeside."

After he had cleared away the supper things I settled down with the visitors' book. There were some excellent accounts of pig-shoots by Currie and his companions, ranging over several years, and with all the usual ups and downs, failures and successes. It was clear that they were written by a man who loved the sport and loved the hills, a keen shot and a good one, above all a very good sport who took his failures with a grin and exposed all his mistakes with an engaging candour. There were little gems of descriptive story-telling that made you feel you were with him in all his adventures, and you got to know his favourite spots by his brief and vivid descriptions and little sketches.

I came eventually to several stories about a mystery pig he called the Old Grey Boar, a hermit who was never seen in company with other pigs or who, as he explained it, had been thrown out by the other pigs because he was too bad-tempered. Now this pig could apparently carry without discomfort all the lead the hunters could pump into him, and he had given them the slip on several occasions when they felt sure they had bagged him. Currie always went out with three companions, but he alone wrote up the day. Finally he mentioned that the Chinese beaters firmly believed he was a Joss pig that could not be killed. They were also afraid of him, for after he had been wounded he terrorised the villagers, especially the grass-cutters, and had killed several of them. I did not pay much attention to the story at the time, but I was fascinated by Currie's general descriptions and sat up reading till after midnight. I think I got pig fever that night, a great urge to roam those hills with a few good companions like Currie and, like him, to find new strength up there. Finding good companions was the rub, and the only one I could think of was Hunter. The others had given up the struggle and would not move out of the Club; the hills were too far out and pig-shooting too much like hard work.

The next day I explored the country around and made myself familiar with the various ranges of hills. To the south was a long range called Chang Shan, on the top of which was a small temple. In between the two main mountains were rolling hills with the main road to Chinkiang twisting through the valley, past a solitary hill like a hog's back, sticking out of the flat country to eastward. This was called Tung Shan, and close to its northern base lay Chakamen, or the beaters' village, as we called it, for most of the beaters lived there.

Chakamen was a busy little village, being a halting place where wayfarers stopped for a meal or a cup of tea. It was typically Chinese, straggling, unkempt and unswept, with trestle tables standing untidily in the narrow street outside the shops and eating-houses where travellers or local patrons would sit down and enjoy their food or tea. The Chinese love the noise and bustle of a street and get as close to it as they can when taking their ease. They appear impervious to smells—to give them a polite name—and a little dust more or less is of no importance.

Through the street went string after string of donkeys, carrying bags of rice or wheat to market, and a stream of wheelbarrow coolies without which no village scene in China is ever complete. They come straining and swaying along the uneven slippery cobbles, muscles rippling and sweat running off them even in the cold weather, and every barrow squealing like a stuck pig.

The Chinese wheelbarrow is entirely different from ours. The wheel is very large and in the centre of the barrow, and on either side of the wheel is a shelf for cargo. They can carry incredible loads because the full weight is borne by the wheel bearings, and it is common to see four pigs going to market in this way, two being lashed to each shelf. With the barrow bearings and the pigs having a squealing match the row is deafening. When I think of a real beast of burden, I think of the Chinese wheelbarrow coolie staggering along. The handle-bars are wide apart, a webbed band from the end of each bar goes over the coolie's shoulders and takes part of the weight, but it requires a fine sense of balance and great strength to push the barrow and prevent it from toppling over. Over the coolie's forehead, above the eye-brows, is a band to prevent the sweat from running into his eyes. That sweatband is the badge of his servitude as a poorly paid beast of burden. Like many others, he is a purely Chinese institution, so common that he is part of the daily scene on any Chinese road, and as such unnoticed except by a fool foreigner with a heart.

There is a small pot of oil dangling from every barrow. It is meant for the bearings, but is seldom used. I think the squealing bearings are regarded by the barrow coolies as a substitute for their own voices. All other coolies have a sing-song in rhythm with their pace, but the barrow coolie, with his eyes riveted on the load and the road ahead, dare not let his attention wander for a moment, neither has he any breath left for singing, so the barrow must provide the only working song he knows.

This was Chakamen as I saw it the first time I went there. Just that one narrow road leading through it, carrying the traffic of the countryside. The beater boss, Tah Gu Tzu, had invited me to tea, and a number of beaters crowded around us. Tah Gu Tzu was very tall and spare, with sharp eyes, and the look of the shikari about him was quite unmistakable. I was talking about the chances of getting pig, which I thought were slim, as there was still far too much cover. He agreed, but at the same time he told me that the whole village would be out during the week cutting grass on the southern slopes of Wu Chow Shan, and by next Sunday there would be one or two gullies well worth beating. I arranged to be there early in the morning, and ordered twelve beaters as there would be only two guns.

There is something very stirring about one's first venture in a new sport. Pig-shooting, I knew, could be very exciting, and I had been busy oiling and cleaning my rifle days before going out. The bullet points had to be filed off to make them mushroom, for the pigs were very hard to kill with a plain nickel bullet.

It was a bright sunny morning when we rode out just after daybreak. The Golden Island Pagoda stood glittering in the first sunrays, and farther west the hills lay warm and inviting. Scouts were out looking for us, and no sooner did we approach Chakamen than we heard the news being shouted in the streets: "Huang Mao lai la!" (Yellowhair is coming!). Like most foreigners I had received a nickname, and with my mop of fair hair I was just begging for a name like Huang Mao. All was bustle in Tah Gu Tzu's house, tea was brought and tongues were wagging.

A big sounder of pig had been seen on Wu Chow Shan. It was easy to see that everyone was excited, for no pig-shooting had been done for a number of years, and this looked like old times again. They were all as keen as mustard, and when Tah Gu Tzu shouted "Tsau la!" (Go!) they jumped up and started off almost at a trot.

It took us nearly half an hour's hard walking to get to the first beat, a gully with thick cover of tall grass, thorn bushes and dwarf bamboo. On one side of the gully a fairly wide swathe had been cut, which the pigs would have to cross if driven out of the thick cover. All we startled there was a hog-deer, which we let run unharmed.

It did not seem to be our lucky day, for we beat cover after cover without result. However, that did not matter. The anticipation and excitement were always there from the beginning to the end of each beat. We had lunch on the sunny hillside and beat our way back towards the bungalow in the afternoon. Then everything happened at once.

One of the beaters pointed excitedly towards a bush, another threw a big rock in that direction and the whole hillside seemed to explode with sound. First the wild, ear-splitting yells of the beaters: "Tsooh! Tsooh! Tsooh!"* and then a mighty crashing in the bushes. Three swathes were cut by heavy bodies tearing through the dense cover at great speed, but nothing could be seen to shoot at. I stood and shivered with buck-fever, excitement and chagrin, watching the swathes moving downhill with increasing speed. Then I saw a great grizzly body, mostly head and shoulders, and fired—a miss apparently: fired again—another miss.

No wonder! The suddenness and excitement had been too much for me. Then I heard Hunter firing. He had a 44 Winchester repeater, firing heavy lead bullets out of black-powder cartridges, which made a lot of smoke. Three shots, and then a yell: "Da huai la! Da huai la!" (He is wounded.) Just after came another shot, and a triumphant chant: "Su la!" (Dead.)

Hunter was higher up the hill, and I went up to inspect his kill, a fine young boar. The beaters, all highly elated, were busy gralloching him when I reached them.

And late in the afternoon, in one of the last beats, luck came my way too, and I did not muff my shot this time. There came the same frenzied yelling and a warning: "Hui tau chy la!" (He has broken back.) Tah Gu Tzu grabbed me by the arm and tore off. We ran like hares through the beater line, making for the top of a small hillock. As soon as we arrived we spotted him, as big as a baby elephant, trotting across an open space.

It was a long shot, but I did not miss this time. He ran a few

* Pig

paces, stumbled, got up again and ran another short distance. Then he dropped and stayed down.

Alas for my baby elephant—he had dwindled considerably in size by the time I reached him. He was only a little bigger than Hunter's, probably two hundred pounds: but it is always like that when you shoot your first wild boar. It is the biggest thing on four feet you have ever seen, the grandest and most ferocious-looking animal in the world, and you are a damned fine shot to have brought him down.

Two boars in one day was something to set tongues wagging in Chinkiang, and next time we went out Harry Singer came with us. From then on the three of us were out nearly every week-end as long as the season lasted. Old Chun at the bungalow became almost human again, for old times had come back to the hills.

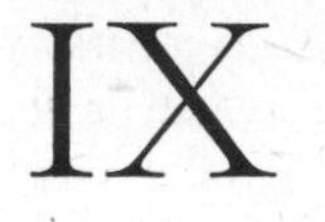

Most people may think that one pig-shoot is very much like another, but, believe me, every time you go out is a new adventure. The mountain boar we were hunting is the toughest, fastest, most cunning creature on four legs and is much bigger than the plains pig of India. The average run of a full-grown boar is about two hundred and fifty pounds, but some of them grow to an enormous size, my three biggest being 395, 400 and 410 pounds: all bone, gristle and muscle.

It was these big brutes that made the sport so fascinating; they were all personalities, extremely wily and very dangerous because they nearly always charged. Although they lived in localities well known to the beaters they were difficult to get and special plans of campaign had to be devised for each of them. Most sportsmen think it an easy matter to hit such a large target even when he is charging at full speed—until they face a boar. Then they find that bullets have absolutely no effect on him, and, unless, like me, they are very lucky, they will never live to face another. After I shot my first boar I haunted the hills every week-end that season, and shot eight in all. It was one of those eight that taught me a very useful lesson.

I had borrowed for that occasion a 30-30 Marlin repeater, with a long magazine running the whole length of the barrel and taking fourteen cartridges. I was standing on a bare hillock and had wounded a boar farther down near the base. He charged me, coming straight up the bare hillside. "What an easy target!" I said to myself, as I opened fire at about a hundred yards. That great shaggy head seemed as easy to hit as a barn-door, and I fired again and again, but still he came on; nothing seemed to hurt him. He was bleeding a lot but going as strong as ever. When he was

ATE 3

Top: The Bund, Chinkiang, Customs House
Bottom: Huang Shan House

PLATE 4

Top: Outside our field dressing station at Ma Chung. Dr. Stephenson at the door
Bottom: Our back premises at Ma Chung. Lightly wounded awaiting treatment

five paces away I had only two shots left. The enormous shaggy head and blazing eyes were terrifying. He was fury personified, and it was now too late to jump aside. I fired when he was almost on top of me, right into those furious eyes, and he stopped dead. He wasn't badly hit, only blinded by the gun-flash and probably stunned. I fired the last shot into his ear as he turned his head, and he dropped in his tracks.

An old hand from Shanghai who was with me on that hunt, watched the last stages of the charge and came up when I was ruefully examining the pig, wondering why I had not been able to stop him. Some bullets had knocked off bits of skin here and there, some had ploughed through the skin of his sloping forehead, most of them had glanced off, and none of them had done any real harm. My companion poked the head with his shooting-stick: "All wrong," he said. "Waste of ammunition, firing long shots at a charging pig—like firing at the sharp end of a bone wedge. You've got to wait, wait till he's five paces away—three is better—then fire down into the brainpan. One shot's enough, but you mustn't muff it."

All very fine, I thought, but who the hell is going to wait till he's only five paces off—"three is better," I mimicked, and turned my attention to the gralloching. But I saw the old hand bring it off later in the day, neatly and cleanly. And I saw he was right.

There is absolutely nothing vital to hit during that headlong rush. The huge head was all you could see, all bone, and sloping backwards. The old hand didn't lift his rifle, even, until the boar was fifteen yards off, and then when he was almost on top of him and the rifle was pointing down, the crack of the shot rang out and the boar dropped at his feet. Therc was a neat hole in his brainpan, a target no bigger than a very small saucer.

It took me a long time before I had the nerve to do that, but once it is successfully done, the whole thrill of that exciting game is concentrated in the moment when you lift your rifle and fire, with the boar almost dropping on your feet. It is like a matador's *coup de grâce*, a fine art and very dangerous, only you are generally alone when you do it, and no discriminating public rewards a first-class performance by showering you with gifts. But neither do you suffer any indignities if you bungle the job. You are just carried off and buried. And here I am reminded of the story of the Old Grey Boar.

Towards the end of November that year, a young Frenchman was carried in on a door by the beaters and taken to the hospital, where he died. He had come from Shanghai on a shooting holiday, and I had the whole story from Tah Gu Tzu. Having drawn a blank pig-shooting the first day, he decided to go pheasant-shooting the next.

As a rule we had buckshot of S.S.G. in the left barrel in case we ran into deer, and that was the cause of the trouble. The Frenchman did not run into deer, but he aroused a huge boar by firing at a pheasant, and then fired the buckshot into the boar at twenty yards. The boar charged, knocked the Frenchman down, broke both his legs, rammed a tusk into his side and tore out some of his ribs. Then he trotted off into the bushes in a rage, for the buckshot must have hurt a good deal.

Tah Gu Tzu was rather evasive when I asked him to identify the boar. There were only three boars of that big size: the Old Grey Boar, the Big Stranger—a newcomer—and the White Boar with the broken tusk.

The Old Grey Boar had not been heard of for a long time, or perhaps Tah Gu Tzu had purposely omitted to talk about him so as not to put any ideas into my head about going after him. I got suspicious and questioned another of the beaters, Mahtzu (the pockmarked). I soon learned that I was right and that the offender was the Old Grey Boar. A week later I was out in the hills again and found the countryside humming with news. The Old Grey Boar had been on the rampage ever since, two grass-cutters had been killed and now the grass-cutters dared not go out in certain localities. To add insult to injury Old Grey had last been seen on Tung Shan, close to Tah Gu Tzu's house, and now Tung Shan was closed to grass-cutting, just where Tah Gu Tzu had his own cutting rights. This, of course, made him lose face in the district. There had been a good deal of gossip about this in Chakamen, and at the food-stalls many rude jokes were made about Tah Gu Tzu and his "guest." To make a Chinaman lose face is an unforgivable sin, and the whole village and countryside were feeling the pinch and were, in addition, very frightened.

I had arranged to go out with Harry Singer early on Christmas

Day. We had decided to go after the Old Grey Boar, in spite of Tah Gu Tzu's objections, and to force an issue. On our arrival the villagers crowded around us and I made a short harangue in Chinese to tell them that we were determined to shoot the Old Grey Boar, or Lao Chu Chu (Old Uncle), as they called him. I ended very grandly: "Ni men doh chi ko-ni men doh hrai pah. I ting yao dah tah!" (You are all eating bitterness, you are all frightened. Surely he must be killed!) There was a shout of approval and all Tah Gu Tzu's opposition wilted under the pressure of public opinion, if it had not already vanished because of his losing face.

He suddenly banged the table and shouted: "Tsau lah, dah Tung Shan" (Get going, beat Tung Shan), and the shout was taken up by the beaters like a challenge. We were off, straight up the hill. The lower part was densely covered with tall grass and scrub bamboo, and half-way to the top was a belt of stunted firs. It was difficult country to shoot over because the field of vision was limited and broken by outcrops of rocks and by trees. I was taking the top of the hill, and Harry placed himself in the fields on the other side to stop the boar's escape in that direction, if possible.

Tah Gu Tzu was my gun-bearer, and Mahtzu, a sturdy little fiery fellow, deeply marked with smallpox, went with Harry. It was not that we needed any one to carry our guns, but their keen sight and knowledge of the country made the bearers invaluable.

I was rather puffed when we reached the top of the steep slope. Below us lay a little gully full of jumbled rocks and isolated dwarf pines. The cover was dense: tall grass, yellow and ready for the sickle, dwarf bamboo and thorn thickets. Tah Gu Tzu was positive that the Old Grey Boar was lying doggo in a little hollow beyond the far ridge of the gully and that he would cross here when driven out. It seemed incredible luck to me to be so close to this great beast, and in the very first beat too. I whispered this to Tah Gu Tzu, and had every reason to reflect on his reply for the rest of the day: "Ha me yu da tah." (He is not killed yet.)

The beaters were now drawing near and we could hear their shouts and an occasional rock crashing through the bushes. The tenseness grew. Every sense was alert and straining, and my knuckles were white from gripping the rifle. Tah Gu Tzu stood like a statue, his eyes riveted on the ridge to the right. Then his hand came up like a flash and he pointed. Something was moving in the dense cover. I spotted it too, and watched it move slowly towards the edge of the large patch of scrub bamboo about fifty yards to the right. The beast itself was invisible and we could only hear a faint rustling and see the thin bamboo stems quiver. I was trembling all over with buck-fever before I had even seen what it was, but I was pretty sure it was a large boar, and the deadly slow invisible advance was getting on my nerves. Then, without warning, a huge grey shape hurled itself through the tall grass of the gully, followed by an ear-splitting yell from the beaters: "Tsooh! Tsooh!" (Pig! Pig!) I just caught a glimpse of his enormous shoulders and shaggy head with big gleaming tusks, but there was no time to draw a bead, for he disappeared in a flash behind a rock, and stopped.

Then came another lightning dash downhill, a sharp swerve to the left, some rapid zigzags amongst an outcrop of rocks, a bound over the ridge on my left and he had disappeared. I just caught a glimpse of him between two fir trees as he cleared the ridge with an easy, even graceful leap in spite of his great bulk. It was a grand sight, and some compensation for his getaway.

It was all over in a few moments; and although I rushed after him down the steep slope until I reached the first open space, it was useless and I had missed my first chance.

He had certainly outwitted us, and as I sat down for a moment to get my wind and inspect my many scratches, I considered his clever way of making use of the cover and thought of what Chun at the bungalow had told me: "He too muchee clever, he have got savvy box alleesame man." Not that I had expected to get him with the first shot in the first beat, but I had not even had a chance of getting him on the front sight.

Tah Gu Tzu stood silently watching the fields below. The boar still had to get past Harry down there, but I could see that Tah Gu Tzu had ruled Harry out of his calculation already, as his eyes were fixed on a distant field over on our left. Then he said, almost casually: "There he goes!" and pointed. The Old Grey Boar was walking quite leisurely through a field, clean out of range, but even at that distance he looked a monster.

He was making for a small village, and soon we heard the people yelling, and saw them scatter. Tah Gu Tzu watched him out of sight, and then said: "He has gone to Chang Shan and we had better move on." We joined Harry and the beaters down in the fields. Harry had heard all the excitement but had not seen a thing. The beaters were jabbering away greatly excited, but Tah Gu Tzu was silent for a long time, looking towards the Chang Shan range and thinking things over. Then he called the beaters and gave rapid orders. They were to start at the extreme end of the range and beat slowly and carefully towards Joss-house gully where we would be waiting for them. Chang Shan is a long range, about a thousand feet high, and Harry was to take the upper beat while I took station half-way between him and the foot of the hill.

It took the beaters three-quarters of an hour to reach us, and they had drawn a blank. Now we started on a gully where Tah Gu Tzu felt sure the Old Grey Boar had taken cover. It was densely covered with fir trees and thick undergrowth, almost hopeless for shooting over.

Tah Gu Tzu took us from one retreat to another, but the cover was so dense and the country so broken that we never got a shot at him. We just heard the frenzied yells of the beaters and the boar crashing through the undergrowth. We dashed off through thorns and bamboo in the hopes of a shot, but he chose the country too cleverly. This game went on relentlessly for over six hours. The beaters were weary and in rags, and were beginning to be demoralised, for the boar was becoming more and more savage and had knocked three of them over. We beat one more gully, and then I suggested to Tah Gu Tzu that we had a little rest. It was after three o'clock in the afternoon, and we had not had sup nor bite since we started. We rested on the crest of a ridge where there was only a sprinkling of fir trees on the slope below us. The Old Grey Boar was on a densely wooded hillock ahead of us but, beyond, we were coming to open country where our chances would be better if we succeeded in driving him away from the pine belts. "If," that was the question.

Tah Gu Tzu figured out the possibilities while we were resting. He was taking no chances after the dance the Old Boar had led us. He told us that he was almost certain the pig would try to break back again, and we would have to be prepared for this. If he did, the gully was the only place where there was a chance to shoot him.

And so it was arranged that Harry should cover the top of the hillock where he would be in a position to watch both the country ahead and the gully behind. I should take the lower position and follow behind the beater line, in case he broke back lower than Harry's field of fire. The rest had done the beaters good and they started off in high spirits, knowing that the worst was over now.

They lined up on the edge of the wooded hillock as soon as Harry was in position, and I followed on their heels. With every sense on the alert I moved along the narrow winding pig path where the going was better than in the rough cover. Tah Gu Tzu was just ahead, striding along with springy, soundless steps. We were nearly through the wood, and something might happen at any moment. Above us the beater line was advancing steadily through the grass and bushes between the firs. Suddenly the two nearest to us halted and one of them started to point ahead, very excitedly. We stood still and waited.

There came a piercing shriek followed by a rumbling noise, half grunt, half roar, and a beater was catapulted down the steep slope. At the same moment I saw the great boar hurtling down the hill and crashing through the bushes with incredible speed.

I caught only a few flashes of him between the trees, and there was not the ghost of a chance to shoot. Bedlam was loose all around for the beaters were yelling like maniacs, and even Tah Gu Tzu was leaping into the air with excitement and shouting and pointing to the gully at the back. I was off like a streak. I had about three hundred yards to cover before I could get to the edge of the gully, and my only hope of a shot was to get there before the boar had crossed over. I ran as I have never run before and when about half-way I heard Harry open fire: Ping! Ping! Ping! Three slow and deliberate shots, but these were followed by a fusillade so fast that I felt Harry had got demoralised. The firing stopped, and I pelted on. When I reached the edge my heart was going like a sledge-hammer and my lungs were nearly bursting. Harry was running down the hill towards me, trying to reload, but dropping most of the cartridges in the excitement. And well he might, for on the opposite slope stood the Old Grey Boar stock-still and looking at us. He was right in the open too, only a hundred yards away, and broadside on.

It was just as if he challenged us to shoot him, for he turned his head and looked at us with indifference. He was magnificent.

I knew I had to act quickly before I fell under the spell of that great beast, and I fired a snap shot at him. The bullet struck a rock a couple of inches above his back. I pushed in another cartridge, drew a deep breath and prayed that my heaving chest would keep still only for a moment. The Old Grey Boar had not even stirred, but looked at me with a fixed stare. Then I squeezed the trigger. The beast made a sudden startled movement, as if stung, and streaked up the hill at a tremendous speed. He was over the top and away before I could reload and get in another shot, and I dashed after him with an empty rifle.

Down the slope I slithered, through thorns and brambles which tore my clothes to bits, and then up the other side as fast as I could scramble. There was a faint hope of a shot if I could only get to the top before he had crossed the next gully. When I reached the ridge I saw at once that I had mistaken the contour of the hill. There was no gully immediately beyond the ridge, but a long stretch of broken country. It was still worth an effort though, for I knew the boar was hit and might not travel fast.

I sprinted on and on until finally I reached the next gully. It was empty. Not a thing in sight, and no movement anywhere.

At first I refused to believe that he had got away after all, and I stood looking and listening for a long time. Then I examined the whole length of the ridge for blood spoor, but there was not a sign. Suddenly I felt very tired and worn out and flung myself down in the grass. Then I thought of the poor weary, tattered beaters and their disappointment, and started to take an interest in my torn legs, hands and face. They were gashed with thorns, but I had felt nothing in the excitement. I looked at the open breach of the rifle and cursed myself for a fool, running after a wounded boar with an empty rifle.

I had expected Tah Gu Tzu to be with me by now and wondered why he had not come. We might still find blood spoor, and there was plenty of daylight left. Then I heard a shout and a triumphant yell which sent me to my feet like an electric shock: "Su la! Su la! Ta tsooh su la!" (Dead! Dead! The great boar is dead.)

As I ran back I could hear the beaters yelling like maniacs and see them dancing a wild dance on the hillside. Suddenly I felt limp and slowed down to a walk. The beaters ran up to meet me, laughing and jabbering, but I did not even hear what they were saying, and for the life of me I could not share in their joy and triumph. Harry and a few of the beaters stood round the boar as I came up, and Tah Gu Tzu was digging S.S.G. pellets out of his side. He looked magnificent where he lay, with his eyes closed and his great shaggy head resting on a moss-covered rock. There was a tiny hole a couple of inches behind the point of his huge shoulder, and a slight trickle of blood on the skin below the hole. I don't know whether I communicated my own feelings to the rest of them, or if it was spontaneous, but they all stopped talking and, standing solemnly round the Old Grey Boar, East and West paid silent tribute to the King of the Hills.

He was carried down to Chakamen with great pomp and ceremony on fir poles, by six beaters and if you have heard the sing-song of the carrying coolies you will have a faint idea of what the procession was like.

The beaters knew they were carrying no ordinary burden, and they sang accordingly. It was a wild triumphant chorus, for the solemn hour had passed, and now they were telling the whole world the great news. Men, women and children rushed out from the villages and joined them. The old headmen came out and kow-towed in thanks, and all were in high spirits. The procession swelled, and it looked almost like an army when we entered Chakamen. Tah Gu Tzu was in the lead stepping out with long effortless strides, for this was his day of triumph, and he certainly deserved all the "face" he could get.

Harry was silent and rather sick with himself for making such a mess of his shooting. He confided to me that when the Old Grey Boar stood there and looked at him he became so dithery that he could not hold his rifle steady. He could see that I had hit him but he did not think my bullets heavy enough to kill, and when he saw the boar disappear over the top at great speed he felt sure we should never see him again.

Not so Tah Gu Tzu. He had marked carefully the spot where the boar crossed the range, had run up to investigate at once and there he found slight blood spoor which led straight to the dead boar only fifty yards farther in. So this was certainly Tah Gu Tzu's day.

It was the greatest excitement they had ever known at Chakamen, and the whole village was packed. The Old Grey Boar lay in state on one of the big trestle tables for all the villagers to see at close quarters. All the beaters were surrounded by the crowd and had to tell them again and again every detail of the day's shoot, and the kill. The story lost nothing in the telling, I can assure you. Every Chinese is a born actor, and each episode of the day was enacted in front of us with priceless graphic gestures and mimicry, as we sat and had tea while our ponies were being saddled.

Then we rode home, but as I looked up at the deep blue dome of Tung Shan, I was touched by sadness as I thought of the old warrior who would no longer roam the hills. I had never felt like that before about wild boar.

CHINA TRADER

I HAD been four years in Chinkiang before I had my first attack of malaria. It was a wonder that I had escaped so long and that I was still alive.

I can only put it down to the iron constitution with which life at sea had blessed me, and the healthy outdoor life I had sought as a means of saving my reason. Few escaped malaria, though, for in the breathless summer nights sleep was impossible under a mosquito net, and without a net four hours' fitful sleep was as much as one expected and generally less than one got because of mosquito bites.

The only real illness I had had was one attack of dengue fever when for four days I endured agonies in every bone in my body, as if a steam-roller had smashed all of them. An all-merciful providence has ordained that one gets dengue only once, but the same providence has been a good deal more lavish with malaria. I had three bouts, all severe, but on the whole I was lucky to have escaped with nothing worse, for ten of the original thirty-five Europeans in the port had died, two were in a lunatic asylum, and two had cut their throats (one unsuccessfully), so the casualty list was very heavy.

However, the worst period was now over, for the Shanghai-Nanking railway had been completed, Chinkiang became divisional headquarters, and a small hospital was built on a hill above the Maloo. It was chiefly for Chinese, but two beds were available for foreigners, and there was an operating-theatre and a nurse. Her name was Ethel Halley, she was fifty-five-ish and all of fifteen stone. It was purely coincidental that she arrived at the same time as Halley's comet, which at that time was greatly disturbing the Chinese masses. There had been a great deal of agitation among the Chinese concerning the railway tunnel which had to be made through the Mud Fort hill, thus angering the feng shui, or spirits of wind and water, and the necromancers had a very busy and lucrative time advising people as to what precautions they must take to avoid the evil consequences.

The coming of Halley's comet left the Chinese in trembling and fear. Here was a sign from heaven that this wanton act of the foreign devils had been noted and disapproved by the gods. Then came an even more sinister sign; a partial eclipse of the moon, that brought every Chinese householder out beating gongs and madly firing off crackers.

What could one do when the people were so incredibly ignorant and superstitious? To the vast majority an eclipse of the sun or moon means that a monster is trying to swallow them, and it has to be driven away by the most frightful din they can make with gongs, drums and crackers. The noise in a Chinese city at such times is deafening, but was one of the things we soon took for granted. But in this case the comet and eclipse were used by trouble-makers to stir up anti-foreign feeling, and two gunboats had to be stationed in the harbour before things simmered down.

Another cause of trouble was that the Chinese were using the permanent way of the railway as a highway, especially in rainy weather when their own mud roads were almost impassable. There was not a single metalled road in the whole province—I doubt if there was one in the whole Empire—and the permanent way was the only place where they could walk dry-shod. Having no idea of the speed of a train, they did not get out of the way in time and were often maimed or killed, and it was for them that the hospital had been built.

We, of the old nursing brigade, often had to assist at operations when Nurse Halley was worn out. One of my first was the amputation of an arm. I didn't mind at all while the doctor was sawing and I was holding the arm in position, but I nearly fainted when he had cut through and I was holding on to the severed arm when it fell away.

A great deal of money was paid out in compensation in the early days of the railway, especially to dependents of those killed, but payments had to be stopped as it was found that the Chinese put their dead out on the line in order to turn an honest penny. I was up at the hospital when Dr. Balean discovered a case that really could be proved, when formerly he had had only suspicions. This corpse was really "high," and the doctor was furious. In the front hall the widow and several children were playing their parts by crying and wailing away in a typical Chinese manner. He was deeply shocked and turned on them and chased them out. After that incident there was a very thorough investigation into every accident.

That same year the Standard Oil Company, the Asiatic Petroleum Company and the British-American Tobacco Company opened in a big way in Chinkiang, and twelve new residents arrived. Two German firms also opened branches and sent up managers. They were after the rapidly growing oilseed business from the interior, sesamum seeds and peanuts mostly, for which there was an increasing demand from Europe. To us old-timers the worst was now over, for what with new people, new activities and constant visitors from Shanghai and Nanking, the Concession and we took a new lease of life.

My only regular visitor at this time was Dr. Stephenson from the American Presbyterian Mission, out in the hills. He was a young doctor practising in the States when he heard of the great need for doctors in the Mission field in China, and joined as a medical missionary. He was not greatly interested in converting the Chinese, but he was deeply concerned with curing them, especially the millions of desperately poor for whom absolutely nothing was done by the Chinese authorities.

On arrival, he found that he was expected to take an active part in missionary work, prayer meetings and other activities which had nothing to do with doctoring, and also that his mission regarded smoking as a sin. He was a heavy smoker and did not like being censured for it. He had unburdened himself to me just after we became friendly, through a chance meeting when I was out shooting. After that he came occasionally for a chat and a smoke and got rid of a lot of steam while furiously puffing at his pipe. He was a man of few words but had a knack of making you understand his long silences, broken only by an occasional short sentence or a word now and then. I was not then talkative myself, for after a few years of life in the Concession talking became a burden and such silent companionship was what one craved.

One evening Stephenson came in as though he were in a trance, hands deep in his trouser pockets and his hat pulled down over his eyes. He sat down heavily and buried his face in his hands. I saw that he was sobbing quietly and left him alone until he lifted his head: "Wife just died," he said tonelessly, "childbirth—girl. Must get back now—girl all right. Wanted you to know."

He struggled up from the chair and walked out as if in a daze. I saw nothing of him for a long time, but I heard that he was devoting himself to his baby and would not let anyone else touch her. He bathed her, changed her nappies, made the food, fed her and put her to sleep in a basket near his bed.

A few months later he came in to see me one Sunday afternoon. "Come out and see the baby," he said. "Finest baby in China!"

He was a different man, and I could see that he had found himself. He was again articulate and told me that everyone in the Mission had been splendid to him after the tragedy. They had even winked at his smoking. He said: "We have got a real he-man out there now, a cowboy from Wyoming who got religion and joined the Mission. Came two weeks ago and smokes like a chimney. He's looking after my girl now; I wouldn't trust an amah with her. His name's Pete, Pete Webster, and oh boy, has he turned the Mission upside down and made them like it! The place is human now. Come and see." In those few minutes he had told me more than he had ever done during the whole time I had known him.

And so I met Pete Webster, or rather, I heard him first. I heard some loud "Yippees!" and the heavy trampling of feet. When Stephenson opened the door there was Pete galloping round the room with a fat gurgling baby in his arms, hair rumpled all over the place, and all in a sweat. He stopped abruptly when we came in and fumbled to get some of his hair out of the baby's grip. Then he handed her over to her father, and we shook hands. He was short, but very powerfully built, with black hair in a big wavy mane and warm sparkling brown eyes, very vital and *all* man. Strong, honest and good, was my first summing up of him, and that he proved to be when, later on, we were tested together under fire.

He was also tender-hearted and gentle, for I saw him bathing the baby that evening, with Stephenson directing, and no woman could have done it with greater care. He had begged Stephenson to allow him to do it as a great favour, and it was strange and rather sweet to see those two men busy over their unusual job.

When the baby was in bed in the adjoining room, we lit our pipes and soon had a fine old fug. Pete was in great form talking about Wyoming, ranching and mining. It was in a mine accident that he "got religion," as he called it, when his life was saved by a miracle while nine of his buddies were killed. He went back to cow-punching again after that, but could not be happy until he had joined a mission and "given himself to God."

Dr. Taft, the woman superintendent of the hospital, came in to inquire about the baby. She shook her finger at Pete and said half-jokingly: "You two will give that poor baby nicotine poisoning." Pete got up and answered with a broad grin, "No, ma'm, she's like me, she likes it! As for Doc and me, we sure are a sight better Christians when we smoke and would be mighty poor ones if we didn't. I've tried it, and if I don't get my pipe I can't pray properly, and then I start cussing like a Godless creature. My religion and my pipe belong together!"

XI

Now came the year of the big famine in northern Anhui Province, when people died by the thousand from starvation and typhus, that dread companion of famine.

As usual, nothing was done by the officials in the early stages when a major calamity could have been averted and thousands from the province took to the roads in a quest for food. When food-ships came steaming into Chinkiang harbour, mostly sent by American and British donors, thousands of Chinese had already died. Starving people cannot wait for food from Europe and America. Help also came from the Chinese Red Cross Society in Shanghai and similar organisations in the Foreign Concessions, but little or nothing from official Chinese and government sources.

It was a great experience in the ways of the Chinese in a calamity of this kind, and my first. At the same time as these mercy ships came steaming in with food, Chinese food profiteers were trying to corner rice and wheat supplies which, when bought, were sold at famine prices up-country. There was also a brisk trade in girls and boys, for the only means left to the starving of saving their own lives was to sell their children. Brothel keepers from many cities were buying girls at fifty cents apiece, and wealthy families bought up girls at the same price or boys at seventy-five cents as house slaves. The normal price of a boy for slave labour was twenty dollars at that time, but starving people were not in a position to bargain.

The great problem facing the Foreign Famine Committees was distributing the food, for which they required a very large staff of foreigners. If distribution was left to the Chinese authorities, most of the foodstuffs would disappear *en route*. What were a few hundred thousand lives to them? Less than the dust. It was my first experience on a big scale of the cheapness of human life. The Chinese man in the street was equally indifferent, and the general reaction to these lavish gifts of food was: "What foolishness is this, and what is the purpose? They are up to no good!" People who give nothing away willingly, always examine the teeth of a gift horse very carefully.

It took a long time for the survivors of that tragic death march to reach Chinkiang. When they arrived they were an incredibly filthy and ragged band of staggering skeletons with staring eyes, no longer human beings. Every open space on the outskirts was soon filled with them. They brought their own shelters, a roll of matting on their backs. The mats were bent and made a miniature Nissen hut the size of a big dog-kennel, into which they crawled on all fours, too exhausted to beg for food.

Missionaries hurriedly erected soup-kitchens and worked untiringly among the survivors, but, even so, many died. They had brought typhus with them, and Dr. Williams of the China Inland Mission contracted the disease while caring for them and died. But his passing, and that of thousands of Chinese, made little or no impression on the populace.

At that time four Chinese were accidentally killed on the railway, and the public outcry nearly caused an anti-foreign riot. The coolies had fallen asleep on the line at night, their heads on the rail, and were all decapitated by the train. Decapitation is a horrible thing to the Chinese, for they firmly believe that they go into the next world headless and remain so. At the same time, and characteristically, they enjoy seeing a man beheaded by the executioner, a show few of them would want to miss.

That year I saw by accident an execution as I came riding through the Maloo. At the base of the first hill was an open space which, I only then discovered, was the public execution ground. It was packed with people, and, being mounted, I could see over their heads.

In the centre was a small open space where a man was kneeling. Another man was pulling his queue, stretching his neck, and then I suddenly saw the executioner with his sword lifted. The whole thing happened so quickly that I did not realise what I was looking at before I saw the head severed with one stroke. There came a loud chorus of applause for the executioner, and then a mad rush of women and children throwing strings of cash into the pool of blood. I was sick with horror, and the scene haunted me for days.

When I came home for my Chinese lessons I asked my teacher why the women were throwing cash into the blood. (By cash, I mean the small Chinese brass coins with a hole through the centre.) He said that they made amulets of them for children and hung them round their necks. Fresh blood from a decapitated man was a very powerful means of frightening away evil spirits, and the gall of an executed criminal, especially a bandit, when eaten made you very strong and brave. Selling this human offal was one of the executioner's perquisites.

I was certainly learning more than the language from my teacher, and that was actually my purpose in studying Chinese, to try to solve a little of this everlasting riddle of the Chinese mind. This study of the Chinese, and particularly of their psychology, was to stand me in very good stead in years to come.

The main thing now was to learn how to handle all these Jekylls who could suddenly turn into Hydes. Take, for instance, a little matter like hiring a rickshaw. A Chinaman would never dream of taking a rickshaw without bargaining about the cost, and would often walk a couple of hundred yards while so arguing. Only when he had beaten the poor wretch down to the lowest possible price would he step into the rickshaw. A foreigner would not dream of screwing down a poor coolie like that, and would just hop into the rickshaw and call out the destination, and he would pay him what he thought was fair. It would probably be twice as much as a Chinese would pay, and the coolie would expect that from a fool foreigner who never bargained or seemed to know the value of money.

The coolies never gave us any credit for generosity; I don't think they even knew the meaning of that word. They were used to being beaten down, but only fools would give away anything extra. If you gave three times the fare, the fat was in the fire. An American visitor was once nearly mobbed because he gave the rickshaw coolie a whole dollar for a twenty-cents' ride. The coolie looked sick and ragged and would be overjoyed, the American thought. But the coolie rose in wrath and indignation. A man who had *so* much money to throw away could certainly afford to pay much more. Only *one* dollar from a rich fool like that. An insult! "Not enough!" he screamed, and a crowd collected at once. A few passing foreigners rescued the American and told him where he was wrong.

When you have learnt about this universal trait in the Chinese character, you begin to understand why China is a country without pity, because generosity is unknown, and the two go together.

Another thing I learnt was never to show any fear of them and never to lose my temper in a dispute, or show any irritation over their inquisitiveness into my private affairs, for in that topsy-turvy land personal questions indicate the utmost politeness.

After inquiring your name, a Chinese gentleman will fire these questions at you:

What is your honourable country?

How old are you?

How many wives have you?

What is your business?

How much money do you earn?

How many children have you?

And so it goes on. I have watched peppery people, unfamiliar with Chinese etiquette, going purple in the face when, through an interpreter, they were asked these questions, and finally demanding angrily: "What the hell has that got to do with you, you insufferable Nosy Parker!" This would indeed be a deadly insult if the interpreters were not also diplomats. They, however, always are.

A knowledge of the Chinese language soon led to a complete change in my fortunes.

One of the big foreign firms in Shanghai, Arnhold, Karberg & Co., wanted to open a branch office in Chinkiang and were looking for someone who could speak the language—a rarity in those days. I applied for the job and, much to my surprise, was accepted. It is hard to conceive of a bigger change than that of an outdoor staff man in the Customs suddenly finding himself in the merchant class. Not only was my pay doubled, but I also got an entertaining allowance, a seven-roomed flat, free servants and four chairbearers resplendent in uniforms of the firm's colours—blue and white and wearing mandarin hats with red tassels. I was no longer supposed to *walk* to the Victoria Park, but had to ride out in state in a sedan-chair together with the other members of the Concession's *élite*: the Consul's chairbearers in white uniforms with red facings, Jardine Matheson's in blue with white facings, Butterfield & Swire's in white and red, Arnhold, Karberg's in white with blue facings, and the other firms' bearers in a variety of colours, each different. The ride was a solemn rite every afternoon.

I had not led the kind of life to make me feel class-conscious or snobbish, and having to ride in a sedan-chair in this procession only made me feel a fool. My old plain way of living, with but a cook-boy to look after me, had to be changed. The custom of the China coast decreed that the least I could do with now was a cook, a boy and a coolie. These three soon grew into five, for the cook had to have a second cook and the boy a number-two boy to cope with parties and visitors.

My flat was over the offices, and there was an endless list of stuff to buy for it: furniture, linen, bedding, china, cutlery, carpets and curtains. That was easy, but there was always one big difficulty. As there was no running water, old-fashioned wash-stands had to be used with heavy stoneware basins, ewers and chambers. These had to be bought at auctions, second-hand, and it was almost impossible to get a whole set. Either the ewer or the basin was broken, and as they were only sold in sets one always had to buy two sets to make up for a missing part. The only thing that never seemed to break was the chamber.

In getting the three guest-rooms fixed up I found myself with three extra chambers, and as I had previously collected three others they became a problem, which was eventually solved by the boy when we had the house-warming party and the guest-rooms were occupied by visitors from the Shanghai office. He decorated the three bed-tables with chamber-pots filled with violets, and I never heard the last of that.

Another thing I had reason to remember was that one of the guests, a Scot from our Shanghai office, proposed the good old Highland toast, one foot on the table. Most of the table gear had been borrowed from other households, an old custom when big parties were given. I knew the glasses were borrowed, but I had never heard of the good old Hieland toast before and thought it rather fun, until I saw the glasses flung over shoulders and smashed. One lives and learns.

I didn't find the *élite* any more interesting than the *hoi polloi*, except for one, a very wild and woolly Irish railway engineer, who was immensely strong and became violent when crossed. He would come tearing into the Club like a whirlwind, haul one of the members up to the bar and force him to drink tumblers of whisky, with the idea of finding out how quickly a man could be made drunk. Another of his foibles was to paint all the members' noses blue with billiard-chalk and enrol them in his Blue-nose Club.

He lived alone at one of the small stations towards Nanking, was as mad as a hatter, but played a wonderful game of cricket. Therefore much was forgiven him, although people often had to jump out of the Club windows to escape his practical jokes. The drop was only eight feet or so, so no one ever got hurt, and it was rather a relief having him there to stir things up a bit. He was also a member of the Customs Club, where he had knocked out the German engineer who had been roaring every night for five years. Now Roaring Rudolph, as we called him, was silent, and there seemed to be something wrong with the place until the new arrival really got going. Even then I missed Rudolph's roars: they were an essential part of the night noises.

In the meantime I was busy every day and all day learning the ropes of this new work and getting to know my compradore. He was a Cantonese named Wu Li Shan, a very dignified man, resplendent in a brocade robe. A fine type, very strongly built, and almost the only Chinese I met who had a humane and charitable heart, the very personification of the exception that proves the rule. He was an active member of the Shanghai Red Cross Society and an indefatigable worker for the Famine Relief Fund. It was he who unburdened himself to me about how hard it was to get the Chinese to subscribe; but he kept on at them and often shamed them into a donation.

From him I also got a good deal of information about the unrest and growing revolt against the Imperial government. I am pretty certain he was a revolutionary himself, for there were meetings nearly every night down in his office and many people came and went all through the night. They were safe from interference in the British Concession, the only place where they could feel secure. Chinese detectives were very busy, but the revolutionaries were too alert. One day a detective working for the Chinese magistrate was found strangled just outside the Concession boundaries. It was no ordinary murder, for he had a fine silk cord round his neck. Kelly, of the police, came and asked me to go with him to see the dead man and, pointing to the silk cord, he said: "No ordinary murderer would waste money on a silk cord. I bet you he was in the Concession nosing around and was killed there. Afterwards he was carried here."

At the same time a very brilliant star was visible in broad daylight, and crowds of Chinese were to be seen standing in silent groups, staring at it fearfully. Something was bound to happen soon. This they said was a sign from heaven.

XII

I CAN still remember clearly the elation and enthusiasm we foreigners felt when the first news came through of the revolt at Hankow and Wuchang in the early autumn of 1911. Sun Yat Sen was quite a hero in our eyes, and his rescue from the Chinese Legation in London through the agency of Dr. Cantlie had made him a very romantic figure. We thought high and noble thoughts about China and the new era that was dawning, and believed that the end of the bloodsucking mandarins was near. In the south, city after city went over to the revolutionary armies. There was nothing to stop them as the so-called Imperial garrisons were only a band of ill-fed, ill-armed coolies. Shanghai went over, then Soochow, and one day the garrison at the Mud Fort in Chinkiang surrendered, all one hundred and fifty of them, and the four ancient muzzle-loading guns were handed over. The Chinese Imperial Navy in Chinkiang also surrendered: twenty sailing sampans with one muzzle-loading bow-gun each.

General Lin, commander of the Revolutionary Army under the supreme command of General Hsu Siao Cheng, made official calls on the Consul and on the Commissioner of Customs. The whole force at their disposal was fifty thousand men armed with Mauser rifles, a few batteries of mountain-guns and one 4·7 gun. So far, their advance had been without opposition, but at Nanking the old Imperialist, General Chang Hsun, was barring their way. He was a fighter and had tough Shantung troops under him, so there was a stiff task ahead and plenty of fighting.

Gifts were showered on the conquering heroes by the Chinese merchants—food, bedding, blankets and clothing—and committees were formed by the merchants both inside and outside the Concession. Wu Li Shan, my compradore, took a leading part and, being a member of the Red Cross Society at Shanghai, he was chiefly concerned with Red Cross work. One day he came to me looking worried and said: "I have just found out that General Lin has no Red Cross unit with his army, not even one stretcher, and of course no bandages or medicines. It is not the custom in the army, his secretary told me, to look after the wounded."

We put our heads together to see what could be done about it, and the result was the Chinkiang ambulance unit, of which I was to take charge. Pete Webster and Dr. Stephenson asked to be enrolled, and Delahunty of the Customs, an old campaigner and ex-trooper, also came and asked to be taken on. The ladies in the Concession (there were a fair number of them by now) got busy making bandages, and the whole Concession was in the war up to their necks, doing voluntary work.

The big snag was the shortage of stretchers which could not be obtained for love or money. I solved that problem by purloining eighty gunny sacks from the firm's stocks and, using bamboo poles as frames, making forty rough but serviceable stretchers. Wu Li Shan had seen only General Lin's secretary, but I went to see the general himself to report and to get facilities for going with the army when they moved. He was the most surprised man in Chinkiang when I told him what we had done and what we were prepared to do.

"But I can't afford to pay for all this. It isn't necessary. These soldiers are only common coolies. If they are wounded I get new ones and discharge those who can't fight. They know that. For those who are killed in the beginning I have fifty-five expensive coffins; *that* surely should be enough, and more than they expect to get! The merchants in Soochow presented me with the coffins and an umbrella for each soldier. They are already pampered enough!" This is, in effect, what he said, but he expressed himself in a much cruder manner. His relief when he heard that the ambulance unit would cost him nothing was very genuine, but at the same time I felt that he regarded our motives with suspicion. He was suave and very polite, but showed his complete lack of humanity when he referred to his soldiers. His assessment of the value of human lives other than his own was the same as that of the mandarins and the well-to-do. The old order had not changed in *him*. However, he promised to send word when the army was moving and to make arrangements for our transport.

I was not a happy man when I left, but I had so much to do that I soon forgot the nasty taste of his interview. It was arranged through the railway officials that the railway hospital in Chinkiang should be used as a base hospital; an ambulance train would be at my disposal, as near the firing line as was safe, in order to transport the wounded back to base, either to Chinkiang or to Shanghai, where there was more accommodation.

Dr. Ziervogel would be in charge of the ambulance train, with one nurse and two Chinese dressers, Dr. Stephenson would look after the front-line dressing station, and I would be in charge of front-line ambulance work, with Pete Webster as my assistant. Delahunty would be maid-of-all-work, and ten young Chinese volunteers were to look after the wounded until they could be moved.

Business was, of course, dead and would remain so until the campaign was over, and it never occurred to me that my head office might object. I had written and explained the position and what I had undertaken to do. Then I got word from General Lin that the main army would move off by train next morning, scouting forces having gone on ahead some time before.

I was ready to ride off to the station next morning, when the mail arrived. There was one letter from my immediate superior in Shanghai, Mr. Erlanger. It stated briefly and emphatically that in these troublesome times I was under no circumstances to leave my post. I stuffed the letter into my pocket and rode off. I couldn't turn back now, orders or no orders. There was a big crowd of foreigners and Chinese at the station to see us off.

I had told Pete to bring his pony too, so that we could cover more ground. A horse-car was attached to the train, half-full of vicious-looking ponies, some of them blocking our way, with their hindquarters towards us. One of them was just going to lash out at Pete, and I shouted, "Look out!" Instead of jumping back, as I expected him to do, he dived like a flash towards the pony and grabbed him by the root of the tail, putting his whole weight on it and pushing one hip right under the pony's hind-quarters. The animal screamed with rage and tried to kick, but could not. Only a few short futile taps was the result, and they soon stopped. The beast was nearly paralysed with terror in that relentless grip, and then Pete gave his rump a hard slap and pushed him to one side to make room for our own ponies. That was just like Pete—and Pete knew horses, but while the tussle lasted my heart stood still.

We had been given a whole third-class car for our party. Nurse Ethel Halley and Dr. Balean were coming with us to confer with Dr. Ziervogel and his nurse about the transport arrangements, while we were to move inland at once to find out where we would be needed and establish ourselves there.

The train crawled, stopped and crawled, and the hours crawled too. The journey to Nanking could be done in an hour, but, when evening came, we had only reached a station call Lone Tree Hill, where we stopped for the night. We used the stretchers as beds, placing them so that they rested on the high-backed seats. It was quite a climb up, and it took two of us lifting and one pushing her weightiest part before we got our Ethel safely parked. She was a good sport and it was all great fun.

Then, being very tired, we were soon fast asleep. In the middle of the night we were awakened by a mighty crash. It was Ethel. I had given little thought to working out the breaking strain of the stretchers: they had looked stout enough to me, but it was now clear that they were not as stout as Ethel's physique demanded. We picked up her ruins and those of the stretcher by the light of our one stable lantern. After that she curled up on one of the seats on her undamaged parts: there was fortunately a good deal of surface to choose from.

We were off again after daylight and a couple of hours later reached Yaohuamen station, where we saw the ambulance train in a siding. We found the whole Shanghai Red Cross party at breakfast, and we joined them and heard the latest news. The ambulance train, decorated with huge red crosses, had tried twice to proceed, but each time it had been shelled from Purple Mountain, where, apparently, the Imperial troops were entrenched in strength in the key defence position.

There was no information about the general disposition of the revolutionaries, but it was rumoured that they were fighting in the area to the south of Purple Mountain. In the meantime all the soldiers on our train were lined up on the station and soon afterwards marched off in a southerly direction. I decided to follow them. The plan was that I should send all the wounded I could find to Yaohuamen station, and the Shanghai party would send them on. The Shanghai party, incidentally, consisted of Dr. Ziervogel and the nurse, with two Chinese dressers; other duties would be undertaken by Mr. Mossop, the Crown Advocate in Shanghai, and by Mr. Strickland of the Salt Gabelle, both volunteers.

We did not waste any time, but marched out more or less into the blue. We were quite a cavalcade. Pete and I rode ahead as scouts, then came one of the Chinese carrying a big Red Cross flag, and after that the rest of the party in single file. We had forty ambulance bearers with us, as General Lin had refused to supply bearers. This was a scouting expedition, and I had arranged for only a couple of days' rations to be taken along, leaving the rest with the stationmaster.

We had enough to carry, anyway, being loaded with stretchers, bedding and medical supplies. As soon as we were established I had planned to get the rest of the food supplies sent out by the stretcher-bearers who took in the first batch of wounded. I was riding Blue Cap, Satan's successor, a very fast blue dun and an excellent jumper. Pete was on a shaggy chestnut and we soon had a splendid cross-country ride in the direction of Purple Mountain, that rather queer-looking, lonely hill, rearing up from the plains to the east of Nanking's city walls.

We all carried big Red Cross armbands to show what we were doing, but we had been warned that the Imperialists would not know what the Red Cross meant and that we could expect to be fired on. It was not long before this happened.

Nearing the eastern slope of the mountain we were met by a fusillade, and we could then clearly see the trenches, in three lines, not very far away. Soon after rounding the eastern spur we heard firing to the west, towards Nanking—rifle and gunfire—then going through a small, dirty village we were met by a few wounded stragglers who gave us work to do at once. They told us that fighting was in progress at the village of Ma Chung, a couple of miles farther along, which had just been taken by the revolutionaries. Most of the wounded were walking cases, but a few had to be sent along on stretchers to Yaohuamen. More wounded were coming in and we were busy for several hours. Late in the afternoon we pushed on and, shortly afterwards, passed through a shelled village where most of the houses were in ruins.

At the next village we were shelled but got through without casualties. There I split up the party, and we went on in small groups. It was nearly dark when we reached Ma Chung and found the village packed with wounded.

The colonel, who was the commanding officer, gave me a low straggling house as headquarters; we moved in, hoisted our flag at the front door and got busy with the wounded. It must have been after midnight before we were finished and rolled up on the mud floor in our Chinese cotton quilts. The sleeping-room was small, and by the time the ten young Chinese volunteers and the rest of us were bedded down, we were packed like sardines. Indeed, it was only by lying on our sides tight together that we could be fitted in. It was a case of "when father says turn, we all turn," if we wanted to turn over to the other side.

There was a counter-attack during the night, and a terrific din with shouts, shots and the clatter of horses galloping about on the cobbled street. The tiles were rattling too, apparently from machine-gun fire, but I was too tired to get up and inquire, and there was nothing I could do about it anyway. I had to talk sharply to the Chinese, though, as they were terrified. So was I, as a matter of fact, but I dared not show it. Being butchered by a lot of savage Shantung braves was not a cheerful prospect, but the attackers were apparently driven back, for we were all intact in the morning.

We were up early, glad to stretch our cramped limbs and get the blood circulating.

We had had little opportunity of examining our quarters when we arrived, and now I found that luckily the house was well suited to the work. Our sleeping-room would have to be used for treating and dressing the wounded in the daytime, being the only room fitted with windows. A big adjoining room would be ideal for stores and could serve as a waiting-room for the wounded, with Delahunty in charge. A courtyard at the back was surrounded by several open-fronted rooms. It was all very dirty and dingy, but I had the rooms and courtyard swept and layers of clean straw spread on the floors of the outside rooms and the waiting-room for the wounded to lie on.

There were several stretcher-cases to be sent off first thing in the morning, and, after that was attended to, Pete and I went out scouting. Our quarters were in the fourth house from the end of the only village street. About a hundred yards away, between us and the base of Purple Mountain, was a small hillock, and along the ridge of that were our front trenches where some half-dozen emplacements had been made for mountain-guns.

All was quiet when we got there, and we had a good chance of looking the country over and noting the enemy positions. The steep slope of the mountain was only two hundred yards away, and the first trench about three hundred yards from our position. It was fully manned, and it was curious to see the men of the two opposing sides calmly looking at one another, without firing a shot. I asked one of our men why they were not fighting and he explained that they had been fighting so much yesterday and during the night that they were tired of it. So they had arranged with the enemy up the hill to take a little rest, and to start again after eating their midday rice. It was clearly a gentlemen's war.

Suddenly a heavy shower of rain pelted down and up came the umbrellas, the usual olive-drab oiled-paper type which each man carried folded on his back as part of his equipment. It was astonishing to look up the hill and see every trench sprouting umbrellas like big mushrooms, revealing clearly the whole defence position.

But nothing could surprise me any longer, for that morning I had seen a squad parading in pink underwear, a gift from the merchants in Chinkiang. The garments were the popular Wright's underwear of thick fleecy cotton imported from England in huge quantities, the same kind that I had been fitted out with after the wreck in the "Patria"* The soldiers were strutting about in what had once been, to me, shameful garments of a revolting colour, because they were too proud of them to hide them under their drab and dirty uniforms.

It was only the rainy weather, which now began, that put a stop to further similar displays. I had seen the Amazon "Dare to Die" corps swaggering through the street with Mauser pistols slung saucily from their waists. Swaggering is perhaps the wrong word for they all had small feet and staggered painfully along the uneven cobbles. I had also seen the display of the coffins in an open space outside the village. They had now dwindled to thirty or so, and pink underwear, Amazons, coffins and umbrellas were almost too much in one day in the front line.

But there were other things too, not so funny. Within fifty yards of our dressing-station was an open space in the street, a small square on the south side where three dead men, roughly-clad country people, were lying with staring eyes. They must have died by slow inches, for their arm and leg muscles had been partially cut through, and their faces gashed in several places. Round them squatted a number of villagers poking their fingers into the gashes and discussing the various cuts as if they were looking at animal carcases. I heard that the dead men were farmers fleeing from the outskirts of Nanking and suspected of being spies.

In the evening four of our stretcher-bearers came back in terror

* Sea Fever

and told me that all the wounded sent in that day had been massacred. A scouting patrol from Purple Mountain had stopped the stretchers and bayoneted all the wounded. The rest of the stretcher-bearers had fled. This was bad news, because from now on I would have to send a foreigner in with each lot as escort. There was another serious thing: we were running short of food, for this party of bearers should have brought supplies back. We were also short of water, as the village wells did not hold enough for all the forces quartered there.

There was nothing for it but to tighten our belts and ration the water severely. To add to our discomforts it poured with rain the whole afternoon and night. As many of the tiles of the house had been smashed by machine-gun fire, the mud floor in our room became soaked and sticky and we spent a pretty miserable night in the mud with the rain pouring down on our bedding. Fortunately, it was too wet for fighting and the two opposing forces sat tight under their umbrellas, so we had a quiet night.

We had no sooner got up in the morning before fighting started, not only at Ma Chung, but on an extended line all along the southern slopes of Purple Mountain. Wounded came in by themselves, so there was no need to send out stretchers. We had quite enough to cope with and it was late in the evening before we finished. I had brought along my banjo at Pete's urging as he thought it would be a good morale stiffener.

We needed it. We were hungry and tired, but the incessant firing and the crackling of the tiles overhead where bullets were constantly finding their mark, made the Chinese boys very nervous and sleep difficult. So I twanged away on the banjo and we sang. Stephenson and Pete had good voices and knew a good selection of sad and gay minstrel songs.

I contributed "Bible Stories," not very suitable for missionaries, but our two volunteers were sports first and missionaries second, so they joined in the chorus:

"Old folks, young folks, everybody come, Join the niggers' Sunday School and make yourselves at home, Bring a stick of chewing-gum and sit upon the floor, And I'll tell bible stories that you *never* heard before."

It somehow became our battle-song, sharing honours with the

favourite of the Chinese, a pidgin-English song which was very popular. It had a jolly chorus:

> "Ai ya ya chin chin chin
> chow chow velly goodee
> my likee him.
> Makee plenty singsong
> savvy by and by
> Chinaman he velly goodee
> laugh ai ya."

Yes, it was good for morale and for empty stomachs. The Chinese were not badly off at all as they could buy unsavoury-looking dishes in the village and rice, of course. We others had eaten only a bowl each of boiled rice since breakfast, and were ravenous.

Early next morning we had a surprise visit from Dr. Brown, a missionary doctor stationed in Nanking, who had been at Shanghai obtaining medical supplies for Dr. Macklin's hospital in Nanking in preparation for the siege, but the sudden advance of the revolutionaries had cut him off. His wife and children were inside the city and he would be unable to join them until the battle was over. At Yaohuamen he had been told about us and thought he could be of use. On his way he had met the missing stretcher-bearers who brought him along to Ma Chung.

I was very glad to have the bearers back, but the food problem was now aggravated because Brown had brought only enough for the day. I therefore decided to go back to Yaohuamen with a batch of wounded and get all the necessary food. We started off, but about half-way we ran into a lot of our own people in retreat, and I heard from them that the enemy had made a surprise attack and carried the key position they were holding. We were now cut off and I had to return with the wounded.

It was not a happy position, but as fighting increased we had so much to do that we had little time for thinking or worrying. Pete had been far afield that day and collected some badly wounded who had been lying unattended in no-man's-land for three days. There were many more there, so I got all the bearers collected and we started off.

Pete had forgotten to tell me that most of them had to be carried back under fire, and we were sniped at the whole afternoon with occasional volleys, but the enemy were poor marksmen. Our big armbands with red crosses were of no use, in fact they seemed to draw the fire, and I heard later that we were taken for officers on account of them. We brought in a number of cases with gangrene, and the dressing-room stank. Again we supped off bowls of rice and went to bed hungry.

This went on for two more days. The third night we heard a rumpus outside. The front door was flung open and there stood Strickland, revolver in hand and poking it in the back of a terrified coolie. We all had to get up to give him room to come inside.

Strickland was in a frightful temper with the coolie who had undertaken to guide him to us but, being frightened by sentries firing at them, had led Strickland completely astray and tried to bolt in the darkness. Strickland had caught him and made him walk ahead, prodding him in the back with his revolver. Now having found us he just pushed him out of the door, and he bolted like a rabbit.

"I have brought food for you," he said; "we have been worried about you and I came to investigate. It's Thanksgiving Night, and I've brought a big tin of turkey." His voice was drowned in a great cheer as we crowded round him and helped him off with his heavy rucksack. Delahunty got the paraffin cooker going, and we inspected our windfall. Besides the turkey there were sausages, corned beef and tinned peaches, and two thermos bottles with steaming coffee.

It was a meal to remember. Pete said grace and we all echoed his amen from grateful hearts. We no longer noticed the dirt around us, the mud on the floor, the reek of iodoform and gangrene; we were all friends together sharing this feast after sharing the risks, the hardships and the work. We finished up with the fragrant steaming coffee, and talked until we could no longer keep our eyes open. Then we rolled into our bedding and squeezed ourselves into place.

It would be too long a story to recount the daily happenings while the grip round Nanking tightened. Our work increased as

5

Top: The shooting bungalow at Wu Chow Shan
Bottom: Wild pig country

PLATE 6

Top: Week-end shooting part
Huang Shan House

Bottom left: The Old Grey
Author (left) and Harry Singer

Bottom right: Tah Gu Tzu and a
boar

the battle extended, and Pete and I spent long hours in the saddle. Certain incidents stand out: seeing the first disembowelled soldier, and some with their genitals cut off and stuck into their mouths. And others to whom death had come peacefully. There was a priest lying fully clothed in his grey robes in the courtyard of his temple, an Imperialist sergeant lying prone behind a mound with his rifle in firing position, drilled through the head.

I noticed a lot of cartridges on the ground with bullets in them and picked one up. It was a misfire, and I found more of them—all misfires. Then I discovered that the bullets were made of wood and covered with aluminium paint. I wrenched one of them off and found no powder inside. Some of the Chinese arsenal officials had made a nice profit out of that.

But one incident stands out the clearest of all. After a heavy day's fighting a cease-fire was arranged by the soldiers on both sides. I had just gone up to our front trenches for a look around when I saw a foreigner walking towards me along the base of the mountain, quite calmly and casually. He paid no attention to the muzzles that followed him, and came apparently from Nanking. It was all very puzzling, and as I walked out to meet him I felt sure I had seen him before.

Then suddenly I placed him. He was a remittance man, well known on the Yangtze. When he had money to spend he blew in at the various ports, remained drunk for days on end and then vanished until his next remittance arrived. Always a gentleman, always friendly and very generous, he was welcomed everywhere, but what on earth was he doing here? I knew the hazards of the country he had passed through and could only wonder at his foolhardy courage. A warm smile greeted me as we shook hands: "Heard you were over here," he said, "and thought I would pay you a surprise visit. I'm over at Tiger Hill forts and the only foreigner there. I felt lonely today, and got a queer sort of longing to hear English voices." I brought him along and invited him to have tea with us, for we generally had a short break in the afternoon.

He could not have been much older than twenty-six, sandy-haired and with good features, though slightly bloated-looking. His eyes were a clear grey and looked straight at you. There was no doubt about his being glad to be with us, and he told us his story and why he was over at Tiger Hill by himself. He thought he would do something useful for a change, so he had invested his last remittance, half in booze and half in medical supplies, and with two coolies to carry his gear he had boarded the train in Chinkiang. When he reached Yaohuamen he was told that my Red Cross unit was on the south side of Purple Mountain, so he decided to go to the north side. He and his coolies went off into the foot-hills towards Nanking, and finally he ran into an artillery unit at Tiger Hill where a kind of fort had been captured by the revolutionaries. They had taken several 4·7 guns too, and when he arrived they were bombarding Lion Hill forts inside the city walls.

He had a lot of cigarettes with him and soon chummed up with the gunners. Every time a salvo was fired, the gunners went into the tunnel and waited until the guns of Lion Hill had replied. He thought it curious that the guns never fired simultaneously, but the gunners told him they had arranged with the enemy that each side should fire in turn, so that they could each take cover after a salvo. But one day they received a salvo just as they were going to fire, and several of their gunners were killed. This was very unsporting of the other side and something must be wrong.

Sure enough, they found out by means known only to themselves that General Chang Hsun himself had spotted that there was hanky-panky going on. He had come down with an executioners' squad and beheaded all the gunners and hung their heads up in bunches on the telephone posts as a warning. New gunners had then replaced them, and the general himself had given the order when to fire.

This fellow himself had been part gunner, part Red Cross worker, and had drunk himself silly part of the time, but he did not like drinking always by himself. "And today," he said, "I just felt I must go and see some fellow whites and hear English again, so I strolled round the western spur of the mountain and came straight here, keeping about midway between the lines, but no one fired at me. They probably don't think I am worth shooting, and I don't doubt that they are right."

He sat and chatted with us for a while longer, then rose abruptly to go. We urged him to stay with us for the night, as he was taking an appalling risk by going back. All the soldiers were jumpy and had itching trigger fingers as the final and deciding battle was drawing hear.

He only shook his head: "No, we are expecting the big show tonight, and I can't let my side down." We followed him part of the way, and said good-bye when in sight of the Ming Tombs. He stalked on quite unmoved and looked indifferently on the black rifle muzzles which suddenly appeared from the trenches. He seemed absolutely sure that he would get through safely. As he waved just before he disappeared from sight, I thought of the contemptuous way he had said: "They don't think I am worth shooting."

He was wrong this time, for he was never seen again, and where or how he died on his lone way back, we never heard.

XIV

It is very difficult to describe a battle, especially the first one you see. What happens before the men go over the top is easy enough, but after the attack everything becomes a jumble of noises and scenes changing so rapidly that you can't follow. You find your eyes glued to things happening near by, and miss what goes on farther afield.

I was lying with Pete in our front trench just before the attack started, and Blue Cap and Pete's pony were in shelter farther back. We had a wide view of the country around, and only a mile or so to the west we looked straight at the high crenellated walls of the Tartar City. The year before I had come through the gate there to go shooting around the Ming Tombs and in the Lotus Lake country. I could clearly see the avenue of mammoth stone animals, camels, elephants and horses, which marked the route of the Ming funeral procession four hundred years ago. A little more to the north and close to the western spur of Purple Mountain lay the enormous mound, more like a hill than anything else, where the coffin had been placed; nobody knew where, for all those who followed the catafalque, bearers included, were executed on their return.

A battery of mountain-guns on our right suddenly started shelling an enemy battery only four hundred yards away, and they replied briskly. We were in the stalls for that, and it was pandemonium. Higher up the mountain the final assault had started. I could clearly see the eastern ridge being carried and then our men advancing along the ridge and sides. The slopes were very steep and those who fell rolled down the hillside which was bare of trees. Little clusters of men were holding out behind outcrops of rock until enfiladed, and I caught myself several times shouting "Look out!" when I saw men sneaking up at their backs to bayonet them. It was now clear that the main and final fight would take place right in front of me, on the western spur at Pa Te Chun, where the Imperialists had a fortified position. If this should fall, Nanking's fate was sealed, for our artillery could then bombard the city from high ground, and the walls would be useless for protection.

A party of "dare and die" soldiers started off for the Tartar City gates, carrying big mines fitted with handles and fuses for exploding them against the gates. Pete and I went back to get our ponies and we had just mounted when a gun went off close by with a fearful bang. This was too much for Blue Cap and mad with fright, he bolted like a streak uphill. He went clean through our battery, over the hill and straight for the enemy guns, buck-jumping all the way to get me off. There was no stopping him until we got the blast of one of the enemy guns from only fifty yards or so and he nearly sat down on his haunches with the shock. Then they stopped firing and I saw some grinning faces watching me try to extricate myself from a very embarrassing position. Our men had stopped firing too as if by mutual consent, while I was doing my circus trick-rider stunt in that narrow strip of no-man's-land.

Eventually I got Blue Cap under control, dug my heels into him and sent him flying back to where we belonged. No sooner had we sailed over the top than the opposing batteries opened up again. After that I had no clear picture of what happened, because our men went over the top with Pete, myself and the stretcher-bearers on their heels. We had both dismounted by then. All I remember are noises and smells: the savage shouts of the soldiers; "Sha! sha!" (kill! kill!), screams and yells, gunfire, rattling machine-guns, the acrid smell of powder, and the curious smell of blood and of the dead. I remember finding a man who had been bayoneted through his cheeks, and whose tongue was nearly severed. All our stretchers were in use by now, and I carried him on my back with his life-blood streaming down my neck. He died before any of the stretchers returned. Then Pete and I stopped the massacre of about twenty men who had surrendered. Walking-wounded were directed towards Ma Chung, and severe cases were collected in one place against the return of the stretchers.

I found one man past help, but he was still alive. When I knelt down by his side to examine him, he looked at me with unseeing eyes and kept on whispering: "Wei sho mo, ta men shi Tsung kuo ren i yang wu. Wei sho mo?" (Why? They were Chinese like me. Why?) The riddle of why he was killed by his own countrymen seemed to bother him until he died.

Then I was called off because the Imperialists were retreating towards the Tartar Gate pursued by our men. Leaving Pete in charge, I followed in their wake taking with me Delahunty, who had suddenly arrived.

We soon found plenty to do, not for the living but for the dead. The moat was full of women who had ended their lives in the slimy waters rather than face the sacking of the city and the inevitable rapine and horror. We hauled them out, one by one, pathetic wet bundles, and placed them on the banks where they could lie on clean grass. They made a picture I shall always remember, those rows of silent figures on the edge of the moat with the massive, sombre and cruel city walls behind them, walls that had seen hundreds of thousands die by the sword in Nanking's long and bloody past.

It was dark before we came back to Ma Chung where I found both doctors working at high pressure, and it was nearly midnight before we got to bed. My right arm was giving me great pain, as I had got an infection through a cut in my hand. The whole arm was badly swollen and the next morning it was nearly useless so I decided to go along with the stretchers to Yaohuamen that day and get my arm attended to. Brown and Stephenson were swamped with work, without having me to worry about.

The hospitals in Nanking would now be available, as we had heard that the city had fallen during the night. This would mean much shorter transport of the wounded, and I left Dr. Brown to attend to that, with Stephenson to help him.

I planned to go to Nanking as soon as my arm was dressed and warn the hospitals there. And so I said good-bye to our little home in Ma Chung, which would soon be broken up. Dr. Ziervogel attended to my arm and, as rail communications with Nanking had been restored that morning, I boarded the first train. At Sia

Kwan station, just outside the city main gate, I got out and made my way to the closed and guarded gate through a seething crowd. The armed guard fortunately knew me and passed me through.

I knew the way to Dr. Macklin's hospital well: from the gate I had only to follow the main road which skirted the forts on Lion Hill. Here every telephone post was decorated with a bunch of gory heads nailed up by the queues—apparently the gunners of the fort. It was rather a shock to realise that I could look at them without turning a hair. After all, beheading was quick and clean. But I had seen so many mutilated bodies that a few dripping heads meant little to me, and I wondered if I had any feelings left. It was with the same indifference that I passed the parade ground near the Naval Academy, which was sprinkled with headless bodies. The trouble was that some of the worst atrocities had been committed by our own men. Was this New China any improvement on the Old? I was full of doubt and misgivings, weary and despondent.

Soon I ran into a horde of looters who, quite unchecked, had cleaned out the houses. There were carts bulging with loot, rickshaws, donkeys, horses, wheelbarrows, anything the soldiers could get hold of to carry the stuff away. At the Naval Academy they were even carrying away the doors and windows as I passed. It was apparently an old Chinese custom, and the new regime was faithfully following in the footsteps of the old.

I called on Dr. Macklin, a short man with iron-grey hair and kindly eyes, and explained the position, and told him that Dr. Brown was at Ma Chung. He told me that Mrs. Brown and the children were safe and well, and I promised to send word to Dr. Brown. They had been through some tough experiences during the siege and especially on the last day, when looting and murder started. The new "bunch," as he called them, were only cleaning up after the Imperialists, and when they had finished, most of the Chinese homes would be bare.

I left him to pay a farewell call on General Hsu, now installed in the Viceroy's Yamen. I had met him a couple of times at Ma Chung, an insignificant-looking little man, who had taken a keen interest in our work. To him, and to most of the other officers, Red Cross work in the army in war was quite unknown, and he had seen it in operation for the first time. He had, however, heard of the Geneva Convention, but had only associated Red Cross work with famine relief.

The Viceroy's Yamen was in the wildest disorder when I arrived. The whole place had been looted clean. Clean is perhaps the wrong word, for every courtyard was littered with books, broken furniture and all the stuff discarded by the looters. The cleaning-up gang were carefully going through what was left, sorting out anything of value.

I met General Hsu's orderly in the main building, at the end of a series of courtyards. He took in my card, and returned saying that the General would see me in a few minutes. A table was laid with tea and cakes, and soon after the General came in. He was all smiles, for it was no little triumph for him to have won the decisive battle of the Revolution.

I stated that I came on a brief courtesy visit to say good-bye and to inform him that nearly four hundred of his severely wounded were being cared for until they were able to rejoin his forces. He was clearly pleased and appreciative. He was in no hurry, he said, as his main work was done. The only thing left now, he added, was to wipe out the Manchus in the Tartar City. There were only a couple of thousand of them to deal with, and that would be soon done; in fact, they should be starting it now. As we were chatting, machine-gun fire suddenly broke out from the Tartar City, followed by a weird, wailing sound that froze my blood.

"They have started," General Hsu remarked. "Would you like to see it?"

I mumbled some excuse, and rose to take my leave. I left the Yamen with that despairing, agonised, wild wailing of the doomed ringing in my ears.

I had quite a shock when I returned to Chinkiang. My boss in Shanghai, Mr. Erlanger, had arrived that day with a man to take my place, a young Frenchman named Chapeaux.

He had read in one of the Shanghai papers that I had been appointed general in the Revolutionary Army and had led the assault on Purple Mountain which won the day. Such is fame. Some benighted "war correspondent" for the *North China Daily News* was responsible for the article. He had "covered" the battle from Yaohuamen, and had interviewed some of my stretcher-bearers.

I did not look much like a general. The back of my coat was covered with dried blood and so was the back of my shirt, which I now had a chance to change for the first time since I had carried that bleeding man on my back, as I had no spare clothing in the field. It seemed that my impetuousness had got me into a serious mess and that my career as a merchant had ended before it was really started.

There were two things only that saved me. The first was that M. Chapeaux knew no Chinese, and my compradore said that knowledge of Chinese was essential, because sooner or later interior buying centres would have to be visited. The second was that Mr. Erlanger was a real sport, who had appreciated the whole adventure. I later took him up to the hospital where he saw the wounded and had a long talk with Dr. Balean.

There was no doubt that our unit had saved the lives of the three hundred and ninety-four severely wounded who had been treated in Chinkiang, apart from the hundreds of "out-patients" who had been treated and cared for in the field. So instead of curtains for me, my shares went up a lot during the day.

In the evening Mr. Erlanger said that he would like to see Nanking before he returned, and I went with him by river steamer that night. We landed early in the morning, and I got him passed through the gate. However, the sight of those gory heads dangling like bunches of onions from the telephone posts was too much for him. He was violently sick, and I had to take him out again and give him a stiff drink at the Bridge House Hotel.

We returned by train, and the same afternoon he and M. Chapeaux went back to Shanghai. I drew a deep sigh of relief. It had been a narrow squeak.

It was difficult to settle down to work in Chinkiang for the next month or so. The work during the Nanking campaign and the life we had led, with all its discomforts and difficulties, was such a complete change that it unsettled me. There something happened every day, there was bustle and movement, but nothing ever happened in Chinkiang that could be called exciting.

The place had suddenly become doubly dull and monotonous although a number of new people, mostly young fellows for the Standard Oil Company and the British-American Tobacco Company, had arrived. It was astonishing how many different types came and went. Some were mystery men whom you never got to know much about. They stayed for a while and disappeared.

This was particularly the case in the Customs Service, where the greatest assortment of individuals could be found. There were men like Smith who dared not sleep alone in his house, and Stenson, the ex-banker, who had shot the man that broke up his married life. Stenson was clearly a highly educated man, and one night, when in his cups, he told me his history. His was the story of a desperately unhappy man, moving restlessly from place to place, trying to forget the past. He had sailed in windjammers, been a miner, beachcomber, journalist, bar-tender, and chucker-out. He disappeared from the Concession after a few months.

In the meantime, life went on. Quite a number of the fellows now had ponies, and we all rode together at six in the morning. The British-American Tobacco Company had rented a house out in the country near the Victoria Park, and we used to meet there every morning and breakfast together after the cross-country ride.

One morning a man turned up from the Shanghai office and

introduced himself as Freddie Schroeder, from Arizona. He arrived from the station carrying a small, battered suitcase with his belongings. His face, especially the nose, looked battered too, but there was something frank and very pleasing about him. We were just starting on our ride, and I, quite innocently, asked him if he could ride and would he care to come along, as I knew there was a spare pony in the stable. Freddie "guessed" that he could get along on a cayuse, but he was used to a Mexican saddle, and didn't know if he could "git" along on one of them English saddles that looked like a postage stamp.

He came along, and we all thought he got along amazingly well on his postage stamp. In fact, he was permanently fixed to it no matter what the pony did. Then, apparently having found the saddle to his liking, he did some amazing trick-riding at full gallop, picking up grass tufts from the ground on either side. He was an ex-rodeo trick rider and bronco buster, and I felt no end of a fool for having asked him if he could ride. That ride was one of the finest and wildest I can remember, jumping over the graves with our necks for sale. Freddie had taken us all by storm, and the longer we knew him, the more he won our affection.

He was a lovable character, very much like Pete in build, only heavier. Wild at times, perhaps, but straight, honest and loyal to the last ditch. And what a friend to have in a tight corner! Strong as a bull, quite fearless and obviously a man who had held his own in many tight places. His nose was battered, but somehow it belonged to that rugged face, and his fine, blue eyes made up for facial defects if they could be called such. It was good to be in his company, and the daily rides became something much more exciting and memorable after he joined us.

The Concession was keeping pace with all the new business activities, and the installation of an electric plant and waterworks with an intake far out in the river made us fully up to date. Gone were the days of oil-lamps, punkahs and contaminated water, and the long stifling summer nights. The heat was no longer to be dreaded now that we had electric fans.

The only trouble was the complete stoppage of export trade since the Revolutionary Army had marched out of Nanking in its advance on Peking. This was during December and January, and the sweep towards the north had paralysed our communications with northern Anhui. It was impossible to know how long the stoppage would last without going up to investigate, and as we got no news from our Chinese agents I decided to go up and see for myself.

The first part of the journey would be comparatively easy, as the Tientsin–Pukow Railway was now operating as far as the Huai River. My final destination would be Pochow, almost at the end of the Ku River, a tributary of the Huai, and how to get there would depend on what means of transportation I could get at the end of the railway. In fact the journey was more or less going off into the blue, for I had no exact idea of where Pochow was; and the compradore, who came along, knew very little more. As I did not care for Chinese food at that time, my cook filled a big box with enough tinned food for a month, which would be approximately the duration of the trip, and away we went. At Nanking we crossed by ferry to Pukow, and there we took the train to Lin Hai Kwan, the terminus.

It had again been a bad famine year, and from Pukow onwards we met pathetic straggling bands of survivors tottering along the dusty roads, all of them emaciated through want and suffering. There were practically no children to be seen. They would have been sold farther up the line to provide a few meals for the rest of the family, for the price of a child was again one shilling for a girl, and this sum would not last long. This ghastly trade went on openly and shamelessly, and the starving sellers were beaten down to the last farthing because they were entirely at the mercy of the buyers. It was of no use that the parents offered themselves, for they were not wanted; only girls for the brothels and boys for domestic slavery were saleable. One by one the children went. They would get food that way, and receive a home of sorts, and the money would help the parents to struggle on for a few more days. The alternative was slow, painful and certain death for them all.

At every station long before we pulled in we could hear the moans and pitiful supplication for food by hundreds of starving wretches. A loud chant of hopeless torment greeted the train, and eyes that glittered with pain, intensely alive in the otherwise dead and expressionless faces, stared at us through the windows. The situation got worse as we proceeded on the journey.

At one station it was bedlam. Hundreds of starving men and women were pressed against the white picket fence, clamouring for food from the passengers. A soldier marched stolidly up and down to see that they did not break the fence or enter the platform. Someone threw a few coppers at the crowd and roared with laughter when they fought like wild beasts over them. There was a sudden press against the fence, and the soldier brought up his rifle and bashed in a face with the butt. I jumped out of the train and yelled at him. White with fury I flayed him with all I could lay my tongue to. He looked at me in surprise and blank astonishment. Then he pointed to the fallen man: "He doesn't complain. He is well out of it! This is quick, and they'll all die anyway. Besides, they might break the fence."

The soldier was right. His victim was well out of it, and the fence was not broken, which was all that really mattered. If I had seen, daily, what that soldier had seen, I might even have done the same. It was something hopelessly beyond individual aid, a horrible mass-destruction of thousands, destruction by slow inches of the unwanted. If the officials deliberately turned their backs on the calamity, what could individuals do? It was impossible to give anything to a few of the sufferers, for they would be attacked by the desperate crowd who would trample one another to death for a few coppers. I tried it once, and they fought like savages. The result was a riot, and only added to their suffering.

It was a relief to get to Lin Hai Kwan and away from it all. My compradore had a friend there, a shopkeeper, and we went to him to make arrangements for the journey. We discussed this matter in a tiny smelly office at the back of the shop. The trip was not going to be easy, for all traffic had stopped on the Ku River. There were some ugly rumours about the state of affairs up in that direction, and he doubted whether he could get a boat to take us. A big and comfortable boat would be out of the question; it would be too conspicuous for one thing, and the owners wouldn't want to risk it. A smaller one, perhaps, if we did not mind a little discomfort and were prepared to pay well. What the ugly rumours were, he did not want to say, but he hinted that the whole district was not healthy at present.

I spent a very uncomfortable night on two planks placed on some empty boxes at the back of the shop. I was told it was better than the inn, which was full of bugs, and, in addition, it was just as well that I did not advertise my presence in Lin Hai Kwan. We spent the whole of the next day trying to get a boat, and finally got hold of a small one with a tiny cabin, more like a large dog-kennel than anything else.

It was fairly wide, and had ample room for sleeping, but as it was only about four feet high, we had to move about doubled up, and the boatman would take us only on condition that I stayed in the cabin and did not show myself during the daytime. At night I could come out and do as I pleased. I did not quite see the sense of these elaborate precautions, nor did I relish being cooped up for days in a place where I could not stand up, but had either to lie down or sit on a hard bench. The boatman, however, insisted that this was essential, and I could do nothing but agree. Not a very pleasant outlook for me, as the boatman said that the trip to Pochow would take about ten days.

We got our gear on board at night so as not to attract any attention, and started off at dawn. The current of the Huai was fairly strong and it was late in the afternoon before we reached Huai Yuen, a small city where the Ku River runs into the Huai. Here we branched off and started on our journey up the peaceful winding Ku. The cabin was fitted with sliding wooden shutters on either side, which I could open slightly and get some air and light. I was also able to see without being seen. As soon as we had passed Huai Yuen I opened them wider until we came to the next village. This was all very exciting and mysterious in the beginning, but soon the deadly monotony and inaction began to pall. There was not a boat to be seen, which in itself set me wondering, for the Ku was usually a very busy river carrying an enormous junk traffic, and in China the cessation of such traffic is a bad omen.

Round about noon I decided to have something to eat, more to pass the time than because I was hungry. I opened the box and took out a couple of tins; mock-turtle soup and kippers. It looked good to me, and it tasted good too, after it was heated up on the little oil-stove. Afterwards I read for a while, in the rather poor light, and then had a nap.

In the afternoon we ran into a long stretch of more or less deserted country, and I opened the shutters wide. There was a fair wind and our high, bamboo slatted sail was drawing well. The water was crystal clear; from the green banks weeping willows bent gracefully over the stream, their long bare branches waving gently in the breeze. Snow-white egrets perched on the drooping willow branches or flew back and forth, mirrored in the clear water close to the banks where the wind made no ripples. The whole scene breathed of peace and seemed out of keeping with our furtive and cautious journey.

After dark I went out on the small foredeck and walked up and down to get the stiffness out of my legs. There was not much room, three paces, that was all, but it was enough. There were only two boatmen on board and they took turn and turn about at the tiller and the oars. They slept in a tiny cubby-hole aft and had to work pretty hard as we did not often stop. The man at the tiller would steer with one hand and push the long oar with the other if the breeze was faint and sailing too slow, and sometimes the other worked the forward oar as well.

Chang, one of the boatmen, was squatting forward, right up in the bow, gazing stolidly ahead. Occasionally he would turn in my direction but was apparently too shy to speak. After a while I went over and spoke to him, but he found it difficult to understand me, for he was used only to the Anhui dialect. I also found it hard to understand his brogue at first, but, with the occasional help of the compradore, we got along after a while. Chang was the hired man and a simple, honest soul. He was very shy, but little by little he got over his shyness and later on in the long night watches he confided to me all his little difficulties and troubles. They were not many, but they were very real, and he found it a great comfort to discuss them with me. He could not do so with the other boatman who was the skipper-owner, who would probably cut him short. It was long after midnight before I went back to the cabin to sleep.

When I woke up and peeped through the slats, it was raining and the wind had turned against us. Chang was ashore with the towing-line, pulling us along. The day seemed endless with nothing to do but read and smoke, and the light was very poor.

At noon I dipped into the box to get something for tiffin. I brought up mock-turtle soup and kippers again.

Suspicious, I started to unpack. First came eighteen tins each of mock-turtle soup and kippers, and I saw a long, horrible vista of days to come with nothing but this diet. Then I found a tin of salmon and one of corned beef, twelve tins of plum and apple jam and two small tins of sardines, which brightened the outlook a little, but not much. . . . At the bottom were four tins of oxtail soup, cheese, butter and biscuits. It might have been worse, but it might have been much, much better. I suddenly took a violent dislike to mock-turtle soup and kippers and vowed that I would throw all the tins, one by one, at the cook when I got back. The following three days I lived on corned beef, oxtail soup and salmon. It was pretty grim I thought. How quickly I had forgotten those starving thousands along the railroad.

One afternoon Chang popped his head in and said that we would soon be at Meng Cheng, the first big city, but that they were not going to stop and would carry on as long as the light lasted. An hour or so later I could see a grey, tall city wall ahead, but no signs of life on the road leading towards the gate. Later I heard the rattle of boat-hooks and the tramp of feet, which told me they were poling the boat along.

Then we bumped into something and stuck. The boatmen grunted and swore, straining hard at the poles. I peeped out and saw numerous human bodies floating in the water. The compradore came in and reported that the river ahead of us was choked with them, and that the bank outside the gate was piled high with dead. He thought the whole town had been wiped out, because the main gate was wide open and there was not a soul in sight anywhere. I got out on the foredeck and the boatmen did not protest: they were horror-stricken. I wanted to get into the town to see if anyone needed help, but it was difficult to get alongside and, when we did succeed, we had to walk over the dead to the gate; there was no getting round them. It was a ghastly feeling treading on lifeless human flesh.

Somehow we picked our way over them and reached the gate. A fairly wide main street lay ahead, but it was entirely deserted and strewn with rubbish. The shops and the houses fronting it had been looted and stripped, and chaos was everywhere as far as we went. We shouted from time to time, but got no reply. Here and there we found bodies in the street, but many more in the houses. Many of them were women and children, some terribly mutilated. Meng Cheng was a city of the dead.

It was getting dark and we could do nothing there, so we returned to the boat. The boatmen had poled their way through the dead in the river by the time we got back, which saved us the ordeal of walking over the pile of corpses once more. And as night spread its merciful cloak over those huddled bodies with the terror-stricken faces, we left the city.

Three days later we reached Koyang, which appeared to be untouched, for we saw people moving about outside the city walls. We did not stop but pushed right on.

For some reason, known only to the boatmen, the danger zone was now considered to be passed, and it was no longer necessary for me to remain in the cabin in the daytime. I don't think they really knew much about the hazards of the trip except, perhaps, that rumours of the Meng Cheng massacre may have reached them and made them very nervous. On several occasions I had tried to find out what they were scared of and why I had to conceal myself, but could never get a direct and satisfactory reply. All they would reply was: "Ping, Tufei, Huai ren." (Soldiers, bandits and bad men.)

I enjoyed my freedom and often used to walk for miles along the banks. The country was flat and monotonous, and the river itself was the prettiest part of it. The country here was fairly thickly populated and yet there was no traffic anywhere on the roads. Even tiny villages had built hastily-constructed mud walls, and deep ditches like moats surrounded them, all freshly made. It looked as if the whole countryside was in a state of siege and yet there were no soldiers to be seen anywhere, nor was there anything visible of which to be afraid.

The last evening before reaching Pochow Chang unburdened himself to me about his biggest problem. He wanted to get himself a wife, but did not quite know if it was wise. His pay was one dollar a month and his keep, and he had saved a little out of that during the last few years. He could buy a nice girl now at Lin Hai Kwan for fifty cents, but if he waited for another year or so there might not be a famine, and he would not be able to buy one at all. Then, if he bought one now, he would have to get a few things together to make a home, and all that cost money.

It certainly was a problem at one dollar a month, and I could see Chang's point. As regards price it seemed to be now or never, but the other considerations were not be blinked at. Of one thing I am certain. He had not told me of his perplexity with the idea of getting money from me: he was too simple and honest for that. It just relieved him to find a sympathetic listener. I left him to get some supper and to think over some way of helping him.

There was nothing but mock-turtle soup and kippers left. I couldn't face that, and went back to Chang to ask him if he could fix me up with some Chinese food. Chang went aft and after a while came back with a big bowl of vermicelli soup and mantou (unleavened bread). It was delicious, and from that day until I returned to Chinkiang I ate nothing but Chinese food.

XVI

POCHOW was a big, untidy place surrounded by mud walls. It was clearly the centre of a large farming area, and all the surplus grain, mostly wheat and sesamum seed, was shipped from there. The river was packed with junks, but they were all laid up and empty until the merchants were sure that it was safe to ship their cargoes down to Chinkiang. The whole foreshore, outside the city gates, teemed with idle coolies who looked at us, and especially me, with awed curiosity. It was clear that they had not seen foreigners before, for I could feel the intensity of their collective gaze.

Leaving the boat, I pressed a dollar into Chang's hand. He looked at it in amazement, as if he did not believe his eyes, and, as the truth slowly dawned on him, he rushed after me and tried to give it back. It was too much, he protested, and I must have made a mistake. Did I realise that I had given him a whole dollar, a whole month's wages? I told him to add it to his savings and left him gazing at it, half in wonder, half in disbelief; when I looked back, a little later, I saw a broad and happy grin on his honest face. I had another plan, of which I did not tell him then. The boat was to take us back to Lin Hai Kwan when our work was over, and I had a surprise in store for him at the end of the journey.

We made our way through a very crowded main street where everyone stopped to gaze at me, not only the people in the street but the shopkeepers who served their customers in the open-fronted shops on either side. The butcher wielding his cleaver stopped with his arm raised, and looked with bulging eyes. So did the oil vendors with their long-handled dippers, the haberdasher with his yardstick, and the tea merchant at his scales.

Every activity seemed to stop until I was out of sight. We were making for our agent's office which we found without difficulty with every urchin in the street offering to show us the way: some were in front, and there was a whole army of them trailing behind, determined not to miss a thing. When we arrived, they streamed silently in and filled the courtyard. They were not like the noisy chattering crowds I was used to; they just stood and gazed without making a sound.

The agent was greatly surprised and delighted to see us. He had large, roomy premises facing the big courtyard on three sides, and he offered me his two best guest-rooms. It did not take us long to settle in, and the smaller of my rooms made a fine, light office. The whole place was swarming with servants: furniture was produced like magic, and in a few minutes my office was fully furnished with a very handsome blackwood desk and chair to match, tea-tables and chairs were placed alternately against the longest wall, and a big, heavy opium couch against the end wall. Finally a large tray with opium pipes, a lamp and all the glittering little boxes and gadgets belonging to the opium tray were produced. Neither of us smoked opium, but it was a typically polite Chinese gesture in case we did.

The whole place was noise, bustle and excitement, for the Chinese love nothing better than to receive unexpected guests. From the kitchen came the incessant clatter of pots and pans and the rapid tattoo of chopping knives and, from the large dining-hall, the rattle of chopsticks and dishes. But through all this the crowd in the courtyard remained unmoved and silent, gazing in through the big windows of my room to see what I was doing, following with unblinking eyes every movement I made.

The agent had invited some of the biggest dealers in the place to meet us and partake of the feast in our honour. It was my first Chinese feast, and a very memorable one it proved to be. Every delicacy Pochow could produce was on the table: bird's-nest soup, shark-fins, bêche-de-mer, black fungus, cuttlefish, duck, chicken and fish made up in a bewildering variety of dishes. With it went unlimited Shaoshing wine and the excitement and uproar of playing fingers for drinks, the favourite Chinese game of forfeits. No business was discussed, for this was only a get-together party and business could wait.

It was the first of a succession of parties, and in between feasts we talked business. I also tried to do some office work, but it was very difficult. The moment I sat down at my desk, the crowd outside pressed against the window with flattened noses and staring, unblinking eyes, watching every movement. I chased them away, the servants chased them away, but they came back at once like mesmerised rabbits. It was terribly trying, as were the concentrated stares in every street when I passed through. There was no hostility, yet the staring got on my nerves more and more as time went on. The looks could actually be felt after the eyes had passed out of sight; that is, I could constantly see them in front and feel them from behind, and they made an impression on me I have never forgotten. And after the staring in the street came the flattened noses and unwinking eyes at the window, day after day for nearly three weeks. Fortunately the work was then nearly done.

We had bought all the sesamum seed we required and chartered two hundred junks to carry it down. We were to lead the "flotilla" in our own boat as far as Lin Hai Kwan, as the boatmen were still nervous of bandits in the Meng Cheng district. There remained only one thing to do, and that was a trip to Yung Cheng to investigate the reason for the stoppage of all traffic between that town and Pochow.

This was one of the main arteries which, for some unknown reason, had entirely ceased to function. By the time we were ready to leave we found that we could not induce a single carter to take us, even for double pay. The reason they all gave was bandits. Then the Magistrate suddenly came to our rescue. He had been very worried about my presence in Pochow ever since I came, for he was personally responsible for my safety. When I called to say good-bye I mentioned that I had to get to Yung Cheng first, before my work was completed, and that my departure would be postponed until I could get a mule-cart to take me there.

He immediately offered me his own mule-cart and a military escort. The cart would take me right to Yung Cheng and back, but the escort would only see us as far as the borders of his own district. It was quite clear that he was determined that nothing should happen to me in his district and, if anything did happen outside, it would be too bad for the magistrate in Yung Cheng who would then be responsible..

We started off early the next morning. The Peking-cart was a fine one with a strong, sleek mule in the shafts and a lively pony in the traces in front, and we had twelve tattered soldiers with old, rusty Mausers as a bodyguard. They tried to present arms as I came out, and one of them nearly bayoneted me in the attempt. What good they would do, in case of any trouble, I could not imagine, but they looked picturesque and added to our "face" as we "processed" out of town. It was a weird sight and a weird journey.

It was my first trip in a Peking-cart, and I have always been willing to try anything once. They are springless and made of very hard wood. You sit on the floor, inside a kennel-like house with a rounded top, and absorb all the shocks and jars. If you are jogging along on a fairly decent road, you just sit and shake like a jelly, and your legs go to sleep. Suddenly the wheel hits a rock, and you hit the ceiling. So perfect is the conductivity that you can feel that rock hit the bottom of your spine; then the pain travels upwards and hits you in the back of your head like a sledge hammer. The mule and the pony were feeling good that morning, rocks and potholes were plentiful and we seemed to hit them all. The compradore took it without turning a hair. Carts *were* like that, he had paid for the ride, and he *would* ride. I got out and walked. The country was flat, the road broad, bumpy and dusty, and absolutely deserted.

After a couple of hours the guards, who were steadily lagging behind, yelled to us that they were returning, and we carried on alone. It was rather a queer sensation to go along on this wide, deeply rutted thoroughfare without seeing a soul as far ahead as the eye could see. Usually, at this time, such a road would be packed with traffic, particularly grain-carts from Yung Cheng and districts beyond.

In the far distance was a village, and we thought we could get some information there. It took us nearly an hour to reach it and we found the main gate shut. The whole village was surrounded by a deep ditch, and there was no bridge across it to the gate. We called out, but got no reply, and finally drove round the place across the fields until we struck the main road again.

There was another village, not far away, and we had better luck there. When we called out, several heads appeared over the mud wall. They wanted to know who we were and what we wanted, but it took us a long time to convince them that we were respectable travellers. Finally, they opened the gates and threw two ropes to us. The ropes were attached to stout poles which we hauled across the moat and placed on top of the bank. Then they put planks across the poles and made a primitive, but serviceable bridge. Once we were through the gates, they dismantled the bridge, hauled everything in and barred the gates.

The villagers clustered round us eager for news. They looked desperately poor, worried and dejected. All of them were farmers who huddled together in villages for mutual protection. It was apparently the way they lived in this part of the country, for I saw no solitary farmhouses anywhere. There were big clusters and small clusters, all surrounded by walls and a deep ditch, all in a state of siege. I asked the reason. Soldiers and bandits they told me: just now it was bandits. First the soldiers came and took all their animals away and nearly all the stored grain. Then came the bandits and almost cleaned them out. The bandits had always been there, but this year they were worse than ever; the soldiers had taken so much that the bandits were desperate because the gleanings were not enough. They had managed to hide a little grain, just enough for food until the winter wheat was harvested in May, and now they were terrified of losing it.

All the villages in the district were in the same plight, as the hidden grain would just keep starvation away until the harvest. What a life and what an outlook! I spoke mostly to the headman, a fine old man with a deeply furrowed and weatherbeaten face. They all seemed to brighten up in our company, and were very glad to talk to us. They were open, friendly and honest, and they had courage too, not only to stick it out in the face of such hopelessness, but actually to fight with hoes, pitchforks and sticks against armed men, for they had already beaten off many attacks. They saw us out through the other gate and fixed the temporary bridge for us. The headman begged us to be careful on the road, for the bandits were all mounted and might be lurking anywhere. Money was no good to these people, but I promised to bring some food back from Yung Cheng, especially salt and fresh vegetables which they required urgently.

The position was the same all along the road, a country besieged and paralysed with every village fortified. In a few places I saw people slide on a pole from the top of the mud walls across the moat to tend a few cabbage patches, cut some cabbages and then climb back again. The main road had originally gone straight through the larger villages, but now we had to find our way round them as it would take too long to wait until we had allayed suspicion and the temporary bridge had been fixed up for us. It was evening before we reached Yung Cheng.

When we first saw it in the distance, Yung Cheng looked a big place with good stout walls. We had some difficulty in getting through the city gates, but I told the soldier on guard to send my card to the Magistrate and we got through. The compradore found a fairly clean inn for the night, and we were just having supper when a runner arrived with the Magistrate's compliments, and asked us to call as soon as we could.

The runner waited until we had finished eating and then showed us the way. The Yamen was a very imposing building with numerous courtyards lit by large paper lanterns and with an armed guard at every door. The Magistrate was in a large room in the last courtyard. He was small, dapper and had a clever face: foxy is perhaps a better description. After the usual lengthy introduction necessary in polite society, we got down to business as quick as is possible in China—that is, very slowly and painfully. It is not what one says that counts, but rather the correct implication of the questions and answers, which is often the opposite of what is actually said in words.

The Magistrate said he was grieved that I should find the country in such a disturbed state and that he would never have forgiven himself if anything had happened to me before I arrived in Yung Cheng. This, I correctly assumed, meant that he wished something had happened to me before I reached *his* district and placed the onus of my safety on him. He then hoped I would stay for some time so that he could entertain me to the best of his poor ability, and asked if I would indicate the approximate time of my stay so that he could make plans. This implied a hope that I would not stay and worry him any longer than was necessary, and he brightened visibly when I told him I was leaving the next day. After nearly half an hour I was able to state my business, which was to find out why nothing had been done to restore the broken communications with Pochow, and when some improvement might be expected. His reply was not very hopeful.

The country was overrun with bandits, and his forces were not large enough to cope with them. He had only two thousand men, and they were only sufficient to hold Yung Cheng. I asked him how it was that unarmed villagers could keep the bandits out and why it was necessary to have two thousand men to defend Yung Cheng when they might be employed to keep communications open with Pochow. He gave me many reasons, none of them valid. It was clear that he was keeping all his forces in Yung Cheng to safeguard himself and his local interests. Before leaving, I ventured a shot in the dark, by suggesting that one thousand men could easily hold Yung Cheng and the rest patrol the Pochow road. This would restore communications and counteract any undesirable consequences of my report to the Nanking government. After all, they could not possibly remove him from office if they knew he had done his best, and I *did* want to see him again when I returned in a couple of months to find out if there was any improvement. He was pondering over this when we left.

The next morning we returned over the same dreary and depressing road. We brought with us salt, vegetables, pickled turnips and some cabbage seeds for the old headman, and from the joy in the village I think they will remember us for years. We reached Pochow safely in the evening.

We left the next morning with our boat leading and a long string of junks following astern. In order to keep together we arranged for certain stopping-places every night. Our boat was small and light and would, naturally, be faster than the others, but every night we stopped and waited for the rest. I spent most of the time on the foredeck with my rifle handy. The current was helping us now and we made much faster time. We passed Meng Cheng at night and found the passage clear, but the city was still silent and deserted. A small Chinese gunboat, a junk with a muzzle-loading gun mounted forward, was anchored just below the city and was the first sign of returning authority.

Chang, my boatman, was now a changed man, with all his

problems solved. He had made up his mind to get married, and had arranged for his mother to keep his girl bride in the beginning. He regarded me as his friend and benefactor for life; it was my dollar which had turned the scales, as he had taken it to be a good omen when he received it so unexpectedly. I was beginning to get quite excited about my return to Chinkiang. I had never thought I could long so much for that place, but I had been in the interior over a month now, and it would be grand to hear English voices again. Most of all I was pining for the dogs.

Stopping every night for the junks was a nuisance, but could not be helped, and the fourth day out, in the evening, we arrived at Huai Yuen. There was no longer any need to carry on with the convoy system: in any case it would not have protected us from attack, as I was the only armed man. However, my presence had given the junkmen the necessary confidence to take them past Meng Cheng, which was all that mattered. Now I intended to push on as I wanted to catch the early morning train from Lin Hai Kwan, and I told my boatman to carry on. He opposed the order strongly. There were rocks in the Huai River, he said, and it was too dark to see them. I thought it was only a common Chinese excuse to have a comfortable night at Huai Yuen instead of travelling in the dark, so I overruled all his objections. He eventually started off, but grumbled all the time. There seemed to be quite a strong current, and we were moving fast when suddenly there was a crash. We bumped hard two or three times, and the boat started to spin.

The boatmen yelled and jabbered and water came spouting through the bottom boards in the cabin. I grabbed the lantern and tore off the loose floor boards. The water was pouring in through a huge hole in the bottom, and I could not get at it at once because the bilges were full of ballast, mostly rocks. I told the compradore to bale with a washbasin, while I heaved the rocks over the side, for we were filling fast and I did not relish a swim. Having cleared the space round the hole, I looked round frantically for something to stuff into it. I saw a bag of flour in a corner, which was just the thing, for the hole was very large, and I slammed it on. Then I put a flat rock on top of it, made the compradore's small cook sit on top of that, and the worst was over.

The compradore and I then baled all the way to Lin Hai Kwan but, even so, we barely managed to keep afloat.

It was pitch dark and bitterly cold when we arrived. The whole town was asleep, huddled under the falling sleet. Before the compradore and I could look for shelter we had to bargain with the boatman for the damage. He needed a whole bottom plank, and five dollars settled that. Then I bequeathed my bedding and stores to Chang. On the way up he had worried a great deal about the high cost of bedding, which was one of the essential items on his list, and now he would be fixed up for years. The stores he could sell at Lin Hai Kwan. Finally, I gave him five dollars for a wedding present. If I had given him any more he would have gone clean off his head.

I also owed something to the other boatman whom I had forced to undertake the last stretch in the dark, and gave him an extra two dollars. Then we scrambled up the steep slippery bank and made for the railway station. There we spent the night in the small, cold waiting-room, stamping about half the time to keep our wet feet warm. However, I thought the last stage of the journey was worth this slight discomfort, for that episode on the river was the only real excitement we had had on the whole trip.

We arrived at Chinkiang late in the afternoon. It was cold and raining hard, but the chair-coolies were waiting at the station and they took us home at a great pace. There is nothing to beat a sedan-chair for comfort if you have four strapping coolies swinging along in perfect rhythm. Even when we passed through the smelly, dismal Maloo, I leaned back with a contented sigh.

XVII

I HAD a great welcome from the dogs on my return, and a telegram from the Shanghai office: "Well done." I am afraid I had stolen a march on our competitors, for no cargo except ours came through from the interior that season and my dereliction of duty when I had gone off with the Red Cross unit was completely forgotten. In fact, it had done the firm a lot of good, as we had got "big face" with the new regime. A letter from General Hsu was waiting for me, inviting me to Nanking to receive the Red Cross of Honour and the Battle of Nanking medals.

The investiture in the Viceroy's palace was a grand affair, but I still had the memory of the Manchu massacre vividly in my mind, and I did not feel greatly impressed or honoured. I was surprised by the scruffy appearance of the officers and men. The queue-cutting campaign had started in Nanking, and I saw nothing but untidy mops of hair. The one and only sign of cleanliness, the shaved ring round the skull and the sleek well-groomed queues, had vanished, and an unlovely mop of bristly, unkempt hair had taken its place. The sole object was to remove the mark of bondage and put the stamp of the New Order on everybody. But the people did not submit to it willingly, for they were exceedingly proud of their queues.

On my return to Chinkiang Dr. Stephenson called on me to say good-bye. He told me that his experiences at Ma Chung had killed his ambition to work for the Chinese and he was returning to the States with his baby girl. He wanted to take his baby back to a clean country among clean people before she could realise the filth and squalor, the beastliness and cruelty of China.

He had sad news about Pete. He was in love and had stopped

smoking because his girl, a devout Christian, did not approve. "She's trying to improve him and has ruined him altogether," Stephenson said; "now he goes mooning around sucking candy, and all the life has gone out of him. But he's crazy about her, so he's a gone coon."

Pete was a "gone coon" all right when I met him a few days later. He talked of nothing but his girl and how unworthy he was of her. I could gladly have wrung that girl's neck.

However, I soon had other things to think about, for we experienced our first riot, a short, but very ugly affair. Some Chinese soldiers had come strolling into the Concession to look around and wanted a rickshaw ride when they had seen enough. The only available rickshaws were two in which women were riding. Two soldiers stopped the rickshaws and started to haul the shrieking women out. One of the Concession policemen intervened and at once a fierce fight started. The policeman blew his whistle, reinforcements came, and the two soldiers were hauled off to the police station, whilst the other soldiers ran off yelling imprecations and threats. I had heard the row from my office and came out, and hearing the soldiers' threats I walked off at once to warn the Consul. I then warned the Chairman of our Watch Committee and was returning along the Bund, when I saw the Chinese fleeing in all directions from the boundary road as some thirty odd soldiers came charging in, ramming magazines into their rifles.

In the deadly stillness I could hear the rattle and snick of the breech-bolts as the cartridges were rammed home. I was the only man on the Bund and I had no intention of meeting that charge defenceless. The soldiers were about a hundred yards off and kneeling to fire. I slipped off into the one and only side street, and did the hundred yards dash in record time. Rounding the next corner I nearly ran down Mr. Twyman, the Consul, who had come to read the Riot Act. I told him hurriedly what was going on on the Bund. He was a very cool and determined man, and his coolness saved the day. He went straight on and I came with him. Rounding the corner we saw a soldier kneeling in the middle of the road, aiming straight at us. Behind every tree were other soldiers with the muzzles of their rifles pointing at us. I am sorry to say I did not feel very brave, but the Consul went straight for the kneeling man and as I tagged along I knew that our lives hung by a thread and that this bold unhurried advance was the only thing that could save us now. It puzzled and unsettled the soldiers, although they still pointed their rifles at us and followed us with the muzzles. Mr. Twyman called out to the kneeling man: "If you shoot, you'll be beheaded! Don't be a fool—put down that rifle!"

The man did not move, and some of the others ran up and surrounded us. One jammed his rifle into Mr. Twyman's chest, another into his back. He never turned a hair, but said quietly, but firmly: "I am the British Consul. If you kill me, you will be executed. Put down your rifles at once!"

At that moment I heard an order being shouted in Chinese. Turning, I saw that an officer had arrived and in the nick of time too. He was nearly breathless from running, and very angry. A few sharp commands, and the soldiers moved away from us slowly and reluctantly.

I breathed once more, and my stomach came into place again. By now the soldiers had lined up, sullen but under control. The officer came over and apologised profusely to Mr. Twyman; then he marched his men off. After they had passed the corner, Twyman mopped his forehead and said "Whew!"; that was all.

I had not been feeling well since my return from the Ku River and now broke out in open sores. Nothing the doctor could do improved my condition, and he was completely mystified by these virulent sores that would not yield to any kind of treatment.

At last he told me to try the sulphur baths at Unzen in Japan, and I went off on sick leave. There is always some compensation for every ill in life, and this sickness not only gave me a much-needed rest and change but an enchanting journey to fairyland, for it was cherry blossom time in Japan.

My first delights were the beauties of Nagasaki Bay, where islands and promontories, fragrant with pines, stretched out from the rocks to look at their own reflections in the still, blue waters. Toy houses sheltered among the rocks and trees, and shrines and temples in red and gold lacquer with massive roofs and curved eaves gleamed as I gazed towards the land. I thought of the old

Chinese legend that the curved eaves were there to remind them of the days when they lived in tents, for those eaves and the roofs looked just like tents in outline. But the most beautiful sight of all was the cherry blossom, pale-pink clouds floating over and among the sombre green of the pines. At Nagasaki I was to take a rick-shaw over the hills to a little fishing village called Mogi, then go on by steam launch to Obama at the foot of the high Unzen Mountains. From there, I would be carried by chair up the long steep mountain track to Unzen. In the summer this route swarmed with visitors from Shanghai and Hongkong; but it was now much too early for tourists, and I had the whole road to myself. I was in no hurry and could linger on the way. It was a strange sen-sation to find myself in a land and among a people where every-thing and everybody were spotlessly clean. The gay colouring of the kimonos, especially those of the children and young women, the clean faces and the total absence of filthy and ragged beggars which crowded the Maloo every day, were a joy, and the neat and dignified appearance of the married women and older people in their dark, almost sombre kimonos made a perfect foil to the riot of gay colours of the young.

I stopped at a little tea-house with a thatched roof on a high bank by a mountain stream where the cherry trees leaned over the banks and the blossoms nearly touched the water. On a rustic bridge children stood silently and watched their reflections in the clear stream while the cherry trees appeared to do so in a quiet eddy, their petals falling like pale pink snowflakes slowly and gently in the still air, to settle on the water and drift away. While I watched them, my mind went back to the fo'c'sle-head of the "Hermanso" and the old bosun who told us about the pale-pink snowflakes at Nagasaki when we sat smoking and yarning in the summer evenings.* And now, sitting entranced and sipping my tea on the veranda of the little tea-house, I had seen them. I asked the waitress if any sailors ever came there. "Not now, dannasan," she told me, "but my father say that many years ago plenty sailors come here from seal-catching ships, drink beer and then go Mogi eat lobster."

I knew that the old bosun had been seal-poaching off

* *Sea Fever*

Kamchatka, and that their main calling ports were Nagasaki and Hakodate, so I felt that I was following in his footsteps when I took the road to Mogi. The first stage was a long fairly steep road winding to the top of the hill, where it was customary to stop and let the rickshaw coolie have a short rest and treat him to a bottle of beer at one of the small road-houses. After that it was downhill at a rattling pace on a road flanked by giant bamboos: clean dainty pillars of delicate green, diffusing their colour like a pale-green mist in the eternal half-light of the groves. At Mogi, fishermen's huts nestled in small clusters round a sandy bay where the wind blew salt and fresh from the sea and called to me from a world I had almost forgotten, or had made myself forget.

The deep blue sea, stippled with tiny white caps, whispered to me again the old magic messages, and I imagined I saw tall ships in the sunset haze. I left an excellent lobster half-eaten and sat there dreaming till the launch came in to take me to Obama, where I spent the night. Early next morning the chairbearers took me up the mountain, some three thousand feet through pine-groves, with wild azaleas dotted on the hillside. The air was fragrant, the vistas and views magnificent until we reached the top. Here I was met by an awful stench of rotten eggs; it was my first whiff of sulphur. The air was steaming from the boiling sulphur springs, and small geysers spouted from the ground where the earth had turned into liquid mud that bubbled, steamed and stank. We had, fortunately, not far to go now, for a short distance off I could see a cluster of two-storied foreign-style buildings, and one of the first was the Unzen Hotel, where I had booked a room.

It took three or four days before I got used to the awful smell, and within a week I did not notice it at all. To take the sulphur baths was quite a simple matter. The hot sulphur water was led into the bathrooms in bamboo pipes straight from a spring. One bath a day was the rule the first week; after that, two. My sores reacted to the healing waters almost at once; the surfaces became red raw, and gave me agonising pains through the nerves being exposed. Then they started to heal, slowly at first, and then with a rapidity that was sheer magic.

In three weeks I was completely cured and ready to get into harness, but it was with very mixed feelings that I returned to China. There were serious outbreaks of lawlessness up country,

ATE 7

Top: The Bungalow terrace garden, third year
Bottom: Shooting guests arriving in camp

PLATE 8

Top: The Big Stranger's last journey

Bottom: Tah Gu Tzu, the author and a "right and left"

and banditry had increased. The new regime did nothing to stop it; in fact the soldiers were living off the country in the same way as the bandits, as they were not getting their pay.

All this information came to me by letter from the Shanghai office and decided me against lingering longer at Unzen, although I could have done with another week. So one fine morning in May I arrived in Chinkiang by the night train, which came in at seven in the morning. Mr. Erlanger was with me to discuss plans with the compradore.

We struck the Ordure Cavalcade as we left the station. Mr. Erlanger turned pale. "Suffering cats," was all he said, as he jammed his handkerchief over his nose. It was a long and very unpleasant ride before we reached the Concession. Then he removed his "mask" and said: "Seems to me that half the population in this goddam place has got diarrhoea, and the other half carries it away. Is this usual or a sudden epidemic?"

"Worse than that," I replied. "It's an institution and part of a daily curse. By the way, I was going to ask you for a fifty-dollar increase of pay."

"Sure, Mike," he said, "I'll make it one hundred—no, wait, I am feeling better; fifty can do!" And fifty it was, only I did not tell him that I had taken him by night train on purpose. I did not want him to miss this "treat", and thought it might soften him a bit, for he was a Jew and gave very little away. If I had asked him in the Maloo, I would have got a hundred. When would I learn the science of tactics?

XVIII

A WEEK after my return I was once more sailing up the Ku River where the scene was transformed. The willows sent green cascades down from the banks, the egrets were in their wedding plumage with long, delicately curved crests, and the fields were golden with wheat ready for the sickle. At Meng Cheng, although the dead had been removed, the city was still empty and had a haunted look.

We ran into a lot of contrary winds, and it took me twelve days to reach Pochow. There, a series of feasts awaited me and I spent three days eating and drinking more than a sane person should. The road to Yung Cheng was now open to traffic, but the very important road from Yung Cheng to Nan Hsuchow was overrun by bandits and no cargo could be sent in that direction to go by rail to Chinkiang, a much quicker route.

My compradore, Wu Li Shan, was with me and he suggested flying the Red Cross flag on our cart. All country people knew that flag from the Famine Relief food-carts, which they had every reason to bless and respect. And so he had one made, and we went off on this uncertain venture flying the Red Cross on a bamboo stick.

The early summer heat had started, and the mud on the road had dried and been pulverised into inches of choking dust. Every cart we met sent up clouds of it, and our own did its best to outdo them all, for we had two animals pulling, a mule in the shafts and a pony in the traces. The pony made so much dust that we could hardly see the mule, and we had to cover our nostrils and mouths with a handkerchief. We had a hearty welcome in every village, and all we met were happy and hopeful, for the wheat was ready to cut, and their food was ensured as soon as the crop came in.

Our friend from the last trip, the old headman, gave us a special welcome, and I broke the journey there for over an hour while we drank tea and chatted. I asked him how he liked the "New Order"and he said: "Very bad! Before, under the Emperor, we only had the bandits. Now we have the bandits with us still, and the soldiers as well. We must feed them and their horses, because they say they protect us from the bandits. They never do any fighting, but sell cartridges to the bandits to get money, for they seldom get any pay. Now they dare not offend the bandits because they do business with them, and we farmers must eat bitterness. We are all happy now because the wheat is ready to cut, but we don't know how much they will take and how long we can keep the harvest." That was the case everywhere, happiness at the sight of the ripe wheat and a secret fear of the future.

We reached Yung Cheng late in the afternoon, and our intention was to investigate the main problem, the Nan Hsuchow supply route. The landlord at the inn, a fat jovial man in his forties, made us welcome. We had his best room, the same which we had occupied before. It was comparatively clean and there were no bed-bugs, a rare thing in a Chinese inn. An inn is always a good place for picking up news from the travellers who come and go, for the landlord is generally well posted. But this time I drew a blank, for no travellers had arrived from Nan Hsuchow for a long time. This was a bad sign.

We had no sooner settled down than a runner arrived from the Magistrate's Yamen with a request for me to call on him as soon as possible. Outside, two soldiers were waiting to escort me, carrying big official lanterns as the streets were very dark.

There is always something very mysterious, eerie and exciting about the narrow streets and alleyways of a Chinese city at night. They are nearly always poorly lit, if they have any light at all, and shadowy figures flit about silently on felt-soled slippers. An occasional squeak from the rusty hinges on a signboard swaying in the wind is the only sound, except the night-watchman's gong warning thieves that he is coming and that they had better cut and run. There is a furtive look about the shadowy figures as if they were either bent on some evil deed, or were being pursued by evil-doers. There is a sour smell of dirt and decay, for the streets are the universal dust-bins, and the pariah dogs cannot clean up every street. They have to concentrate on the shopping streets or they would starve to death.

But we soon came into the shopping quarters, where there were crowds of people and lights from flares and lanterns. My escort became very important, shouting to people to get out of the way: "Djeh Guang—Djeh Guang—Da rin lai la!" (May I borrow your light—may I borrow your light—The Great Man is coming!)

The Chinese are given to flowery expressions, and "May I borrow your light" is one of them. It means you are standing in my light (or way), get out! To say that "The Great Man" was coming, gave the soldiers "big face" by making people believe that they were escorting an important person.

At the main gate of the Yamen I was met by the Magistrate's secretary, who escorted me round the sides of the various courtyards. There was, of course, a perfectly good path straight through the court, but in the land of evil spirits and ghosts this path is only for the evil spirits, who cannot turn corners. By going along the sides of the courtyards you turn many corners and the spirits cannot follow you. All this is carefully thought out to the last detail in Chinese architecture.

At the end of each courtyard was a high foundation for a fine room with stone steps leading up to it, one flight for a right-hand approach and one for the left. Between the two staircases was an incline of smooth stone slabs in direct line with the centre path. Having no steps, the evil spirits and ghosts could not mount them, and were trapped. These ghost staircases were a common feature in all buildings with courtyards. I was thinking about these architectural peculiarities as I walked along and wondered if they had some connection with Chinese mentality. The Chinese always approach matters, no matter how small, by turning as many corners as possible. You have to follow them patiently through all the twists and corners of the courtyards of their minds before you reach the matter you came to discuss. A direct approach is out of the question.

I was thinking particularly of the Magistrate then, and the impending interview, for I knew that my approach to the matter under discussion would have to be just as devious as the roundabout way I had come.

He looked a good deal more pale and worried than he had the last time I had seen him, probably from too much opium and the Nan Hsuchow situation, which, he knew by my presence, would require action on his part. After many very polite and false starts, we came to the issue.

The bandits had concentrated on new pastures after he had taken military measures on the Pochow road, and he had not sufficient men to patrol both. Therefore the Nan Hsuchow road was now controlled by bandits. I pointed out that he had still a thousand men in Yung Cheng, doing nothing but protecting his own wealth and that of the rich merchants, while thousands of the people were suffering from lack of business and unemployment. That stung him into a violent denial of being wealthy, or that there were any rich people in his poverty-stricken city. To that I only remarked that if the soldiers had nothing but poverty to guard, they would be much better employed on the Nan Hsuchow road so that business could revive and bring prosperity back to Yung Cheng. He was lying, of course, for he was reputed to be a very wealthy man, and he knew I knew he was lying, which worried him considerably. In a land with so many human vultures, personal wealth is something to be carefully hidden by a smoke-screen of protestations of poverty. He lifted his tea-cup to drink, the usual sign that the interview was over. It was now time to let him know what I had come for, and, as I rose to go, I remarked casually that I was going on to Nan Hsuchow in the morning to investigate the conditions. If I had pulled a revolver on him, he could not have been more alarmed.

"On no account," he stammered. "On no account. It is too dangerous, and I'll be held responsible for your life."

"There's not much to worry about if I have an armed guard," I replied.

"No use, no use, they'll shoot the guard to get their rifles. I lost twenty-five rifles that way last week. The men were escorting the wife of an officer in Pochow; they were all killed but two, and the lady was captured and is held for ransom."

I did not want an escort under any circumstances, as I would be safer without, but I would have a hold over the Magistrate if he refused, which I expected him to do. "Very well," I said, "I don't want to embarrass you by insisting on this. I only request you to order the guards to open the east gate at three in the morning when I start. I am sure I shall be safe if I go through the worst part of the road in the dark. The road is deep in dust, so the cart will make no noise. Hui lai chien!" (Au revoir.)

"Hui lai chien—I loh ping an!" (Au revoir, and may your road be peaceful!), the unhappy man stammered, for I had really left him in a cleft stick.

I returned to the inn and conferred with Wu Li Shan. He was one of the very few Chinese I had encountered who had great physical courage. He was game, even keen, to go with me, and I felt that it was the adventure itself which appealed to him, perhaps doing something which everybody thought impossible, an unusual trait in a Chinese.

As for me, I was just the incurable elephant's child, full of "'satiable curiosity." This was undoubtedly a case of finding out what the crocodile had for supper. We sent for the mule driver to tell him to have the cart ready by three in the morning. We learned that he had disappeared with his gear, leaving a message that he had a wife and family to consider and dared not go out with us. Wu Li Shan got busy finding another man, and I was quite surprised, when he returned after a very long absence, to hear that he had succeeded. He said the man was too stupid to realise the risk, but that he knew his job.

I never feel at my best in the early morning, and three o'clock is the last straw, but it was a case of needs must. We piled our gear into the cart and rumbled off in the darkness through empty streets to the east gate, where the guards opened the great massive barrier for us and then closed it with an ominous hollow bang after we had passed through. We made an awful clatter on the flagstones of the causeway, but not for long, for we soon reached the dusty road and our progress was almost soundless.

We had the same team as before, a fine mule in the shafts and a lively pony in the traces. The only sounds were the soft patter of hooves, the creaking of the cart and the mutterings of the driver. He was cursing the darkness, and when I shut him up sharply he started to talk to the mule, complaining bitterly of my rudeness.

His remarks were so strange that we soon realised the man was crazy, and it was almost impossible to keep him quiet. Suddenly he let out a yelp and said he had dropped his tobacco pouch somewhere. He wanted to stop the cart and go back and find it, and wailed when I made him drive on. Then we had about half an hour of blessed sullen silence, till he yelped again and said he had lost his pipe. More loud wails and protestations were voiced when I made him drive on. I had to shake and threaten him by turns to make him keep quiet, and under the tension and irritation the time dragged on like an eternity. I was feeling more and more jumpy.

It was a mad drive with the village idiot in charge of the cart, but we had made good time and dawn found us well on the way with Yung Cheng out of sight. Ahead lay the broad winding road through miles of golden wheat and scattered villages with just the roof ridges sticking up above the mud walls. The driver now clamoured for a smoke. I gave him a big cheroot, something he had never seen before and, as he did not know what it was, he wailed that I was mocking him. Then I lit it for him, and very suspiciously he took a few puffs, grunted contentedly and, after a few more puffs, tucked it safely into the bosom of his thick wadded coat without putting it out. A few moments later the cotton wadding caught fire and smoke came drifting up. Even that did not make him suspect the cause, until the smouldering cotton touched his skin, when it took both of us to hold him down and put out the fire. Half an hour later he had another smoke and did the same thing again. It was the only diversion we had on that grim trip. The sun came up strong and hot, burning fiercely, while the dust smothered us in suffocating clouds.

I spent the whole of that blazing day on the shafts, with my rifle within reach but out of sight. Occasionally golden orioles would flit from one scattered tree clump to another, but they were the only sign of life. The reflection of the sun on the golden shimmering wheat became almost unbearable, and the road seemed endless. And with me all the time was the strain of watching the fields on either side, expecting at any moment a bullet or a volley.

In the early afternoon we made a brief halt in one of the villages, but it took such a long time to rig up the temporary bridge across the moat that this was the only stop we were able to make. There we got all the information we needed about the hopeless state and complete paralysis of the whole district. The villagers were thankful that the wheat was ready for the sickle, and they would take good care that they were not robbed this time. They had no animals to haul in the harvest, and in any case it would be too risky to leave the gates open for carts to go in and out. They would have to resort to the safer way of sending the harvesters across the moat sliding on poles, and hauling the bundles of wheat over the walls by ropes.

Farther along, we saw this weird method of harvesting going on in several villages, while watchmen scanned the surrounding country from the rooftops. The joy of having food for the future months was clearly the predominant feeling, and all faces looked remarkably happy and cheerful as the precious bundles were piled on the edge of the moat.

With the setting sun came relief from the heat and glare and our luck held good. It was dark when we arrived at Nan Hsuchow, and the city gates were closed. As the guards refused to open them we found our way down to a little cluster of huts near the railway station. In one of them we shared the floor with a donkey, a pig and some chickens, but we could have slept anywhere. At six the train came in, but we were at the station long before that and soon after we arrived we were joined by a Jesuit priest from Nan Hsuchow. He looked at us in great surprise, and asked where we had come from. When I told him, he first looked incredulous, then he shook his head and said: "Madness. You are very lucky people to be alive." He spoke emphatically, and it suddenly dawned on me that the providence that looks after sailors, fools and drunks was still looking after me.

Before leaving I made provision for our crazy carter. First I paid him for a new coat and gave him five dollars for his one day's work. This would keep him in comfort for a couple of months, and I expected the road would be safe long before that. I felt certain that the Magistrate in Yung Cheng would be up and doing, as I had hinted that if the Nan Hsuchow traffic was not restored very shortly I would have to take the matter up with the authorities at Nanking.

The cart and team belonged to our agent at Pochow, and we took it by train to Lin Hai Kwan, where it was sent back to Pochow by junk.

My visit to Yung Cheng bore fruit. The fear of investigations from Nanking made the Magistrate bestir himself and the Nan Hsuchow road was opened to traffic again.

The bandits must have moved to new pastures where no foreign devils made life uncomfortable for them by making the authorities put down a scourge that made life unbearable for the country people. Business was increasing by leaps and bounds, and I had no occasion to visit Pochow and Yung Cheng again that year.

XIX

When I returned home in the evening of the following day I found a stranger installed in my flat. He was Mr. Ottewill, the new Consul who had come to take Mr. Twyman's place after his transfer to Wuhu.

Mr. Ottewill explained that the Consulate was being painted and redecorated, and, as most of the woodwork was being Ningpo varnished, he had to sleep outside to avoid varnish poisoning. He had been told in the Club that I had several guest-rooms and most visitors put up at my place, and he had come along and installed himself. This was the custom of the port, there being no hotel, and my servants had orders to look after unexpected guests who might arrive when I was away.

Mr. Ottewill, a small man with twinkling humorous eyes, told me that every time he entered the sitting-room he had to play musical chairs with the dogs before he could find a chair to sit on. The dogs were all very friendly and jumped all over him when he came in, but the moment he moved towards a chair, the dogs made a mad rush to get into their own chairs and establish their ownership.

We had a long talk about the political situation, for the second revolution was already brewing. He was extremely well informed on Chinese affairs and had taken part in the Legation battle during the Boxer trouble. He predicted, and rightly, that there would soon be fighting against Yuan Shi Kai.

The Emperor had abdicated only a few months before, and Yuan Shi Kai was shortly after elected President of the Republic. There were, however, many disagreements between him and Sun Yat Sen's party, the Kuomintang, and matters might come to a head at any time. I found it impossible not to be drawn into these political cross-currents and became acutely conscious of impending events. The up-country lines of communication which were immensely important to the merchants were precarious and worrying because of the incompetent local officials. It was necessary to be constantly on the alert, and my old carefree existence was at an end. I had returned with the feeling that all was well, but only if there were no major changes. Fighting would upset everything. However, it was good to take up the daily morning rides again, and Freddie's exuberant yippees on the wild home runs were enough to drive dull care away.

I got married in December of that year. Like most of my other ventures, it was done on the spur of the moment after a short chance meeting during a trip to Hankow. My wife was a Clarkson Russel from Elgin, but she had been brought up in Sussex and had lost her burr. I cannot conceive of anything more terrifying to a woman than taking over and coping with a lot of bachelor's servants, more or less used to "gang their ain gait" as long as everything looked good on the surface.

Feng, my cook, was adept at making things look good on the surface, and my daily inspection of the kitchen brought no serious slackness to light. My check was, perhaps, rather cursory, but I hate poking about to see if everything is washed "behind the ears" so to speak. Dusting and other things in the house received scant attention from me. But with women it is different. They are of two types. There are those who never go inside the kitchen at all, and save themselves no end of bother and irritation: there is also eternal peace in the house, and the servants stay to a hoary old age. There are others who spend too much time in the kitchen and exploring the house for dust, or poring over accounts, checking and weighing everything. The result is ructions all round, frequent changing of staff, generally for the worse, endless trouble in training new servants, and no improvement. My wife was of that latter kind, and wanted the house and kitchen as clean as a new pin. Like many others she did not realise that the Chinese are so dirty that one who can pass a cursory examination is a gem beyond price, and that no living European, not even a Scot, has ever been able to stop a Chinese cook from getting the better of him or her in the household accounts. The only thing one can hope for is to prevent the squeeze becoming too big. To get more work out of them than suits their tempo is equally hopeless

I only wished that all wives coming out to the Far East in those days had learnt and benefited by Kipling's lines:

"Now it is not good for the Christian's health to hustle the Aryan brown,
For the Christian riles, and the Aryan smiles and he weareth the Christian down;
And the end of the fight is a tombstone white with the name of the late deceased,
And the epitaph drear: 'A Fool lies here who tried to hustle the East."

but these battles went on in every household where a European standard of cleanliness was insisted on, and they were lost from the start.

There was a story going the rounds in those days, of a mistress who suddenly came into the kitchen and found the cook cleaning lettuce leaves with a dirty old toothbrush. She gave him a furious talking to, but the cook got very indignant, and replied: "What for Missy bobbely (scold) my? This no belong Missy's toothblush, belong *my* toothblush!" This would have been the reply of every Chinese cook under similar circumstances.

It did not take long before my cook was caught out. He had a very long and sharp thumb nail, and my wife caught him grating lemon peel with it. He was very surprised when he was dismissed. He had always used his thumb nail to grate lemon peel, only I had never discovered it.

By now the business had grown so much that we had to use part of our flat as offices, and it was necessary to look for another residence. All the houses in the Concession were occupied, but there was a big house to let out in the country beyond the Victoria Park, on the slope of a hill named Huang Shan. It belonged to an old resident who had built it to retire in, but he lost all his money, and the house had been vacant for years. It was a palatial place built in Chinese-temple style, with a Japanese house tacked on to it, his wife being Japanese, and it had about twenty acres of park and gardens, tennis lawns and an ornamental lake. No one wanted to live there because of bandits, and it was also a meeting-place for a pack of wolves, but the house and grounds had been kept in good order by two gardeners.

We moved out in the spring when the place was at its best and really delightful. The grounds had been planted with masses of cherry blossom trees, single and double, flowering shrubs, and for the first time in years I saw daffodils, violets and primroses—all imported, of course. There was also a fine show of tree peonies.

I had the telephone installed, which was essential, but it proved to be a great nuisance as the Magistrate kept ringing me up for news of the movements of the bandits—generally late at night. There were several raids on neighbouring villages, always at night, and the whole countryside was in an uproar with the banging of gongs, screams and yells, so that it was difficult to sleep. We were never attacked, but I always had a rifle by the bedside and a revolver under my pillow. The two gardeners, Lao Chow and Lao Wang, lived close by. The former, who was the number one, had a fine brick house, and the gossips said that he had feathered his nest thoroughly at the owner's expense, as he was the go-between when the land was bought. He was hated by the villagers, who accused him of buying the land very cheaply from them and making a large profit on the transaction. He was a very good gardener though, and kept the grounds beautifully, with Lao Wang and two water coolies to help him.

I expected the bandits to have a go at us, but they never did. Lao Chow told me that it was known all over the place that I had shot many wild boar and, therefore, that I was a very dangerous person. But they tried to get me in another way.

One evening I had been working late in the office and came riding home in the dark. I always rode fast; Blue Cap had a fine turn of speed and loved going all out. I was about a hundred yards from the front gate when he stopped dead and nearly had me off. He snorted and shivered but would not budge when I urged him on. I peered around but saw nothing, and thought he was being temperamental. I turned him round and trotted back a little distance, then wheeled and gave him a good slap with the hunting crop. But exactly the same thing happened again.

I dismounted and examined the bushes by the roadside, but found nothing. Thoroughly mystified I mounted again, and then I suddenly saw what it was. A wire was stretched across the road level with my neck and, but for Blue Cap, it would probably have been my last ride. I have every bit as strong an objection to being decapitated as the Chinese, and reported the matter to the Chinese Magistrate. The following day three "braves" came out to take over guard duties. The Chinese soldiers were always called "braves" then, as they had the character "brave" on the front and back of their jackets.

They were quartered on the village where the wire had been found, but did not stay very long. Every night they patrolled the boundary fences of my grounds, marching in solemn state, the leading brave carrying a big lantern to warn the bandits of their approach so that they could clear out in good time.

I think they had been there about a week when something happened to bring their duties as my protectors to a sudden end. It was a stifling hot evening with the temperature well into the nineties. Sleep was impossible, and we sat on the veranda smoking and watching the fireflies glittering in the bushes outside. Up on the hillside the patrol was marching slowly along in Indian file, the big lantern giving just enough light for me to see the three braves. Suddenly I saw a spurt of flame, heard the sharp crack of a rifle shot and the lantern went out.

There were loud cries for help, followed by sounds of a wild stampede through the bushes on the hillside and terrified shouts from the three braves. I took my rifle from the bedroom and went back expectantly to the veranda. Nothing happened, and all was still again. But not for long, for a fearful hullabaloo came from the servants' quarters, and soon afterwards my boy came in with my three protectors, all talking in chorus and all very frightened. They had been fired at, actually fired at, and the leading man had dropped the lantern, leaving them in pitch darkness at the mercy of the bandits. And now they dare not go back to their billets for fear of being attacked. Would I allow them to sleep in the servants' quarters until daylight?

I let them stay on, and two hours or so later the village where they were quartered was raided and an old woman was killed. She was beating the alarm on an empty kerosene tin to warn the countryside when one of the bandits shot her through the head. The incident proved to be the end of the three braves' military careers, but I often missed their comic-opera patrols. The Magistrate sent me a bill for fifteen dollars for protection, and I sent a contra account for thirty dollars for protecting my protectors. The Magistrate did not appear to be a humorous man. He never replied, and left me to protect myself.

I had malaria very badly that summer, and the attacks came on so suddenly that I always had to have Blue Cap saddled and ready to mount at the office door. The first symptom of an attack was a sudden ache in my eyes, and I knew that within ten minutes I would be delirious and unable to keep my seat in the saddle. Three and a half miles in under ten minutes takes a lot of doing for a pony, but Blue Cap always got me there in time. Huang Shan House will always be associated with that wild dash from the office, the fever raging within me, my skin creeping with cold and my teeth chattering with ague.

By the time I reached the gate of Huang Shan my grip would have gone and I would be swaying in the saddle. The trees along the drive would spin round and round and everything become a red blur. I would only vaguely remember being lifted out of the saddle by the servants and seeing my wife on the steps. Then oblivion possessed me until I awoke, weak as a kitten after an all-night sweat bath. It would be two days before I could stand and three before I could get back to the office, riding sedately in a sedan-chair. I think it was then that my love of gardens and flowers was born, for I spent the days of my convalescence in the garden under a shady tree, watching Lao Chow and Lao Wang tending the flowers. Lao Chow told me that when Mr. Starkey was living there he got fresh seeds from England and America every year. Now he had only the seeds he had saved and no fresh supplies had arrived since his old master lost his money ten years before. He went into the cellar and brought out a lot of catalogues from famous seedsmen in England and the States. They were all profusely illustrated in colour, and became my constant companions in the garden during that summer and, when winter came with long, dark evenings, they helped me to spend many happy hours by the fire. It was as if they filled the house with the fragrance and colour of their flowers as I dreamed and planned the garden for the coming year.

We had heard nothing of the wolf pack during the summer

and thought the story a myth, until suddenly, late one night in the autumn, we heard their weird uncanny cry close to the house. It came from a small hillock above the tennis lawn, and in the moonlight I saw shadowy forms moving off silently between the young pines.

What I appreciated most while living there was watching the seasons through and seeing the farmer at his daily toil. The rice harvest was gathered in September and October, the happiest time for the Chinese farmer, for he had already harvested the wheat in May, and this was his second crop. All the cutting was done with sickles, and the sheaves were stooked and carried in on bamboo poles to the threshing floor. There, a stone roller with corrugations cut in it was drawn back and forth over the sheaves to separate the grain from the straw and loosen the husk. Then the sheaves were gathered and banged on bamboo slats to remove any grain still left. All the grain was now swept up on the threshing floor for the winnowing, and two or three men went to work with long-handled wooden shovels, throwing the grain high up into the air. The wind did the rest, for clouds of dust and husk blew away, leaving the grain clean and ready to be stored. Finally the rice fields were ploughed and the winter wheat sown; and one field, a different one each year, was planted with broad beans.

When spring came, the whole countryside was fragrant with the scent of bean flowers, and the beans were ready for harvesting in April. In May the wheat was gathered, and then the biggest job of the year started. The fields had to be flooded and prepared for the rice, which had already been planted in seed beds.

Water-wheels were rigged up from the irrigation ditches and worked as a tread-mill by one or two men, or by an ox or a donkey. It was a killing job that went on for hours on end, day after day, until there was at least six inches of water over the fields, which were banked all round to form shallow reservoirs. Then those grey, hairless and monstrous-looking animals, the water buffaloes, were set to plough them.

Then one would see all the fields dotted with men and women planting the rice seedlings. Every plant had to be set by hand nearly equidistant. It is all done by eye, but so sure and practised are the planters that every row is as straight as if it were drawn with a ruler. The whole of China's vast ricelands are planted like that every year; and in the south twice a year, for there they grow two crops of rice in a season.

From now on there is "only" weeding and more water-pumping to be done until harvest-time in September and October chores that keep the farmer busy twelve hours a day.

I DON'T know how I managed to keep out of the Second Revolution in 1913 and the second battle of Nanking, but I missed that altogether.

I was no longer thinking high and noble thoughts about the New Order; on the contrary, I had found it a change for the worse so far as the population was concerned. The countryside was swarming with soldiers doing nothing in particular except placing an extra burden on the people, who had, at any rate, escaped this hardship under the Manchus. The evil which the Nationalists had come to remove was still there, as ugly as ever and untouched, and the only visible signs of a change were the absence of queues and the ankle bands which had largely disappeared, chiefly by the forceful application of the new law.

A struggle for power was now going on which had split the country into two camps, the North under Yuan Shi Kai and the South under Sun Yat Sen's party, the Kuomintang. But a struggle in such a vast country is felt only when the conflict is brought to your door. The nearest it came to ours was Nanking.

An army was approaching from the north under General Chang Hsun, the same Imperialist general who had defended Nanking in 1911. An attempt was made to stop his advance at Pengpu, on the Huai River, which had become a collecting centre for oil-seeds. My firm had large warehouses and a cleaning plant there, and I had to run up to see what could be done to save a cargo of a couple of thousand tons. The task appeared to be hopeless, as the Kuomintang general, Li, had made some of his defence positions and established his headquarters just behind our warehouses, trusting that General Chang Hsun would think twice before he fired on foreign property. This was, of course, a typical Chinese way of reasoning, of which I had had some previous experience. General Li had also seized the railway, and no cargo could be moved without his consent.

I took my problem to Mr. Ottewill, who, luckily, knew General Li personally and was on very good terms with him. He gave me a letter to him and with that in my pocket I left for Pengpu. The result was quite remarkable. Five hundred soldiers were set to work loading the trucks, and within two days the cargo was removed out of danger to Pukow on the north bank of the Yangtze. While the last bags were being shifted from the warehouses the two armies were sniping at one another across the Huai River, and I was glad to get out of Pengpu before fighting started in earnest.

What was even more remarkable than getting the cargo moved, was that General Li never charged me anything for the use of his labour. It was still a gentlemen's war, apparently, and I can only regret that General Li was beaten. Chang Hsun swept on and took Nanking. In revenge for his defeat in 1911, he handed the city over to his soldiers for three days' rapine and looting, three days of untold horror and savagery. Once more the poor innocent townspeople suffered the loss of everything that could be carried away, and once more the moats and wells were filled with women suicides.

The fall of Nanking was a serious blow to the Kuomintang, and a set-back from which it took years to recover. Yuan Shi Kai was now master, and, whatever may be said of him and his political ambitions, one thing must not be forgotten. He was one of the few Chinese statesmen who did not carry on anti-foreign propaganda and, while Viceroy of Shantung during the Boxer trouble, he protected the foreigners against the Boxers. Indeed, every foreigner in Shantung owed his life to him.

In the meantime life in Chinkiang went on unruffled by all the political turmoil; the billiard-balls clicked, the cicadas buzzed and the camel in the Club bar plodded wearily through the burning sands. However, there had been great changes in the last two or three years, and the Concession now had a good deal of social life. There were several young married couples, frequent tea- and dinner-parties, and occasionally a third-rate singer would come from Shanghai and give concerts in the Customs Club.

We were getting gay. The waterworks had made a tremendous difference to the health of the port, and the psychological effect of the constant arrival of new people and the regular train service was beyond belief.

We were no longer a community of morons but of live human beings. There were even a number of children, always a source of wonder to the older hands. Out at Huang Shan we gave a series of tennis parties during the summer and autumn and had many house guests from Shanghai. Strange to relate, Chinkiang was now becoming a health resort, particularly in the autumn and winter when the hills were at their best, for Shanghai people, tired and jaded from too much social life. The summers were always the same, though, three months of stifling heat and long sleepless nights.

In the autumn of 1913 my compradore was transferred, and I got a new man, Cho Yik Tong. Cho was, like most compradores, of Cantonese extraction, but had spent many years in Chinkiang. He was very thin and had a beaky nose (rare amongst the Chinese), very bright beady eyes, and was chirpy and bird-like in his manner. He was a very much married man, having two wives, two concubines and so many children that he knew the names of only a few of them. The way he kept track of them was rather ingenious. The three oldest boys by his number-one wife he called by name, the rest he numbered.

I often called at his house, or rather two houses joined into one. It was a very large foreign-style place, built to his own plans. There was an enormous hall near the entrance, packed with children and amahs, where the number-one wife received us. The number-two wife was seldom present, as most of the household duties fell on her. Although very handsomely furnished, the hall looked like a rabbit warren and the noise was deafening. We would spend a few minutes there, but, as we generally had business to talk about, Cho would take me through a double door into his sanctum sanctorum, a large and very handsomely furnished room, in the adjoining house. Then he would lock both doors and not a sound could be heard. His two concubines lived above on the first floor, but there was no staircase, so we had absolute privacy and quiet in his sanctuary.

He was a merry soul and a very clever business man, so he had accumulated much wealth. His principal hobby, apart from concubines, was curio-collecting, chiefly blue and white Kang Hsi porcelain, and, after we had talked business, he used to show me some of his favourite pieces.

It was through him that I came to know Lao Chang, the itinerant curio dealer, a delightful old rogue, whose visit to my office became a weekly event. He was perhaps sixty, tall and stout, with a scanty white pigtail and a drooping white moustache; he was always very dignified and deferential. After sending in the office boy to find out if it was convenient to see me, he would come in with some heavy bundles, bow and inquire if I was well and happy. Then he would squat down and undo the bundles with a deliberate care worthy of the "priceless treasures" he was going to let me see. He was a perfect showman, and even the rubbish he often carried was handled with such delicacy that it became enhanced in value.

It would take him nearly half an hour to arrange his exhibition on the floor, and in the meantime I went on working, for it would never do to show any interest in the articles before all was ready; and even then the old gentleman would often have to cough discreetly once or twice before I turned round.

There they were, all beautifully arranged: ginger jars, vases, bowls, snuff bottles, bronzes, brassware, embroideries and rugs—mostly small prayer rugs or saddle-cloths in lovely colours. I often wondered how he got all that stuff into his bundles.

Bargaining in China is a fine art if carried on with anything like the native astuteness and finesse. It is, perhaps, the most beloved pastime in the country. The Chinese would rather sell at a minimum profit after a long and stiff bargaining bout than sell at a big profit to one who does not know the rules: in the latter case they always blame themselves for not asking much more, for greed is one of their besetting sins.

Lao Chang was no exception. He would ask the most outrageous prices for articles with the air of doing me a favour, and I, in turn, would make an equally outrageous counter-bid, with the air of doing *him* a favour. It was essential never to let him know what I was really keen on, but to carry on a spirited bargaining for things I did not want, taking care to keep my bids too low.

This was a necessary chastening process, which generally ended in a deep sigh of regret and disappointment: then, slowly and sorrowfully he would pack up his whole collection while I went on working. He was a wonderful actor, and could put more reproach into a sigh than other people could put into words.

But I had to be adamant, for that was the game. At the door he would give a discreet cough and I would turn to him with a polite: "Tsai djen!" (See you again.) He would then invariably come back and say: "Great man, perhaps there are some things which you may have overlooked. It grieves me to leave you without satisfying you." With that, he would squat on the floor and undo his bundles once more, and start all over again: time meant nothing to him, this game of bargaining everything. It was a slur on his salesmanship to leave without selling me *something*.

Again I would start bargaining for some article I did not want, and again it would end in a deadlock. And for the second time he would reach the door in a thoroughly dejected frame of mind, judging by his looks.

Then I would say, "You have taken a lot of trouble and I don't like to see you go without having done any business with me, but I really can't afford to pay your prices."

"Great man," he would reply, "nothing would please me better than to oblige you!" And once again the bundles would be undone and the display arranged.

"I only want a cheap article," I would warn him, "just to please you, for I do not really need anything. What about that thing over there?" This time I pointed to the rug I really wanted.

Lao Chang said, with hurt dignity, "That *thing*, as the great man chooses to call it, is a very valuable Mongolian saddle-rug, worth at least forty dollars, but I will sell it to you for thirty, although I will lose money," adding unctuously, "better to lose money than to spoil friendly relations."

"A pity," I replied, "for it is at least ten dollars too much, and I cannot afford to pay your price."

With a deep sigh he started to pack up his bundles again, leaving the rug to the last. As he made for the door, he said hopefully: "Twenty-nine?"

"No."

"Twenty-eight?"

"No."

"Twenty-seven fifty?"

"No, but I'll give you twenty-one!"

Having come down as far as was prudent in one day, and having got me up one dollar, he bowed himself out, perfectly happy, knowing that we would come to terms sooner or later. I bought the rug a few days later for twenty-three dollars, but even so I had paid a little too much for it, for I never flattered myself that I had got the better of a Chinese in a bargaining match.

That is how I bought my first saddle-cloth from Lao Chang: a beautiful rug in blue, ivory and rose, and one of the few souvenirs I still possess from my Chinkiang days. The old gentleman was nearly in tears when he parted with it—at a tremendous sacrifice, he said, which he would only make for a dear friend. On no account must I breathe a word to his other customers in the Concession about how cheaply I had got it.

"Please do not be so hard-hearted another time," he said, as he bowed himself out, "as to let me eat bitterness twice for a friendly act."

My twinges of conscience, if any, did not last long. Kelly, of the police, rang me up next day: had I bought a saddle-cloth from Lao Chang for fifteen dollars?

"No, I paid twenty-three for it. Why do you ask?"

"Well, well!" He chuckled. "I have the old rogue in the cells. He was selling that cloth on commission, and the owner was dissatisfied with the price of fifteen dollars, which Lao Chang swears by all his gods was the price you paid. It ended in a free fight, and I locked them both up. The old man was using filthy language."

I am afraid I strayed from the path of righteousness, for I went round to the gaol and told the owner that I had paid only fifteen dollars and that he could have it back for that price. No, he did not want it back, he was only checking up on Lao Chang, and now that I had established the latter's honesty he could only offer his profound apologies and pay the fines for the dealer and himself. Lao Chang accepted the apology with the mien of a saint who wanted only a halo to complete a picture of innocence personified. Kelly, being Irish, had averted his eyes from the British scales of justice, and fined the owner two dollars.

As the owner bowed himself out, he remarked: "If I had not made passion and suspicion rule my conduct, I would have made a profit of five dollars; now I make only three." Lao Chang also made a profound bow before leaving and said, turning to me with lofty dignity: "Great man, my sacrifice in the matter of price has brought you to my aid in this sordid affair. Justice has been done, and I have not suffered for my generosity!" He didn't even wink—nor did I.

After he had closed the door, Kelly sat and looked at me for a moment without saying a word. Then came an emphatic: "Well—I'll—be—damned!"

Such incidents brought home to me how hopeless it was for the average foreigner really to understand the Chinese and their points of view. I realised that there is an active or latent Lao Chang in nearly every Chinaman and that this game of roguery, wrapped up in flowery speech until it is smothered in politeness, is part and parcel of the daily intercourse from high diplomacy to the daily bargaining.

To lie is a fine art, and to be caught out in a lie is no shame at all: on the contrary, it is a shame to expose a liar and make him lose face. Every Chinese would have complimented Lao Chang. They would argue that he had done all the work, for which he was entitled to eight dollars, while the owner received five for doing nothing. Only a fool would have told the truth under such circumstances, or indeed under any circumstances, for the advantage is always with the liar.

It is this acceptance of the fact that everyone tells lies which is one of the chief characteristics of the Chinese mentality, and you are expected to know that they are not telling the truth. For centuries they have been engaged in an incessant battle of wits in their struggle for existence, a real life-and-death struggle in which the art of lying is one of their chief weapons. That is where we white men, with our inherent respect for truth and honesty, are at a tremendous disadvantage in our dealings with them.

That was one of the first things I had to learn and appreciate out there. Transactions had to be done Chinese fashion, and that was the main reason why I had come to Lao Chang's rescue, for I was indebted to him for learning a good many subtleties. The important point was that I had saved his "face" when most foreigners would have exposed him. By observing all the rules of the game I had gained a good deal of "face" myself and earned the distinction of being referred to as "lao hang dja" which, roughly translated, means an old hand at the game. This was a distinct advantage, because the Chinese dealers in future spared me from the long preliminaries imposed on those they regarded as inexperienced in their ways.

I must confess that I have always liked cheerful rogues better than earnest and respectable people, and so I got on very well with the Chinese. I had long since given up the idea of being an example of sobriety and rectitude to them and having high and noble thoughts about our mission amongst them.

No one could have set a finer example of self-sacrifice, of charity and devotion, than the missionaries. Tending the sick in mission hospitals, caring for waifs and strays in mission orphanages, teaching in mission schools, distributing food to the starving in times of famine, and working like trojans during typhus and plague epidemics. If anyone deserved love, respect and affection from the Chinese people, they did. I am thinking particularly of those valiant men and women who buried themselves for years in some God-forsaken Chinese town, cut off from civilisation and their own kind, to teach the people God's love and sacrifice and our Christian way of life.

All too many of them—and their children—have been murdered, and under the most revolting circumstances. It was, in many cases, no more than the absence of rain and fear of crop failure that would decide the fate of the missionaries in out-of-the-way places. Each one of those men and women had rendered a greater service to the Chinese people than any Chinese I have heard of, and their reward was death. We are poles apart from the Chinese and feel and think on diametrically opposed lines. For that reason we cannot judge them by our standards or expect them to conform to them, even those educated abroad, for at the moment they return they have to revert to type or perish.

It is not surprising that four hundred million people, left in stagnation and neglect for hundreds of years to fight bitterly for survival, should, of necessity, have developed a character and standards in keeping with life as they have had to live it. The colossal ignorance and superstition of the masses and the corruption and conceit of the officials have swept such virtues as love and charity away, and the severity of their struggle for existence has given hate and greed and suspicion a prominent place. With so many, many millions of them thinking and feeling alike, the exceptions are smothered by the rule.

XXI

A FEW hundred yards from Huang Shan House, a little higher up the hillside, stood a deserted white bungalow. You could see it for miles because the hill was absolutely treeless, whereas Huang Shan House was completely hidden by its own park. The bungalow had been built by a former secretary to the Chinkiang Municipal Council, named McGregor, who left the same year as I arrived, and who sold it to a Shanghai pilot named Captain Watson. Watson used it as a week-end bungalow in the shooting season and kept a caretaker, old Taiping Joe, as he was called, to look after the place.

I used often to drop in for a cup of tea and a chat when Captain Watson and his wife were there, and enjoyed the magnificent view from the veranda. To the north there was an unbroken vista of the whole countryside, a wide sweep of the Yangtze with Golden Island Pagoda on the left and Silver Island and Consular Bluff on the right. To westward lay Wu Chow Shan, Chang Shan and Tung Shan, and in the far distance a high mountain named Kao Li Shan. The view was so fascinating that one did not at once notice the fact that the house had no other attractions. No attempt had been made at gardening or brightening up the bare hillside, probably because it looked so hopeless. There was no soil, only a steep slope of a kind of shale deeply furrowed by gullies where nothing would grow except a few stunted bushes, some rough hill grass and two trees which McGregor had planted near the house for shade. Because of the exposed position and the light construction of the house, the eaves were anchored to the ground with stout wires; otherwise the first typhoon would have blown it off the hill.

If I passed when the Watsons were not there, I generally

stopped to have a chat with Taiping Joe. He was a dear old soul in his early sixties with a bronzed, wrinkled face, a small white moustache and a very short white pigtail, which he had managed to save from the queue cutters.

Taiping Joe, as his name implied, was a child of the Taiping rebellion. His father had served under the Taiping leader Tien Wang (Heavenly King) and, together with the last few thousand of Tien Wang's loyal troops, had been butchered when Nanking was captured in 1864. Joe did not want to talk much about those days or about his home life. In his simple way he told me the reason. When he was fifteen he had seen his mother killed while she and he were searching for his father's body on the battlefield, and he himself had been cut down and left for dead. But there was one topic he never tired of: the execution of the traitor Tung Wang (Eastern King) and twenty thousand men, all of them beheaded on the parade ground. He had seen it, for his father had been one of the two hundred executioners detailed for the job.

The first time he told me about it, I pulled him up about the number. "Surely you mean liang chien (2,000) and not liang wan (20,000)?"

He laughed at my ignorance. "Don't you know that Tien Wang appointed four kings under him, the North, South, East and West Kings, each with an army of twenty thousand men? There were two hundred executioners, and each of them had to chop off one hundred heads, cha pu doh (more or less). They received extra pay of one ounce of silver for ten heads, and my father brought home ten ounces of silver. *Anyone* can figure out that it was twenty thousand and not two thousand." Joe was quite indignant.

When I looked up the history of the Taiping rebellion I found that Joe was correct. The Eastern King and twenty thousand of his men had been beheaded as a warning to other would-be traitors.

One week-end the Watsons came and found that Taiping Joe was not at the bungalow. Inquiries were made in the near-by villages, but Joe had not been seen for several days. The following morning when the coolie went to the well to draw water for the bath he came running back terror-stricken and said that there was a body in the well. The corpse was hauled out and proved to be poor old Taiping Joe's body with half a dozen knife wounds and severe burns in the armpits. He was reputed to have some money hidden away, and red-hot irons had apparently been applied to make him tell where it was. The criminal was never discovered.

The Watsons were shocked and grieved. Mrs. Watson became so nervous that she returned to Shanghai the same day, but the Captain stayed on and arranged for the funeral with my gardener, Lao Chow, to whom he paid the necessary money. I was very shocked and grieved too at the tragic end of the dear harmless old man.

Lao Chow knew the address of Taiping Joe's son, who was advised and turned up shortly after. He was engaged as caretaker and moved into the servants' quarters, but the Watsons never returned because Mrs. Watson was frightened of sleeping there. The bungalow was put up for sale, but nobody wanted it. The Chinese shunned it, being afraid of Joe's ghost, and said it was haunted.

One summer at Huang Shan House had convinced me that it was impossible as a summer residence. It was essentially a winter house, and Mr. Starkey had always spent the summers in Japan. The many trees kept the breezes away, and all the verandas were enclosed. Midnight temperatures on the verandas ranged between ninety and ninety-eight degrees, moist heat at that, so there was no chance of getting more than a couple of hours' sleep. We often went up the hill for a breath of cool air, and one night we went over to the white bungalow and slept in long-chairs on the open veranda. It was delightfully cool and refreshing and a real wind trap.

The summers were always a big problem, for we had no summer holidays, and this was my eighth year in Chinkiang. Every summer meant three months of constant sweat baths, day and night, with bouts of malaria when I would sweat clean through a thick horse-hair mattress and leave a pool on the floor. It kept your pores open and clean, of course, but that was not much of a comfort. All clothing had to be changed three times a day, and sheets and pillowcases once a day.

It would, therefore, be wonderful to have this bungalow for the summer, even if I had to buy it. The trouble was I had only three hundred dollars in the bank and I could not very well offer Captain Watson that amount. My wife, being a Scot, had no such qualms about it. She argued that Watson would never be able to sell it to anyone else, his wife would never dare to come up again, and that they would be glad to accept my offer, and as it was roughly furnished, we could move right in and spend the rest of the summer in comfort.

She was right, and within a week the bungalow was mine. It was rough and ready, but a few bright curtains and rugs made a wonderful difference. The nights were delightfully cool, and for the first time in all those years I could enjoy unbroken sleep and awake refreshed in the morning.

By unbroken sleep, I mean sleep unbroken by the heat. We were, on the other hand, often awakened by bandit raids as the house lay so open on the hillside that every sound could be heard in the stillness of the sleeping countryside. The loud barking of dogs was the first sign, followed by a bedlam of screams and yells, the frantic tocsin of the gongs, and the sharp cracks of shots.

Soon after the first alarm, village after village sounded the tocsin until the whole countryside was in a turmoil. The farmers were at the mercy of the bandits, as they were not allowed to have firearms, nor did they ever receive any help from the authorities. The soldiers were kept in town, and on no occasion did I see a patrol.

At the big house we heard only the near-by raids as the sounds were deadened by the many trees, but here, in the bungalow, the noise was often ear-splitting and sleep was difficult as long as the raids lasted. But the novelty soon wore off, and then we slept on through the whole show, my Winchester automatic within easy reach. When the autumn came we were so fond of the place that we stayed on. I had to do something to the floors though, as the wind came whistling up through the boards, making the rugs wriggle about in a weird way that was most disconcerting to watch. Linoleum cured that, and when the winter came the house was snug and warm.

But the bare hillside, gaunt and sterile, was an eyesore and a challenge. I think there must be a gardener hidden in most of us, and at the first opportunity he comes popping out like a Jack-in-the-box.

There were about two acres of land round the house, and not a level piece big enough for a flower bed anywhere. The only possibility was to make terraces. I got hold of Lao Chow, and we made a rough plan of how to set about it and where to hew out the terraces. The shale was not very hard and yielded to picks and mattocks. It was the slack season for the farmers and they were only too glad to take on work like this for twenty cents a day. The next morning twenty of them were hard at work, and in about a week the first terrace was finished and big enough for a badminton lawn.

A big retaining wall of turf blocks was built to dam up all the shale dug away, making each terrace wider, and before the winter was over most of the terracing was done. We then dug big holes to receive trees and flowering shrubs, beds were dug out of the shale and, for a couple of weeks, the labourers carried soil up from the fields and filled the holes. Every evening I spent happy hours with seed catalogues and wrote out long order forms. The early spring brought four hundred roses from England and enough seeds to stock a garden ten times the size. Then came bulbs from Holland, azaleas, deodars, cherry blossom trees, maples and japonica from Japan, and spiraea, flowering plum and sweet-scented witch-hazel from local nurseries. And as a sign that this was really a garden, I had a white picket fence put up by the front entrance.

There are few joys equal to that of making a garden, of watching the seed beds greening, the buds swelling, and the first sweet peas pushing their way through the soil. To me it was doubly fascinating, because it was like seeing a desert springing into life, for the whole dreary hillside had been transformed. The turf retaining walls were now green banks, and the badminton lawn was a pleasure to look at.

I shall always remember that early spring in my first garden, each day bringing new surprises and new pleasures. I also remember it for another reason, because I had the narrowest shave of my life with a wounded wild boar. The chief actor was the famous Hermit of Sia Shu Kai, a very vicious brute who had defied all our efforts to get him that season. I had decided to spend the Chinese New Year holidays under canvas out in the pig country farther west than Wu Chow Shan, and had chosen Sia Shu Kai.

Two friends came up from Shanghai to join me in the shoot, and we formed quite a cavalcade on horseback and donkeys and with a dozen bamboo-coolies carrying the tents, provisions, bedding and pots and pans.

For two days we beat every one of the Hermit's favourite haunts but drew a blank. On the third day we saw nothing until late in the afternoon, when a large boar broke cover and I dropped him with a lucky snap shot. He was a magnificent beast of nearly four hundred pounds, but it was not the Hermit. That evening the cook had a treat in store for us; he had roasted a saddle of wild pig, gipsy style, in a self-basting tin buried in charcoal embers. It had been hanging fourteen days, and I don't think I have ever tasted anything quite so good.

We had to return in the evening of the next day, and were anxious to meet up with the Hermit, as it would be the last chance that year. We started bright and early in the morning, after breaking camp. The country was not like that of Wu Chow Shan; there were no mountains, only rolling hills thickly covered with grass, bushes and bamboo. The bamboos grew so thickly in places that you could get through the groves only by following the paths, or rather tunnels made by the pigs, and it was impossible to walk upright because of the thickly interlaced branches. You had to crawl through them on all fours, slowly and carefully laying the rifle on the ground with every move forward. It was dark in there, even on the brightest days, as the foliage lay like a thick mat above you and it always gave me a creepy-crawly feeling going through these death-traps, often a couple of hundred yards long.

There was a good chance of a head-on collision with a sounder of pigs or, what was worse, a collision from the rear, as it was impossible to turn. A mere man is poorly equipped to meet wild pig under such conditions; his only weapon, the rifle, is useless, because you cannot kill a pig in that position. You can only pray hard that no pig will come your way, or write yourself off if one does. It always gave me a distinct inferiority complex, and I drew a deep sigh of relief when I saw the blessed daylight at the end of the tunnel.

This did not seem to be our lucky day, however hard we tried. Late in the afternoon when we had reached the last hill

TE 9

Top: Tientsin harbour
Bottom left: "Smiley" and Elizabeth Rosemary
Bottom right: Elizabeth Rosemary and Up-a-tree Cottage

PLATE 10

Top left: Hand-cleaning wool

Top right: Chief wool sorter

Bottom: Left to right, wool merchan
and Wang, Pi Hsin Tsai the Compra
and Paul Pi

and the end of the shoot we drew another blank, and I was moving slowly downhill when I saw a movement in the tall grass lower down on my right. It was so slow and stealthy that I did not think of pig but, nevertheless, walked back soundlessly keeping my eyes on the moving grass.

The animal, whatever it was, moved very slowly towards a ridge, without making a sound. I followed it on the higher ground, fascinated and mystified. Tah Gu Tzu had joined me and I could see him quiver with excitement. The movement continued over the ridge, where the cover was thinner, and revealed a shadowy form which I suddenly saw was a huge boar, streaking downhill as if shot out of a gun. We tore off in a wild dash. It was the Hermit.

Reaching higher ground, I saw him galloping towards the cover at the base of the next hill. I flung a snap shot at him and saw him stumble, but recover immediately and disappear into cover where he was lost to sight.

The next time I saw him he was nearly three hundred yards off and crossing the next ridge. I took careful aim and squeezed the trigger. He made a sudden jump and disappeared. The light was failing, and it seemed a hopeless quest to follow. However, he was hit, and I never left a wounded animal without doing my utmost to find it. We took an easy way up the hill and followed a narrow track. Tah Gu Tzu walked just ahead of me looking for tracks or blood spoor. On either side of us was dense cover, mostly brambles. On the left, just ahead, I could see an opening with some mud puddles, a likely spot for picking up his tracks, but with darkness creeping on us I did not think there was the slightest chance of getting him. Suddenly Tah Gu Tzu froze and pointed with a shaking finger to a mud hole just ahead. Following an unearthly scream that nearly froze my blood came a frightened yelp from Tah Gu Tzu who jumped back and cannoned into me. Fighting for balance I saw, coming for me, an enormous grizzly head with gleaming tusks and blazing eyes, roaring with rage. I fired as I fell. He was almost on top of me then, and I felt a sharp pain as I hit the ground.

The breath was knocked clean out of me, and all went black as a great weight settled on me. When I came to I was surrounded by beaters and Tah Gu Tzu was lifting the head of the dead boar off my chest. I got up shakily, feeling as if a steam-roller had hit me. The only visible damage was to my right arm, which had been pierced through by a sharp bamboo spike when I fell. The Hermit was being gralloched, and I staggered over to look at him.

He was hit twice in the shoulder and had rolled in the mud to stanch the bleeding and plug the bullet holes. By some miracle the last shot had found the brain; but then, I have always had more luck than sense.

We nearly lost the last train from Sia Shu Kai that evening through my arriving so late. The others had pushed on as they had to be in Shanghai the next morning and they prevailed on the stationmaster to keep the train waiting until I came.

Prevail is perhaps the wrong word. They put their baggage on the line in front of the engine, sat down on top of their bags and defied the driver to run over them. It only delayed the train half an hour or so, and what was half an hour in China in those days?

However, Mr. Tuxford, the divisional chief in Chinkiang, was quite cross with me the next day when I met him in the Club, and I had to give him one of the Hermit's hams before he was mollified. He was a bit of a stickler regarding the time-table; it was the Shanghai Express we had stopped.

XXII

OLD Taiping Joe's ghost never troubled us at the bungalow, but the servants were very worried and gave notice because they were frightened at night.

It was rather curious, for the well in which he was found dried up and the Chinese said that the water dragon was angry because Joe's spirit was not avenged and therefore could get no rest. I kept Joe's son on as water-coolie, and he performed some mysterious rites by the well, assisted by a necromancer, which ended by throwing in handfuls of rice. This, apparently, appeased Joe's spirit, for after that the servants were no longer frightened.

I bought another couple of acres of land and made a tennis lawn with two grass courts, and a large vegetable garden below the house, where the ground was less steep and easier to level. The garden was coming on apace and there must have been subterranean water which seeped into the holes made for the trees, for they grew phenomenally fast. I had planned to get as much colour into the garden as possible the first year, with bulbs, flowering shrubs and annuals and that spring the whole hillside was gay with crocus and daffodils, azaleas and forsythia—the last named grows wild in China and is called Chi dan huangtze (yellow of egg).

The extraordinary thing was that the garden had completely banished the sinister look of the house. For it had looked sinister before, standing abandoned on that sterile, unkempt hillside, and it was no wonder that the Chinese shunned it. But the magic of a flower garden had changed all that, and the house, in a brand-new coat of white, now smiled at you through bright chintz curtains, where formerly it had scowled savagely.

Later in the year the bungalow became famous because of the

roses in its garden. I never thought at the time when I ordered them from Cants in Colchester that there, on that bleak haunted hillside on the far-away Yangtze, the first English roses in the whole of the Yangtze valley would fill the air with their fragrance. It had been thought impossible to transport them so far but I had had them sent out in the winter via the Canadian Pacific Railway, and out of the first four hundred I lost only two. There were masses of the most exquisite blooms even the first year, and people came from miles away to admire this rare sight—especially Chinese, who are great flower lovers. The abbot and several monks from a monastery at the back of Huang Shan were frequent visitors. The Concession people came and took back armfuls for their vases, and shooting friends came from Shanghai for week-ends.

I am sure Dean Hole would have rubbed his unbelieving eyes if he had been transported to my rose garden during the first year the ramblers bloomed. From every bank cascades of red, white, pink and yellow fell in a riot of colours that could be seen a mile away. And he would have known every one of them by name, because they were his own favourites, selected from his own book.

There was even a hedge of English sweetbriars filling the air with fragrance after rain; and moss roses, Lancaster and York, La France, Malmaison, W. A. Richardson, Gloire de Dijon, Frau Karl Druschki, Maréchal Niel and Silver Moon, all beloved names to him, and most of them blooming for the first time in China.

That everything grew like magic was due chiefly to Mahtzu, my old boatman. He put me on to a guano deposit on a lonely rock near Silver Island where hundreds of cormorants had nested for centuries. He would take a large sampan down and fill a couple of dozen sacks with guano which he delivered to my garden.

Curiously enough, the Chinese never made use of those rich deposits, saying it was too strong and burned the plants. They used only night-soil in liquid form, which they splattered all over their plants. This was one of the reasons why it was dangerous to eat salads and fearing dysentery and other communicable diseases one never touched them, except after washing them in Condy's fluid. Even cooked cabbage and other greens, though safe, were far from appetising when you knew how they were grown, and in the Concession we were entirely dependent on Chinese market gardens. These produced quite a lot of strawberries, but few had the temerity to eat them, and by the time they had been soaked in Condy's fluid and brushed clean, there was little flavour left.

I used the guano sparingly in dry form as a top dressing in the vegetable garden and on a huge bed of strawberries, and in liquid form on the roses. It worked miracles, and we had delicious salads and tomatoes in such abundance that big hampers were sent in every day to friends in the Concession.

There is nothing like a garden to anchor one down, and the moment you begin to till your own bit of ground your own roots go down into the soil where you plant the first tree or bush. So it was with me. I had always thought that my roving spirit would be the last to succumb to the lure of a garden, but then I had also thought that I would be the last to stick the life in Chinkiang for years on end, until I found an outlet for my restlessness in wild gallops cross-country and the excitement of boar-shooting.

The dogs played their part too. Now we had six, and the latest arrival was Jock, an Airedale pup of only six weeks. Jock was a real personality from the time I got him, a born guardian angel and companion, almost human in the way he understood every word you said to him. He had the courage of a lion, yet was as gentle as a lamb. He was unlike any pup I had ever owned, for, from the moment he arrived, fat and a little awkward on his feet, he seemed to know that he was there to protect us—a very important and serious job.

He was never silly or irresponsible like other young puppies; never played with the other dogs or allowed himself any frivolity. He was quite grown up in manner, and his face showed the tremendous responsibility he had taken on. He would hardly ever leave our side and looked on the servants with great suspicion. When he grew bigger and I wanted to take him out with the other dogs for walks, he refused to go farther than the garden gate. I would call and call, but the only response was an apologetic wag and an agonised look in his eyes that told me: "Can't you see that my job is to look after the house? Goodness knows what may happen when you are away, or what the servants may be up to!" Then he would go back and take up his sentry-post on the top step of the front staircase. He would let no one into the house from outside, even visiting friends, and he would not allow the servants to leave the house or enter the rooms until we came back.

He was well over six months old before I managed to take him out with me pig-shooting, and then I had to haul him out on a lead. Once out of sight of the bungalow, he settled down and cantered happily alongside Blue Cap all the way to Wu Chow Shan. For the first time he had a chance to show his mettle. A wounded boar had taken cover in a dense patch of bushes, and I was advancing for the kill on the bare hillside when the boar winded me and came roaring out to attack. Jock was standing near me when he saw the great beast coming straight for us, and the next moment he was off like a streak. I felt sure he would be killed and yelled to him to come back, but nothing could stop him.

He avoided the vicious side sweep of the boar's tusks by leaping high, and then he fastened his teeth in its front leg. The boar crashed down and they rolled over and over, Jock hanging on like grim death, although he must have been nearly crushed by the great weight of the beast.

It was almost impossible for me to shoot for fear of hitting Jock, but by running close up to them I managed to put a bullet into the boar's head. Jock was still hanging on, and it took some time before he would let go. He sat and coughed and spat out hairs for a while, the breath having been knocked clean out of him, but he was very pleased with himself as he sniffed the dead beast, wagging his tail excitedly. Then he came over to me, sat down and cocked his head. I shook hands with him solemnly and said: "Thank you, old chap, you are a *very—clever—doggie*!" He always loved to hear me say that, and to shake hands.

XXIII

We had moved to the bungalow in 1914, but we were so far away and so occupied with the difficulties created in our own sphere by revolution and counter-revolution, that the rumblings in Europe made very little impression on us.

My firm, however, was registered in Berlin, and the outbreak of the First World War made it necessary for the partners to declare themselves. Two of the German partners left for Berlin, but the two Arnhold brothers, who had been brought up in Britain and were British citizens, liquidated the firm of Arnhold, Karberg and started their own firm of Arnhold Bros., registered in Hongkong as a British firm. They were sons of the founder and held most of the shares, so the whole China business was taken over by them.

The firm had wide ramifications with important branches and large staffs in Hongkong, Canton, Tsingtau, Tientsin, Peking, Hankow and Chungking. Chinkiang was the newest and smallest of the branches. After receiving the registration certificate from Hongkong, I registered the firm at the British Consulate and business went on as usual.

A few valiant souls in Chinkiang gave up their jobs, paid their own fares home and joined up. However, the great majority of us thought that the war would be over by Christmas and that it would be a waste of time and money to go home all that long way.

We were too far removed from European affairs to be able to grasp the real importance of the struggle and too near the internal strife in China, which increasingly affected each one of us. Conditions up-country on our long lines of communication were becoming more chaotic as the control in Peking weakened and ambitious war-lords became stronger. Spheres of influence were being formed by the various generals serving Yuan Shi Kai, and lawlessness was increasing.

The bandits in our district were getting bolder every day and one night they attacked a little village below my bungalow. For the first time they fired up in my direction as a warning to me to keep away and I heard bullets whistling through the air. It was raining, but I did not wait to dress. I threw on my dressing-gown, put a couple of magazines into my pockets, grabbed the automatic and started off down the slippery path. Half-way down to the village I saw spurts of flame coming from a small shed in the outskirts.

I stopped and fired a few rapid shots at the place, then quickly moved farther down and waited. The firing stopped instantly, then four shots were fired and I heard the whistle of bullets a little higher up the path. They were clearly firing at the place where they had seen the flashes from my rifle. I let them have the full magazine, moved, then slipped in a new one, and fired again. I was aiming over their heads, intending only to frighten them. As I was using dum-dum bullets, a hit anywhere in the body would have meant a very serious, if not a fatal wound. It was not my job to kill them, but I wanted to teach them the lesson not to fire at my bungalow again.

The yelling from the village stopped suddenly, but now the yelling came from the shed. "Kwei pao, wai guo ren fang chang!" (Run away quickly, the foreigner is shooting.) I was used to the darkness now and could see shadowy forms running away.

I was just going after them to let them have the remainder of my last magazine, when I was suddenly mobbed by a crowd of hysterical men and women who wanted to thank me for their deliverance. I had arrived just in the nick of time, it seemed. There had been about twenty robbers in the band, but only a few of them had rifles; the rest were armed with swords and spears, and all had blackened their faces. It was impossible to get a coherent story, as everyone was shouting at the same time with the children howling and the dogs barking. I cut them short and went home to get into dry clothes and back to bed. However, the village was never raided again while I was there.

I am afraid that pride in my garden led me to devote more time to it than I could really spare, but it was a great joy to me during the long, hot summer, when shooting in the hills was out of season. Most social activities in the Concession also ceased during the summer, and it was very rarely that we went there in the evenings. When we did go, we presented quite a sight. Taiping Joe's son and the groom always insisted on coming along as bodyguards, each carrying a lantern and a big executioner's sword, both of them looking very valiant and awe-inspiring. I always had my Winchester in the sedan-chair.

On the one and only occasion that we met two men on the road, our bodyguards dropped their lanterns and ran. The two men turned out to be terrified farmers who had been delayed in the city and were returning, in fear and trembling, to their village. This was unusual, because after dark every road was deserted, and no one dared leave their village. Only the bandits were about.

The same state of affairs was prevalent throughout the country, and farther north it was unsafe to travel even in broad daylight. I was naturally kept well posted by our agents up-country, where river and canal traffic had come to a stop. However, rail shipments, the only safe way of transporting cargo, were increasing, and we did not feel the pinch too badly.

During that winter the notorious bandit, White Wolf, ravaged three provinces north of the Yangtze, leaving a trail of burning villages and misery behind him. He rode at the head of only two hundred men but outwitted and outfought the whole Chinese Army, which became the laughing-stock of the country. The military commanders had other fish to fry, an operation much more important than to defend the people. They were busy consolidating their own positions, because Yuan Shi Kai's power was waning and there were prospects of good pickings in the subsequent battle for power. Yuan Shi Kai was planning to make himself emperor, realising, no doubt, that China could be ruled only by a despot and that the republican form of government would lead to chaos, for there were too many factions, and too many unscrupulous self-seeking political and military leaders to satisfy. Most of the leaders were, of course, bitterly opposed to Yuan as emperor, for that would mean the end of their own power. Now they banded themselves together.

We in Chinkiang were remote from all this jockeying because the tension was in North China. However, very little of political interest happened even in North China without the Chinese in Chinkiang knowing of it. The "whispering galleries" of the East always brought news of impending storms, and they had been very busy whispering for months past. But the ravages of White Wolf were very much our affair as he was operating in Northern Anhui across our supply routes, and junk traffic soon came to a standstill. I felt, too, that I had a personal knowledge of White Wolf for I bought a souvenir of him that nearly cost me my life.

Two of his ponies had been captured during a brush with soldiers near Nan Hsuchow, and I bought one of them through a friend in the Tientsin-Pukow Railway. Bandit, as I called him, was a very fast bay, but of a nervous disposition. As a friend was coming up from Shanghai for a week-end, I rode down to the station to meet him on the Bandit. I had tied him to the picket fence on top of the high embankment and, after seeing my friend to the sedan-chair, went over to mount my pony. I had just got into the saddle when the locomotive, only a few yards away, gave a sudden snort that frightened the Bandit out of his wits: he made a wild leap into a willow tree, and one of the branches caught me across the chest and tossed me high into the air.

I fell on my back on top of a pile of rocks and fainted. Coming to, I tried to get up but found I could not rise. For a frightening moment I thought that my back was broken and that I was paralysed. Then I rolled over on my side and found I could do that all right, and also that I could get up when lying prone, which had been impossible when lying on my back. I was badly shaken and in great pain. My friend had gone off in the sedan-chair without noticing the accident: the pony had disappeared.

Soon afterwards a coolie brought the Bandit back and helped me into the saddle, for I *had* to ride, having no other means of getting home. When the doctor came to examine me he found that four ribs were broken within half an inch of the spine.

There are times when a little thing like half an inch makes a big difference.

XXIV

In 1915 I was due for home leave, having served five years. I had spent ten years in Chinkiang, with only one holiday when I went on sick leave to Japan. I planned to leave the following spring and got busy making arrangements to find homes for the dogs and ponies. The five well-trained pointers were easy enough to place; but Jock was more difficult, as we did not want to leave him in the Concession. Eventually two missionary friends, the Richardsons, offered him a home in their compound out in the country beyond the Mud Fort. The ponies were taken over by the British-American Tobacco Company Mess.

That left Bobby, a young fawn given us that year by some friends going home on leave. The original gift was a pair which arrived in a crate during the early summer. I did not want them to be confined and opened the crate in the garden so that they could run off if they wanted to as they were quite big enough to look after themselves.

They came tripping out, and one of them, sensing he was free, went off like a streak up the hill and was soon out of sight. The other leaped daintily over to me, sniffed my hand with his coal-black nose and started to lick my palm. I gave him bread and milk at once, for he had come all the way from Pukow. He soon finished this off and licked my hand again. Then he tripped around in the garden and made himself at home. I had tied up the dogs, who were all quivering with excitement and blood lust, as they had pulled down many a deer before. I took them, one by one, on the lead to be "introduced." The fawn was not at all frightened, only very curious and anxious to make friends.

It was a bit difficult to make the pointers understand that they must be friends with an animal they had always hunted in preference to any other game, but with Jock it was different. He understood the situation at once and caused himself to become the fawn's guard and protector. He also made the other dogs understand the fawn's position in the household. In no time Jock and the fawn were licking one another, to the other dogs' amazement, but it took them a day or two before they really understood and became friendly. During that time Jock never left the fawn's side, and they even slept together in his kennel. We called him Bobby and he soon answered to his name. Jock would let him share his food, but Bobby did not care much for it and only nibbled a few grains of rice out of politeness.

Soon he was romping round the veranda with all the dogs, and hardly ever left the house. Every morning at seven, while I was having my morning tea, he came and licked my hand, to remind me that he wanted his milk. When he grew bigger he would play around in the garden with the dogs, and later on out on the hillside. They played a kind of hide-and-seek with great enjoyment. Bobby would run off and hide himself under a bush or in the grass higher up the hill, choosing his hiding-place with care. The dogs would wait in the garden for several minutes, and then start on the trail after him. They were like children over this game.

The time came when Bobby would no longer stay in the house but found himself a lair out on the hill. However, every morning at seven he came for his bowl of milk. He would drink it, lick my hand and play around for a few minutes with the dogs. Then he would disappear again and it was clear that he had found other interests. October came and with it the rutting season, and one morning, when I was out in the garden earlier than usual, I saw him coming down the hill in the company of another deer. They stopped a couple of hundred yards away and it looked as if Bobby was inviting the other to come with him, but the stranger refused to go any nearer. Bobby came on alone, had his milk, licked me and then went away again. A few minutes later I saw them scampering off together, higher and higher up until they finally disappeared over the ridge. He never returned after that morning, and the problem of finding him a home was solved in the happiest possible way.

We left by train the following spring. The Pukow Railway at that time had been completed as far as Tientsin, where it connected with the Manchurian and Siberian railway systems, so that one could step into the train at Chinkiang and be in direct rail communication with Europe. The journey took us twelve very wearisome days, in a stuffy, over-heated *wagon-lit* carriage from Harbin as far as Moscow.

When we reached Moscow I discovered that the usual route across the Baltic was closed because of U-boats, and that we should have to go by rail through Finland as far as Torneå. Passengers there had to cross the Torneå River in sleighs over to Haparanda, then board a Swedish train for Stockholm, Oslo and Bergen, from where steamers took them across to Newcastle.

The whole Siberian journey was dreary and monotonous at that time of the year; Moscow was cold, grey and unattractive notwithstanding the magnificence of the buildings, and the people were mostly pinched and ill-clad. St. Petersburg was brighter and as we stayed a day there it was possible for us to attend high mass in St. Isaac's Cathedral and listen to the magnificent choir. I had never before heard such wonderful voices, nor have I heard the like since, and it was no wonder that this choir was world-famous.

In St. Petersburg our small party, bound for England, was joined by Hugh Walpole and Captain Sir Frederick Sykes who was returning from a diplomatic mission. We also had in our compartment a cheery, bluff sea captain named Wake, returning to retire to his native Cornwall.

As soon as we arrived at the Finnish frontier station, Bielostroff, where the train made a long stop for the usual thorough examination both by the Police and Customs, a Russian officer entered our compartment and inquired: "Captain Wykes?"

"I am Captain Wake," replied our companion, "not Wykes." The Russian apparently did not know a word of English and seized the captain cordially by the hand. He was escorted out with great ceremony to a reserved room where champagne and caviare was served, and his baggage was whisked through into the Finnish train.

The rest of us, including Sir Frederick Sykes who should have been the guest of honour at the reception, had to undergo two separate and severe examinations of everything we had with us. This lasted nearly two hours, and while Sir Frederick fumed and swore and waved his diplomatic passport in vain, the sound of revelry from the reception room was growing louder and louder. Finally, Captain Wake and two officers came rolling out arm in arm singing "Tipperary" and a guard of honour presented arms as the sea captain stepped into the carriage and joined us.

The Russians, when they finally discovered their mistake, were not in the least inclined to entertain Sir Frederick. They had all fallen for "Captain Wykes," who undoubtedly had a way with him.

I had no chance of stopping over in Christiania, where I had spent part of my boyhood, as I had to go to London on business first, and we had just time enough to catch the S.S. "Venus" in Bergen. Two days later we were sitting in the train for King's Cross.

It was a curious feeling coming from my remote corner of Asia, where for years I had been completely out of touch with the outside world, right into the very heart of the British Empire.

If I had slept as long as Rip van Winkle, the wonders of London could not have seemed greater. For years I had seen only a handful of Europeans, and it was almost frightening to move about in London's streets, packed with white people and vehicles. Imagine my awe at the wonder of the shops: in Chinkiang there were two provision stores, that was all—Foo Chong and Chong Hsin, and if you met three people on the Bund, apart from a few Chinese, it was a crowd.

I realised with a shock that I had lived eleven years in China, eleven years out of the world, and I realised too that I had thought and done nothing about myself in relation to the War, when men were dying in their thousands in Flanders. There were men in khaki everywhere, especially at the railway stations, either coming home on leave or going back. I saw the Red Cross trains, too, and ambulances with their tragic burdens; men in their blue hospital clothes in invalid chairs, and on the benches in every park. I suddenly felt very small and rather ashamed.

I registered as an alien at Brixton police station, where the sergeant, rather rudely, asked what I was doing in England having a holiday in war-time. A recruiting sergeant equally rudely asked me why the hell I thought I could join the British Army. I was a neutral and this was their war, not Norway's. It was no use my trying, for they were not anxious to take on any neutrals. It was clearly a gentlemen's war, and the rules were being strictly observed.

We returned to Norway late in the summer. My parents were dead, but I had my brother in Trondheim to visit and he had arranged a deer-stalking holiday on Hitra, one of the islands off the coast. There were also two trout-lakes to fish. I shot the two stags allowed me, and fished and ate trout till I was nearly sick, but my heart was not in it. In October we left for China again by rail, and fourteen days later we were back in Chinkiang.

I thought Jock had gone clean off his head when I came for him. He was sitting on the wall watching the road, where Richardson told me he had sat every day since I left. He spotted me at once and with a bound he was off the wall and streaking towards me, yelping with joy. My garden looked lovely, but had lost its magic. Nothing was the same any longer. I had realised that there was a war on.

That winter I shot fourteen boars and worried the life out of the British Military Attaché in Peking to be allowed to join up. It was the spring of 1918 when at last I succeeded. I sold the bungalow and all I had and we went back to England via the Pacific and Canada. But I arrived too late, the War was then nearly over. A wire from the firm reached me in London offering me the job as assistant export manager in Shanghai and we returned almost at once. It was Hobson's choice for me, for I had very little money left.

The next four years I would rather not touch upon. Shanghai is not China, and I felt out of touch with events while I was there. A tremendous fight for the control of the country was going on north of the Yangtze, but I was too tied to my desk to investigate for myself. And Shanghai was the birth- and burial-place of my infant son.

In 1923 I left for Vancouver Island, where I bought a small ranch. We were expecting another child by then and I wanted it to be born in a white man's country. Jock, whom we got back again from his temporary home, came with us.

In March 1923 Elizabeth Rosemary was born on the ranch at Mt. Newton outside Victoria, but the year we spent in that wonderful island is another story.

Part Two

North China

CHINA TRADER

I

I WAS milking Jeanie McNab, our squint-eyed goat with a crumpled horn, early one November morning. It was Indian summer, the sun streamed down forming rainbow-coloured mists over the fields of the adjoining farm. A whistle of wings vibrated through the air, and I turned to see half a dozen pheasants come planing down from the forest higher up the hill to their morning feed in Hagan's farm. They glittered in bronze and gold as they passed. The gate clicked, and the postman came up to me with a telegram. I took it from him, wondering from whom it might be. It was from Shanghai and read, "Offer you post as manager important department Tientsin. Reply soonest. Arnhold."

I signed for it, finished the milking and took the pail into the kitchen. Then I went down to the orchard to think things over.

The young fruit trees had only just come into bearing that year. A few chickens were scratching about, all that an epidemic of roup had left me out of two hundred and fifty white leghorns. I had not expected the ranch to pay, but my losses had been unduly heavy.

It was a wonderful life in a wonderful country, but it led nowhere for a man with very limited means. Sooner or later my own slender resources would peter out, and another big fly in the ointment was the chores, household chores, especially washing up. My wife and I were both accustomed to having a house full of servants to wait on us and here we had to do everything ourselves and run the ranch at the same time.

Elizabeth had given us a very anxious time too. We nearly lost her, but, thanks to Jeanie McNab, we had found in goat's milk the only food she could keep down. My wife was worn out, and in desperation I engaged a Chinese servant, Ah Sing, at forty dollars a month. We spent a whole blissful week just watching him work, our main recreation after every meal being to leave the kitchen door ajar so that we could listen to him washing up the dishes.

He actually seemed to like it, but he was Chinese which no doubt accounted for it. Of course I could not go on paying for this pleasure indefinitely, and it was clear that I had reached the crossroads. But the main problem for me was the lack of brain work. During the last few years in Shanghai I had led too busy a life, with my brain constantly working at high pressure, to bury myself indefinitely in the country. I went back to the house and talked things over with my wife, and in the afternoon I telegraphed my acceptance.

Two weeks later, accompanied by Jock and Jeanie McNab, we were on our way back in the "Empress of Asia," ploughing through those dreary grey wastes and clammy cold mists of the Northern Pacific off the Aleutian Islands. It is a cold and weary journey even in the summer, and in the winter it is a nine days' battle through high seas, snow and fog, with the howl of the siren vying with the shriek of the wind.

We arrived in Yokohama to time, in spite of the weather and a couple of hundred tons of ice on deck. Even the shrouds were massive pillars of ice. At Kobe we joined the "Chojo Maru" bound for Tientsin.

The journey through the Inland Sea was a sheer delight and more than made up for the Pacific crossing. The maples were still in colour and the many islands looked like mounds of copper and gold standing out of an incredibly smooth blue sea. Then came the run through the narrow straits of Shimonoseki, a glimpse of Moji and Shimonoseki town and then out to sea, bound for the Gulf of Pechili.

We anchored outside the Taku Bar early in the morning, and my heart went down into my boots. A dust-storm was blowing, the air was yellow and the cold wind cut me to the marrow. Through the dust haze I looked at Tongku, the most God-forsaken sight I had ever seen.

A gaunt, ugly salt refinery reared its revolting head above some mean buildings, and beyond lay a dun-coloured plain dotted with big mounds of salt. Tongku lies on the northern side of the mouth of the Hai River. On the opposite side are the Taku Forts of Boxer rebellion fame. We were waiting for high water before crossing the Bar and proceeding up the river to Tientsin. The landscape did not improve as we steamed up the winding shallow river, on either side lay a horrible, dreary alkali plain, dun-coloured with withered grass and dappled with white where the soda oozed out of the ground. There was not a hill in sight nor even a slight natural rise in the ground, only the salt mounds near the mouth of the river and an occasional brick-kiln to break the dreary flatness.

But the run to Tientsin through this abomination of desolation did not take long and as we came alongside the wharf I could see people waving to us. They were Mr. Wolfers, the manager —he was one of the "royal family," being a nephew of the Arnhold brothers—and his wife, whom we knew well from Shanghai, and they escorted us to the Court Hotel, where rooms had been booked in our name. Even Jeanie McNab had been provided for and she was taken to Mr. Wolfers' stables by his mafoo, or rather it was Jeanie who took the disgusted mafoo, dragging him along at a brisk trot. She was glad to be off the ship, and was feeling her oats. She was even more pleased than we were to be at the journey's end.

II

THERE were three Concessions in Tientsin, the British, French and Japanese, the former German and Russian Concessions having been taken over by the Chinese. Wedged in between the three was an area of no-man's-land, with dirty streets and mean buildings, a real slum quarter full of opium dens, brothels and gambling joints. The Chinese, with their fine sense of humour, had named this district the San bu kwan, "the three don't cares" because being Chinese territory, it was not under the care of the British, French or Japanese, although contiguous to their Concessions.

Tientsin was opened to foreign trade in 1860, and first became notorious on account of the shocking Tientsin massacres in 1870. These were caused by the common belief that the foreigners kidnapped Chinese children and gouged out their eyes to use them as medicine.

It was not a sudden riot but one which had been brewing for some time, and the Chinese authorities, far from doing anything to stop the unrest, appear to have fostered it as usual. The riot began on June 21st, 1870, and the French Consul immediately made his way to the Chinese Special Commissioner, Chung Hou, to ask his aid, but this was refused. As the Consul left he was killed by the mob and Chinese soldiers.

In the meantime the mob had broken into the French Consulate, murdered Councillor Thomassin and his newly married wife, the Abbé Chevrier and a Chinese priest. At the same time the hospital and orphanage of the French Sisters of Charity was surrounded and set on fire and all the sisters were dragged out, stripped and horribly and shamefully mutilated, and then cut into pieces which were thrown into the burning building. More than a hundred Chinese orphans perished in the flames of the hospital; the French Consulate and the Catholic Church were also burned down.

Altogether twenty-one sisters, three priests, a French merchant and his wife who gallantly tried to aid the sisters, and five other civilians perished in these riots. The murdered civilians were stripped naked and so shockingly mutilated that some of them were unrecognisable.

The unrepentant Chinese government wriggled for months from the demands of justice, but was eventually forced to take action. Twenty more or less guilty smaller fry were beheaded, but the two instigators, the Prefect and Sub-Prefect, suffered only banishment to Amur Province with twenty-five others.

Following the massacre came the Boxer trouble when Tientsin was surrounded by fanatical mobs and the men, women and children faced starvation and massacre.

As I have said before occurrences such as these should be borne in mind when one hears people talking about British gunboat policy and Unequal Treaties. The appalling risks and unspeakable atrocities which were endured by the pioneers and those who came after them made equal treaties impossible and gunboat protection essential.

Foreigners in China were a mere few compared with the hundreds of thousands of Chinese living abroad who could work and trade and grow prosperous under foreign protection, without fear of molestation. I am thinking particularly of the Chinese in Malaya, Burma, the East Indies and Australia. In the United States alone there were close on one hundred and fifty thousand Chinese at that time. When they returned to their own country the only places they could go to were the foreign Concessions, because these were the only districts in the whole of China where their possessions were safe.

The main thoroughfare in the British Concession in Tientsin was called Victoria Road. There stood the Gordon Hall, built in memory of General Gordon and hallowed by memories from the Boxer trouble when the women and children were sheltered there and it was the last bastion of defence if the Boxers should break through. When I arrived the Hall housed the Municipal Council and the Police, the guardians of law and order.

I always felt that every British Concession in China, with its strong blend of duties and rights, fairness, rigid justice and tolerance, was a miniature City of London. The same civic spirit was evident, and an extra touch of pride, for the occupants had conjured up on alien soil, and often out of waste land, cities like Shanghai, Hongkong and, in a smaller way, Tientsin.

Tientsin was built upon a low alkali flat, often covered by flood waters: dykes were built and the level of the ground gradually raised by pumping river silt on to the land. What Tientsin was like in the early 'sixties when it was first opened I cannot imagine, but it must have been pretty grim. Even in 1921, with every imaginable amenity, it was a very trying place to live in. For ten months in the year not a drop of rain fell, and the dryness, the everlasting wind and dust, played havoc with one's nerves. It was blazing hot in the summer, up to one hundred and twelve degrees in the shade, and then the rains came and turned the place into a steam-bath for two months. In the winter, temperatures were sub-zero and the wind cut like a knife, with perhaps one or two light snowfalls to bring relief from the drought for a week or so.

It was a miniature modern city with clubs, societies, cinemas and a cosmopolitan population. As in all other British Concessions, the various nationalities worked freely and without restriction at whatever trade they were engaged in, so long as they did not run foul of the law. They had always shared in all the rights and privileges, without discrimination, but whenever there had been any threat against these rights and privileges, the onus of defending and upholding them had fallen on the British Consul, the Municipal Council and the Police, and often on the British and American armed forces. I am afraid this fact has often been forgotten.

The city did a big trade out of all proportion to its size. Three minutes by car would take you to the end of Victoria Road, which was the whole width of the British Concession, and in five minutes you could drive the whole length of it, along Race Course Road. Yet it was the centre of the inland trade as far as Tibet and Turkestan, and the only port which served this vast hinterland.

One did not need to go far before one discovered that wool was the mainstay of Tientsin. The trade centred in a comparatively short stretch of the Taku Road, and every road leading to this part of the Concession would be filled with carts piled up with bales of wool. There were horse-carts, mule-carts and mixed teams of coolies and mules pulling side by side, all bound for the various large warehouses and cleaning plant. Practically the whole of this trade was in the hands of British firms, and by far the largest investments were in scouring plant, willows (cleaning plant) and hydraulic presses to clean and pack the wool for export. The British were the pioneers of this trade and had built it up from the very beginning. Next in importance came raw cotton, which was press-packed for export in the same warehouses. These two industries alone gave daily work to thousands of Chinese coolies, sorters and pickers.

If one passed through Taku Road at noon one would find the whole street crowded with workers who came out to buy their frugal meals from the travelling food vendors. The food offered was an astonishing variety of dishes ranging from toasted grass-hoppers (in season) to large slabs of heavy date pudding and fried dumplings sizzling hot from the deep pans. A favourite method of buying was to gamble for it with the vendor, who carried marked bamboo sticks in tin tubes. I am afraid the odds were heavily in the vendor's favour, for he nearly always won. The coolies seemed, however, to get a great deal of pleasure from this chanciness and drew their "hand" with the tenseness of poker players. Within half an hour they had all vanished into the dusty warehouses and left the streets clear for the carts and rickshaws.

In a port like Tientsin you could more or less choose your own life. There was more elbow room than in an out-port, but, even so, you were more or less confined to the limits of the Concessions. The extreme limit was the Race Club and Country Club, just outside the boundaries. Beyond was a bare, flat alkali plain with good riding for those who did not mind being smothered in dust, and a canal for boat picnics if you did not mind being eaten up by flies. These were the main pleasures to be found outside the boundaries, and with fierce civic pride, Tientsinners ignored the dust and the flies and seemed to enjoy it all.

For those who really fretted behind the invisible bars, there were opportunities of exploring by car the "Dark Continent" beyond the boundaries. There were no roads, only deeply rutted cart-tracks, and nowhere one could go was of any great interest. But you could find old, deserted brick-kilns, in isolated spots where you could be alone for a few moments and make believe that you were on a hill, which itself was worth a long bumpy drive.

The material advantages of life in Tientsin were obvious if you were not of a restless disposition. I was born and bred in the mountains and could never be happy in such surroundings. I was born restless, too.

Fortunately I had come to take charge of the wool department of Arnhold & Co., and was able to find escape in the deeply interesting work. The department was in a bad way, due to bad management, and it was left to me to work it up again. It did not take me long to discover that I liked the wool trade with as much intensity as I disliked Tientsin.

This trade meant politics, wars, camels, bandits, caravans, Mongols, Sarts, Turci, Tibet, Kokonor and the romance of the whole of High Asia. The lines of supply ranged from the tiny network between widely scattered nomad camps a thousand and more miles from the nearest railhead, to broad unbroken streams of camels which brought their loads into Paotow, Kweihuacheng and Kalgan. Strings of yaks came down the high mountain passes of Tibet carrying the bales through deep snow and down dizzy slopes where no other animal could survive the rigours and the altitude. This cavalcade went to Tangar in Kokonor and thence to Sining on the Yellow River: from Sining the bales continued down the river on rafts and inflated ox-skins to Paotow, the terminus of the six hundred miles of railway line to Tientsin.

From Kuldja, Gu cheng, Urumchi and Hami in Chinese Turkestan, long strings of camels came across the Gobi desert, some fifteen hundred miles, and a four to five months' journey. Along the old Marco Polo trail and every other desert trail they came, all making for the railway and eventually for Tientsin. When the Mohammedans in Kansu were on the warpath the Tibetan trade routes were affected and also the Turkestan caravan trails. Then came local wars, nearer home, which put the railway out of action, and the bandits got busy on the incoming caravans. Or perhaps some defeated war-lord retreated into Mongolia or Kansu and made hay with the supply lines there. Anyway, something was always happening in that vast turbulent hinterland and life was never dull.

The representatives of native dealers and traders dropped in at my office daily and told me what was going on in the interior, from the latest political events and their probable effect, to the doings of Sun Mo Ling, the bandit, or the latest moves by the Russians in distant Chinese Turkestan. The informant might be a Chinese, a Sart or Turci tribesman, or a former Russian officer who had fought his way across China from Siberia and now did business with the scattered bands of White Russians who remained in the interior.

In this way I could keep in close touch with events in my vast territory, especially as I was in the happy position that the natives spoke freely and openly to me. Indeed, my work was full of interest and fascination as I established contact with vivid personalities and the strong pulsating life of the turbulent border.

After reading Marco Polo's travels it was impossible not to feel the fascination of that country, and it grew on me as I realised that my daily work not only covered his trails, but innumerable other ancient routes, as changeless as they were old, because they had not been invaded by machinery. The yak still reigned supreme on the Tibetan mountain passes, the camel in the Gobi desert—and wherever they went ancient traditions and modes of living and thinking and the simplicity and dignity of the past went with them.

My earliest work in Tientsin made me realise this very soon. My firm had sent an expedition led by a Russian ex-officer into Tibet to buy wool, and I had access to all the reports. These covered every stage of the journey, but there was one very curious and noticeable quality about them: they changed in tone as the party got farther and farther away from civilisation. Starting in the form of the usual business letters, they became more and more coloured by the life and surroundings, until business matters almost disappeared and made place for descriptions of wild mountain scenery, hardships, dangers and difficulties. Finally, the expedition met with disaster. It was attacked by Golokse tribesmen, two men were shot, and the pack animals were seized and driven off. The description of the attack and subsequent events read like pages straight out of Hakluyt's *Voyages*. A few of the natives escaped and ended up in Lhasa under the leadership of the Chinese manager, who remained there and married the daughter of a high Tibetan dignitary. The whole attack had been arranged by the villainous Chinese manager, who let the Goloks take most of the supplies and trade goods while he got away with all the cash and enough food to see him through to Lhasa.

There were several reports from the Chinese business manager, covering the journey to Lhasa, after the attack. They contained the best word pictures of the Tibetan mountains and passes I have ever read. I remember one brief description of the Moon Mountain which was particularly beautiful. He was certainly a man of parts, and in spite of all the reports about him, I hope he lived happily ever after.

Chinese expeditions of this kind had been going off periodically for centuries past, but the Chinese were too experienced to carry money. The leaders were invariably either partners in the enterprise, or old trusted employees who had proved themselves on previous occasions. These Chinese caravan traders were, perhaps, the most daring and enterprising in the world. They wheedled and bribed their way through the war-torn districts, eluded, bribed or fought bandits, and then disappeared for months into the back of beyond.

Their gains were enormous, but the risks were great, and it took a very stout heart to carry on the business year after year. They went out with silk, tobacco, tea and finery and returned with wool. Wool was carried back for two reasons. In the first place it was about the only thing the nomads of the country could offer in exchange for tea, tobacco and cloth. Secondly, wool was more or less the currency of the country and the only kind of currency which could be carried, in safety, through the lawless territories. It was also the only bulk cargo obtainable as freight, apart from furs which it would be too risky to carry back.

All this traffic was undertaken by Chinese private enterprise, as no foreign firm would risk business which could not be covered by insurance. My own firm's expedition to Tibet had been a costly lesson.

It was only natural that as my knowledge grew of this vast territory which was my field, the work should become more and more absorbing and interesting. Learning the characteristics of the various kinds of wool from different parts of Central Asia was a study in itself, and I spent weeks in the warehouses among the Chinese sorters, breathing in sufficient wool dust to kill almost anybody but a Chinaman. But it was the only way to learn, and it was my job to see that the standards were kept. The department had been almost ruined by my predecessor, and I had to restore the reputation of our brand, or "chop" as it was called. I had a natural knack of getting on well with the Chinese, and this was the reason why the department, the most important in Tientsin, had been entrusted to my care.

I soon had the Chinese overseers' full co-operation, and they showed me all the tricks of the trade. At home I read practically every available book about Mongolia, Tibet, Kansu and Turkestan. And so, little by little, I came to look at these shabby, burlap-covered bales in a different light. Every bale would tell its own story by its shape and the little bits of wool sticking out where the burlap was torn. The bales might contain the off-white long tasselled strands of the Tibetan wool, and a similar type of pure white from Zaidam in Kokonor. Mongolian wool, and camels' wool from Edsingol and Uliassutai on the edge of the Gobi, the peculiar grey from Turkestan and ball wool from Shansi. For me, each was a direct link with the various parts of my vast "empire," and they were all destined for the carpet mills of America to be turned into beautiful rugs for beautiful homes.

As for the camels' wool, it was curious to think that most of the "British Warms" were "born" on the caravan trails of the Gobi, for that was the only place in the world where camels' wool fine enough for weaving into cloth was produced. The Gobi winters are so bitterly cold that only the Bactrian camel, with its thick, silky underwool, can survive them. This coat is shed in May and comes off in big flakes. An important collecting centre for this wool was at Pei Ling Miao (Temple of the Skylarks) in Inner Mongolia, because this locality was a great feeding-ground for camels to get them into condition for the long desert journey.

There were three main routes for the caravans: the Urga trail from Kalgan to Urga, and then on to Uliassutai, in the extreme west of Outer Mongolia; the Kweihuacheng route from the ancient caravan centre in Sui Yuan province, to Hami and Urumchi in Chinese Turkestan; and the Paotow Ningshia–Lanchow route from the terminus of the Kinsui Railway to Western Kansu and Kokonor on the Tibetan border. It was estimated that at least half a million camels were engaged in the caravan trade, which was the only means of transportation possible in that part of the world.

These ancient caravan trails formed my favourite study, especially the old silk trail used by Marco Polo and last traversed by Younghusband. Since his time the trail had been abandoned owing to the difficulty of finding water-holes.

I found a kindred spirit in the office in one of my colleagues, Owen Lattimore, who, later on, made the journey along the silk trail in Younghusband's footsteps and reached India. It was a great achievement, and made him famous.

Lattimore was a brilliant Chinese and Mongolian linguist who, during the last war, became President Roosevelt's adviser on Chinese affairs. We spent many an evening together planning that first journey of his. It required great courage because he had done practically no travelling of this kind before and had very little money. I would have given anything to have made that journey myself, but I was no longer free to go off into the blue.

But I could do it in my daydreams, and I am afraid that my mind often strayed to the caravan trails of High Asia. I was living more and more in a make-believe world of my own, and there I found relief from my dusty and exacting duties and the flatness of Tientsin. I had found a house in the ex-Russian Concession. The roads, now that the Chinese controlled the district, had gone to pieces through lack of repairs and the whole place had a shabby, down-at-heel look which contrasted sharply with the splendid roads and spick-and-span appearance of the foreign Concessions.

My house was also on the wrong side of the river, and to get home and back I had to go either over the river by ferry, or drive by car through the French Concession, over the International bridge and along the so-called Russian Bund with its wonderful collection of potholes. But the house had a garden, a feature that was almost unobtainable in Tientsin, so we put up with the other disadvantages.

The main social centre in Tientsin was Kiesling and Bader's Café in the ex-German Concession, which had a roof garden. The two German partners were famed for their delicious cakes, and their place was always packed in the afternoons. Other meeting places were the Race Club and the Country Club a couple of miles out, with fine buildings and every social amenity. Racing was the chief pastime and most of the firms had their own stables and jockeys. The Arnholds were racing enthusiasts and had stables also in Hongkong, Shanghai and Hankow.

Between six and eight in the morning, the racing fraternity could be seen out at the racecourse drinking tea on the grand-stand and watching the ponies do their training gallops. I was more keen on riding than racing, so I spent most of my mornings riding cross-country. One thing that could be good in Tientsin, was the air. It was so dry and sparkling that it was almost intoxicating, but one noticed that only on windless days; when the wind was strong, one could hardly breathe for dust.

III

I DON'T know whether one could call the wars in China at that time civil wars, because politics, ideology and patriotism were not the causes. The wars were rather private ones between military leaders for the control of as large a slice of the country as they could grab, and for its extension as far as possible afterwards.

This period was called politely The Wars of the Tuchuns (military leaders), and was in full swing when I arrived in North China. The war-lords had started in a desultory way in 1916 after Yuan Shi Kai's death, but the struggle spread and grew in intensity as time went on. The contenders seemed to follow a set formula. The first step was to grab a railway line, or part of one. This meant not only revenue but also cheap transportation; there was an unwritten law among the war-lords that rail traffic should never be interfered with because without it they would be severely handicapped in the game of beggar-my-neighbour. Trains came and went through the opposing camps, the war-lord in the north taking the revenue from all south-bound trains, and vice versa.

When the railway was under control, every city was assessed at so much as contribution to "war funds" and the money was invariably paid because failure to do so meant the looting of the city. Then the war-lord's printing-press started to turn out worthless paper money which was enforced as legal tender throughout his territory. The soldiers were paid in this paper currency, as were all supplies to the armies. The whole countryside swarmed with soldiers in dirty grey uniforms, living off the country like locusts.

We were very close to all this in Tientsin, where the war-lords

ATE II

Top: The Peking–Tientsin "Autostrada" is nothing but a deeply rutted cart-track
Bottom: Temple of the Sons outside Kalgan

PLATE 12

Top: Wool caravan arriving at Kalgan

Bottom: The primitive ox-cart is the principal cargo carrier on the Mongolian border

had their palatial houses and their harems and strutted about in their comic-opera uniforms. Yes, it was all very comic opera, for very little blood was shed. It was so much easier to buy small opponents over than to fight them, and the big rivals could be mastered by the simple expedient of buying over the high officers and their men who were holding strategic key positions when any real fighting had to be done. Some of the obscure officers rose to wealth and fame by changing sides several times, and were able to start in business on their own in a big way.

Every man was for sale at a price; and to simplify the problem of taking over large bodies of troops at the minimum cost and trouble, each man simply changed the calico armband he had fastened on to his sleeve by a safety pin and put on the band of his new master. This band was the only insignia the soldiers carried to show whose men they were, the uniforms being identical throughout the warring sections; cheap grey cotton cloth in the summer and the same stuff padded with cotton wadding in the winter. This armband business was a very practical solution to the problem of changing sides quickly, but the Chinese are essentially a practical people.

The whole business would have been comic opera had it not been so tragic for the country people. Growing crops were trampled down by the armies, stocks of grain were seized as well as farm animals and carts for transport services, and as many men as were required. There can be few examples of man's inhumanity to equal the heartless and wicked exploitation which went on in North China during those years. The country was bled white, because when one war-lord retired from business or was defeated, his paper money automatically became valueless. A new one took his place and started to print *his* paper money, and so it went on. I shall never forget those pathetic queues of ruined Chinese waiting for hours outside the Chinese banks, only to be told that there were no funds to redeem the bank notes they had brought.

One could always predict the retirement or imminent fall of a war-lord by watching his bank. They invariably had their banks within the foreign Concessions because it was the only safe place for their money. Indeed the main offices and vaults of the Chinese Government bank, the Bank of China, were in the foreign

Concessions and never in the adjoining native cities. Worst of all, the soldiers were never paid off but left to fend for themselves. The argument was that they had their rifles and ammunition, and what better equipment could a man have to make a fat living in a country where the people were at their mercy?

That was the beginning of the rapidly growing bandit menace in North China. Business went on as usual because the war-lords depended on rail receipts for a large part of their incomes, so that we had few transportation difficulties.

It would be impossible to give a true picture of life in Tientsin in those days without mentioning all this, because we were living in an increasing turmoil of strife, with bigger and bigger forces taking part as time went on.

Among the war-lords who came and went Wu Pei Fu was perhaps the one honourable exception, and it was a sad day for North China when this honest fighter was defeated through the betrayal by his ally, Feng Yu Hsiang, the so-called Christian general.

I watched Wu's last fight in the summer of '26 from Peitaiho on the sea coast. Chang Tso Lin's Manchurian troops were pouring through the high mountain passes beyond Shan Hai Kwan, but Wu was holding them back until he was attacked in the rear by his own ally, Feng Yu Hsiang. Wu retreated fighting on two fronts, and gunfire was drawing nearer and nearer Tientsin day by day.

They were anxious times for people living in the ex-Russian Concession outside the protected areas, as the main objective was the railway station which was only a few hundred yards off on our side of the river.

The eliminating bouts of the comic-opera armies were over by 1925 and the big fellows were now starting. The smaller fry had either retired to their palaces or had been eliminated, and the main contenders were the Big Three—Chang Tso Lin, Feng Yu Hsiang and Yen Hsi Shan, Governor of Shansi.

The thunder of big guns and rat-tatting of machine-guns made sleep difficult. Refugees were pouring into the Concession and nearly every day, on my way home in the car, the Concession bridge was choked with defeated soldiers from one faction or another seeking sanctuary. They were being disarmed by British and French soldiers, as no armed men were allowed inside the Concessions.

To get through them in a car was slow work, crawling along foot by foot, steering with one hand and pushing men with rifles and Mauser pistols off the running-board with the other.

The Border Regiment was stationed in Tientsin then and was later relieved by the Lancashires. Sunday church parade was one of the big events, when the men came swinging along Race Course Road to Gordon Hall, where the service was held, and the strains of "John Peel" sent the blood tingling through your body.

We had an armed Chinese policeman patrolling the street near the house; he was an ex-soldier and a great favourite with Elizabeth Rosemary, now aged three. They used to have long discussions about the war situation in Chinese, and Elizabeth became quite an expert on the various kinds of guns we heard. She was also very well informed on what was going on behind the scenes and often surprised me by knowing a good deal more than I did.

The Chinese love children and will confide in them a great deal more than in grown-ups. I prided myself on getting more information out of the Chinese than most people, but Elizabeth got a good deal more and seemed to know the language better than I. We called the policeman "Smiley," and it was a strange sight to see the two of them walking hand in hand in earnest discussion of the war situation.

From our veranda, we could watch the incoming trains packed with refugees from the battle areas. People were riding on the engines, on the buffers and the running-boards, they were hanging on to the door-handles, and the roofs of the coaches were packed. A sergeant and five British Tommies held an outpost a hundred yards or so from the house to keep out demoralised deserting soldiers and installed an ingenious device for this purpose. They erected a series of notice-boards with arrows and a Chinese inscription: "Soldiers! Follow the arrows to safety!" Needless to say, the arrows skirted the Russian Concession and led to the river where a ferry-boat took them across to the other side, well clear of the other Concessions. Hundreds were playing follow-my-leader every day, unpinning and throwing away their armbands. The Tommies called their post "Calico Corner."

They were splendid fellows, full of fun, and brought a feeling of security we never had before. Once a week they invited Elizabeth to "inspect" their dug-out, and she was delighted when, on approaching, the sergeant's stentorian voice rang out: "Squad! Prrresent Arrrms!"

There followed the sharp tap of hands on the butts, the double slap of the grip round the rifles, and the rigid salute of the sergeant. Elizabeth would return the salute solemnly and "inspect" them, having been schooled by the sergeant. On one occasion she saw that the boots of one of the men were dusty and took out her little hankie, bent down and wiped them clean. Then she straightened up and said: "Looks better now, don't you fink?"

The "inspection" was always followed by a small tea-party at our house where Elizabeth presided and the soldiers came in two groups.

Feng Yu Hsiang had a brief spell of lording it in Peking after stabbing Wu Pei Fu in the back. His hymn-singing troops often marched through the ex-Russian Concession to the strains of "Onward, Christian Soldiers," in spite of the fact that Feng was now rabidly anti-Christian.

His regime did not last very long. Once more the guns were thundering around Tientsin as Chang Tso Lin advanced with a big and well-equipped army, and more showers of armbands littered "Calico Corner." I forgot to mention that the Tientsin Golf Course was situated in "Calico Corner," and that play was often difficult when hundreds of soldiers drifted across the fairway littering the greens with armbands.

Chang defeated Feng thoroughly at Tientsin and later chased him out of Peking. Chang was now the new master in North China and had a very firm grip of affairs. With Feng's defeat our difficulties really started for he was retreating along our main communications. He had made a stand at the Nankow Pass in the high mountain ranges beyond Peking and astride the railway line which carried wool supplies from the interior. He broke all precedents by refusing to allow trains to leave his territory, so that business was brought to a standstill. It was, in fact, no longer a gentlemen's war.

I had very large quantities of wool stored at Kalgan, Kweihua-cheng and Paotow and a good deal more was expected by caravan from Chinese Turkestan and Tibet. The most serious part of the new development was that no forecast could be made as to how long the stoppage would last.

I had been looking for an opportunity of visiting our Chinese agents up-country, and this was my first chance. The difficulty was that, on account of Feng's rabid anti-foreign policy, no passports were being issued to foreigners to cover interior districts; in fact all foreigners in the interior had been warned to evacuate as their lives were in peril. Tientsin and Peking were full of evacuees, and ugly rumours were circulating of impending massacres of foreigners in unprotected places. It was therefore with rather mixed feelings that I started on this journey into the unknown. First I had to try to get a pass in Peking, having failed to obtain one from the British Consul General in Tientsin. Owen Lattimore was then the firm's manager in Peking, and if anyone could wangle a pass it would be him. He was doing the Government contracts and would be in contact with the highest officials.

It would be a very cold journey, and it would be necessary for me to wear the customary sheepskin coat and fur cap of the border country. These garments give you a villainous look and make you inconspicuous because they are worn by the common people up there in the winter. The commoner I could look, the less notice would be taken of me. I was accompanied by my personal assistant, Paul Pi, nephew of the compradore, Pi Hsin Tsai, and a very unwilling starter. He was frankly and honestly terrified of soldiers and even more so of bandits.

We were bound for the border country around the Mongolian plateau, which had always been notorious for banditry, and at that particular time, Sun Mo Ling, the most dreaded of all bandit leaders, was very active. His speciality was kidnapping and demanding high ransoms. If the families of his captives were slow in meeting his demands, a finger-joint or an ear would be sent to them as a reminder that his patience was at a low ebb.

He was capable of shocking even the Chinese. For the release of some of his captives he had demanded sums which the families were unable to pay. They paid all they had, and were told to come to a certain place to receive the prisoners. The rendezvous was at the foot of a high cliff, and as soon as they had arrived they saw, to their horror, the prisoners being hurled from the top of the cliff. Not one of them survived the fall. A note from Sun was pinned to one of them: "Don't expect whole bodies when you don't pay the whole ransom."

Paul Pi's uncle, the compradore, was reputed to be very wealthy but also very mean, and Paul told me that he was terrified of being taken by bandits, for he was sure that his uncle would refuse to pay the ransom however many finger-joints were sent to remind him. For this reason he was not a very cheerful companion.

Lattimore put us up in the firm's palatial house, an ancient and beautiful building, or rather series of buildings and courtyards formerly owned by a Manchu prince. He expected shortly to be relieved, having resigned in order to undertake his desert journey to Turkestan and India. But even all his efforts to get me a pass were unavailing. Both the British Embassy and the Chinese authorities refused to grant it. We were discussing what to do next when Lattimore suddenly said: "I wonder if George can help us. He's coming tomorrow and he always puts up at the Wagon Lits Hotel. Besides, it is Saturday and the weekly *thé-dansant* is rather fun. The whole of Peking will be there."

"And who is George?" I asked.

"You'll find out tomorrow," was the reply.

CHINA TRADER

IV

SATURDAY dawned with one of the worst dust-storms that year. I had felt the previous day that very trying tightening of the nerves and jumpiness which most of us experienced before a dust-storm. We made our way to the Wagon Lits through clouds of yellow dust and an icy blast. The massive palaces of the Forbidden City loomed up like ghost castles in the yellow half-light, and in their soft shadows there streamed on towards Hatamen that weird traffic found only in Peking: rickshaws, camels, motor-cars, pedestrians, trams, bicycles, Peking-carts and motor-buses, in a wide two-way stream. Down the road leading to the glacis of the Legation Quarter came strings of smart cars, all making for the Wagon Lits.

The large downstairs reception-rooms were crowded with dancers, and nearly all the side tables were taken. The place was much more crowded than usual as it was race week and most of the racing people from Tientsin had come up. There were besides many who had arrived from inland points on account of the evacuation order. They were now able to enjoy themselves in safety, and at the same time have the rare pleasure of dancing to a good band. Lattimore had booked a table and was busy pointing out to me the most notable people when he suddenly looked towards the door and said: "There he is, just coming in."

A giant of a man, in a greasy sheepskin coat, stalked into the crowded room. He was head and shoulders above the crowd, he stood for a moment, hands on hips, watching with a grin the antics of a very sleek young man in the throes of the Charleston.

He was still grinning when he came over to our table and, grabbing a passing boy, ordered two dozen sandwiches and tea.

He must have been six feet two, and had immensely broad shoulders; he was fair-haired, with friendly blue eyes, and his weather-beaten, dusty face shone with honesty and good humour. "This is George," said Lattimore, "and here is my friend Ras." I shook the biggest hand I had ever seen, and George beamed at me. Then he took off his sheepskin coat, threw it against the wall and sat down.

"A cigarette for the love of Mike!" was the first thing he said. "I ran out of smokes yesterday. Been riding in a troop train for forty-eight hours, living on sardines and stale bread. And you won't get another word out of me until I have eaten my sandwiches." The boy had just arrived with them, tiny little squares which George swallowed two at a time. Lattimore laughed at him: "If I were a society reporter in the *Peking and Tientsin Times* I would have some startling headlines in the Monday number: 'Wild man from Mongolia invades *thé-dansant*—dancers stampede.' Where from this time, wild man?"

George chuckled and said with his mouth full: "Ordos desert, Paotow and thereabouts—sticky job, with Feng's men gunning for me. I have some bad news, but wait till I have finished." This did not take him long. He lit a cigarette, inhaled deeply, and said: "Bad business about Lieutenant Knowles. Murdered in the hills west of Nankow pass. Feng has been driven out of the pass and is retreating westward. Knowles probably ran into his lot and was scuppered. Martinson, the missionary up my way, has been murdered too. Got the evacuation order too late and was killed at an inn. Just dragged out of bed and shot. I got Hulda Malmgren out safely. She was ill and could not leave when the evacuation order came. I had to ride at night to reach her station, lay doggo all day and took her with me the following night. She was very ill but rode like a man, and not a whimper from her the whole of the long ride. Great girl, but I am afraid she's got T.B. badly. I put her into the American Hospital before I came here."

Lattimore and I were taking in every word. We were shocked to hear of Lieutenant Knowles's murder. He served in the Peking Legation Guard and was on a long shooting holiday, when the situation suddenly became tense. Every effort was made to warn him, but in vain. It did not look very encouraging for my trip, but I asked George about the chances of getting through without a pass and of coming back alive. George grinned: "Don't worry about a pass here. They won't ask to see it before you get to Kalgan. You can easily get a Chinese pass there. Just board a troop train westward and leave it at Kalgan. Feng has been driven out of there now. You'll find Rustad, Mamen and Butler in the B.A.T. Mess there; my brother John is at Kweihuacheng when you get as far west as that, and Tony Oberg is about in there somewhere. Stick to Chang Tso Lin's troops and you'll be comparatively safe. It is Feng Yu Hsiang's men you have to avoid if you want to keep alive!" He rose and picked up his coat. "Sorry, chaps, I have to leave you. I need a bath and a shave and then I'm taking the night train to Tientsin. Cheerio!"

That was the first time I met George Soderbom, one of the fine persons who lived and worked in that wild border country of the Mongolian plateau. You could almost count them on the fingers of one hand: George and his brothers, John and Gus, Tony Oberg from Saratsi, all in their early twenties, and born of Swedish-American missionary parents at Kalgan. In Kalgan itself were Rustad and Mamen, both Norwegians, and engaged by the British-American Tobacco Company, and Butler, an Australian. The doyen of them was Larson, the "Duke of Mongolia," whom I had met in Tientsin, a legendary figure on the border who spent the winters in Kalgan and the summers in Mongolia.

Lattimore and I sat and talked for a while and he told me of his plans. I was surprised to hear that he had recently got quietly married, and that his wife was away preparing for their journey. It was an astounding plan which had to be kept very quiet.

Lattimore was shortly proceeding to Kweihuacheng, where Arnhold's agents had procured camels for his journey. The animals had to be hidden because Feng Yu Hsiang's men were seizing camels right and left for their transportation service. His wife, Eleanor, was later on to go via Siberia to the station nearest to the Turkestan border and then travel to Urumchi where they planned to meet after Lattimore had crossed the desert. They would then continue the journey together, cross the Karakorum Pass and spend a belated honeymoon in Kashmir.

The journey up there had worried him a bit, but the latest news brought by George indicated that the trip was feasible. He was now only waiting for word from Kweihuacheng. He had secured his passes before the present emergency stopped their issue, but whether a pass would see him through or not was quite another matter. As we were talking George returned looking very well groomed, in fact almost a different person, but it was clear that the collar irked him. We arranged to meet at Kweihuacheng if possible, in the near future.

The next morning I boarded a troop train at Hsichimen station. Most of the passenger coaches appeared to have been to the wars, for the windows were smashed, seats stripped of their coverings and stuffing, and peanut shells littered the floor. Both Paul Pi and I travelled light having only the indispensable bedding roll. My shaving kit and soap were tucked into one of my big pockets, the other being full of cigarettes.

Finding a coach that was not too full I barged in as if the place belonged to me, put my bedding roll down on the seat and perched on top of it. Paul Pi took the place next to mine. The soldiers paid us very little attention until I lit a cigarette, when I noticed a few of them eyeing me enviously. I handed a pack round and their faces lit up. There were about eight of them in my corner, and the cigarettes broke down their reserve and we were soon chatting away. Three of them were sergeants, and I explained to them that I had only a limited supply of cigarettes and could not possibly give all the soldiers in the coach smokes, or we in our corner would not have enough to last us to Kalgan.

This diplomacy worked well, and established our party on a more solid personal basis. Half an hour or so later the train started with a jerk. The journey had really begun and no snooping inspector had appeared to ask for either ticket or pass because this train was not controlled by the railway authorities.

The train skirted the Western Hills, and soon the massive ranges we had to cross loomed up in the distance. A bitter, cold wind came through the broken windows and would have made the journey almost unbearable had it not been for my sheepskin coat and fur cap; but outside the sun shone and the sky was clear after the dust-storm. I was filled with suppressed excitement and a good deal of elation at having made a start. The unknown beckoned, and my blood tingled as never before when I looked up towards those mighty mountains rising sheer from the plains.

Beyond that barrier, with its jagged peaks stabbing the clear, blue sky, lay the land I had dreamed of for so long. The slow ascent of the train was almost torture and my impatience grew as we neared the top. There must have been some fierce fighting here, for the mountainside was littered with war material, gun carriages and ammunition trucks abandoned by Feng in his retreat. We stopped at Hei Lung Chiao (Black Dragon Bridge) where the railway breaks through the Great Wall and there is a most magnificent view.

As far west as the eye can see are mighty masses of mountains, and along the ridges and peaks the Wall winds its way like a giant serpent until it is lost to sight. One blinks unbelieving eyes at the massive structure of the Wall, which is thirty feet high and nearly as broad at the top, where armies could march and horsemen gallop eight abreast. Up the steep slopes of dizzy peaks and down the rugged mountainsides it meanders through this vast rocky wilderness for one thousand five hundred miles.

Historians relate that it was planned and completed in its original length of one thousand two hundred miles by the Emperor Shih Huang Tih. It was so well built that it stood for one thousand seven hundred years before the first repairs were necessary during the Ming dynasty, when a further three hundred miles were added. The original work was done by one and a half million men, criminals and impressed labourers, guarded by three hundred thousand soldiers. The Wall was started in 228 B.C., and took ten years to complete. Owing to the peculation and corruption of the officials looking after the commissariat the labourers starved to death by the thousand. A Chinese historian has placed on record that only one cartload of grain arrived out of every one hundred and eighty-two sent. The rest had been sold *en route*.

The labourers' conditions were so low that sickness claimed even more victims than starvation, and all those who died or were too sick to work were thrown into the soft earth core of the Wall and stamped in with the filling.

I thought of this when for the first time I looked on the Wall, making its ruthless and defiant way towards the West, trampling down all one's preconceived ideas of what man can do. For me, it seemed to exude a sinister aura of suffering and misery from the thousands who were buried within it and formed part of it.

The Chinese point with pride to the Great Wall as a monument of their ancient culture, confident that the dust of human bones within it is well concealed and forgotten.

The train arrived at Kalgan late in the evening. It was raining hard, although this was the so-called dry season, and streams of water came down through the bullet-riddled roof over the station. The streets, which usually are ankle-deep in dust, were now a dismal morass of mud, flanked by drab, dripping buildings.

Our rickshaw coolies splashed and slithered along but, fortunately, it was not a long journey to the B.A.T. Mess. There were no hotels in Kalgan other than Chinese inns which were notorious for their bugs, and George had told me to go straight to the B.A.T. Mess where they always put up visiting foreigners.

For obvious reasons I had not telegraphed them that I was coming. We had our own offices and Chinese agent, of course, but I did not know the address. I need not have worried about arriving uninvited for I received a very warm welcome from my two countrymen, Rustad and Mamen.

I knew big and burly Mamen in Tientsin, but had not previously met Rustad. Butler, the Australian, was also a stranger, but not for long. It is curious how quickly you get on terms with strangers in these out of the way places, especially in China, where white people are a rarity when you get away from the beaten track.

Another newcomer I met in the Mess was a tall young Dane named Haslund, who had spent some time in Outer Mongolia. He belonged to that happy band of Danish adventurers who had trekked in old Boer style into the wilds of Mongolia in a search for farmland. They had had a very hard struggle to get established, and when the worst was over, and they were beginning to see the fruits of their labour, a revolution fostered by Communist agitators broke out, and they were driven out of the country. The whole of Outer Mongolia was now under Communist control, all the Chinese and foreigners having business there had been driven out, and the frontiers were closed. I knew, of course, that a revolution had taken place, but I had not known until now the full extent of Moscow's grip over Outer Mongolia. The capital, Urga, had been renamed Ulan Bator Khoto, Red Hero City, which was sufficient proof of who was master there.

We sat and yarned over our whisky-sodas until late. Things did not look too good for the future, and Kalgan, which had been doing a big trade with Outer Mongolia, was faced with very hard times. Banditry was rife and on the increase. Nevertheless it takes a great deal to ruffle such men, and they were a very cheery crowd.

Next day brought fine weather, and I had a look around the town. I use the word "town" purely as a courtesy term, for I have seldom seen a place that looked less like a town. Houses just "happened" here and there like a rash, as did the streets. Mr. Li had said in bygone years, "I want my house to stand there and the road to go thus." Mr. Huang said: "And I want my house here and the road there." Then came Chang, Wong, Ma, Wu, Feng and the rest and they put *their* houses and roads thus and thus. Kalgan was originally a frontier trading mart and still retained the character of one after it blossomed into a small township, chiefly because of the important caravan trade with Urga, and even Siberia.

Kalgan lies three thousand feet above the sea and at the foot of the Mongolian plateau, two thousand feet higher up, and is reached by a steep pass from the West Gate, one of the few passes through the almost sheer escarpment. It is surrounded by wild mountain scenery. There is a more or less straight main road leading to the North Gate where a dry river bed provides open-air storage for the traders' cargo, mostly wool, hides and skins. In this road shops are built on high embankments on both sides. Practically every other shop is a saddle shop, or displays riding gear and kit, riding whips and flywhisks, headstalls and the heavy iron stirrups of the border. Customers, mostly Mongols, in greasy plum-coloured or yellow robes, waddle painfully along, clearly out of their element, as they loathe walking even a few yards, or doing anything that cannot be done in the saddle. They walk with a peculiar stiff and awkward gait as if every step gives them a pain, always leaning a little forward as if they are still in the saddle.

I returned from my sightseeing in time for tiffin, and Rustad, having located the address of my agents, gave the rickshaw coolies directions: "Come again, any time," he called out as we left.

If the Emperor himself had come, he could not have received a finer welcome than I from the moment I entered our imposing compound on the outskirts of the town. Mr. Li, big, stout and jovial, did the honours, for I was the first manager in the firm to visit the Kalgan offices and this was thus a very special occasion. Li had three district managers and a large staff under him, and the office and residential buildings were commodious and pretentious in a Chinese way. Behind the buildings was an enormous walled compound of several acres where a whole caravan could unload into the warehouses, in fact it was a typical border caravanserai on a big scale.

All was bustle and excitement, with cooks and servants scuttling around preparing for the feast of all feasts. Tea and cakes were served in the big reception hall, and, after the inevitable long exchange of courtesies, Li explained the situation.

Kalgan was dying as a trading centre since the Urga caravan trail had been closed by the Bolsheviks, but he had found other fields to exploit in Inner Mongolia and our own trade had suffered little, if any harm. All westward rail traffic had come to a dead stop, and it would take a year, he thought, before normal communications would be possible. The Kalgan wool trade was not particularly affected by this, as camels were used to bring cargo from the interior and it was still possible to get rail freight to Tientsin from Kalgan. The chief difficulty was farther west where the main business was done and all shipments by rail had been stopped on account of a private feud among the generals regarding the division of the freight receipts.

Part of the line there was held by Chang Tso Lin's men, and part by Yen Hsi Shan; hence the trouble. In Kalgan the line was under the undisputed control of one of Chang Tso Lin's generals who, with commendable forethought, had started his own transport company with a distant relative in charge. I got to know quite a lot about the private affairs of these generals who were conducting the biggest private war since the revolution.

There were about half a million men in the field, and the bandits were having a high old time. Never before had they been able to get ammunition so cheaply and in such quantity. The Shansi troops had not been paid for several months and recouped themselves by selling cartridges to the bandits. Officers responsible for buying ponies from Mongolia for the large cavalry forces now bought them much cheaper from the bandits, who got them for nothing by raiding the Mongol camps up on the plateau. Everyone was satisfied with this ideal set-up except the Mongols.

While we were chatting, guests came in to pay their respects and partake of the feast in my honour, or rather the series of feasts lasting three days. I then had to endure another three days of return feasts arranged by the guests, all prominent merchants, including the manager of the General's transport company, a very jovial soul with a big paunch and an enormous capacity for food and Shaoshing wine. A Chinese feast with, say, thirty different dishes is the biggest test that even the most robust digestion can undergo, and an orgy of them, like this one in Kalgan, would ruin most foreigners for life. Not only were the usual Chinese Shaoshing wine and Kaoliang provided, but gin, whisky, brandy and liqueurs were available in prodigious quantities, and every delicacy of the north, including the famous Peking duck, was served. This duck, the most delicious of all dishes in China, is also the most ruinous to the digestion, because one invariably eats too much, and it consists mostly of fat. Stewed shark-fins are equally fatal. When you have gone through the long list of different fish courses, and meat, pork, game, mushrooms, ham, ancient eggs, bêche-de-mer, chicken and sundry other dishes, you reach the stage the Chinese call "chi bu sja fan chy." You cannot force any more down. The Chinese have an enormous capacity for enjoying food and good company, and are wonderful hosts. Of course such a feast takes hours, and there are pauses for a walk around or to smoke a pipe of opium. In between there are hilarious and noisy games of forfeits, the losers having to empty their wine cups.

Most of the guests remained on the battlefield that night, as they were unaccustomed to foreign spirits and had underestimated their potency. Among them was Chun, the transport manager, who insisted on becoming my blood brother. I have a hazy recollection that we pricked our fingers and squeezed some blood into a wine cup and drank it. We were then the only two left on our feet.

Some unearthly snarly squeals woke me the next morning. I was feeling ill and tried to go to sleep again, but the queer noises continued. Then I looked out and saw that the compound was full of camels and two of them, huge hairy beasts they were too, stared at me as if I was something unclean. Camels always look at one like that, but it was the first time I had looked a camel in the face at close quarters, and I thought it worse than pink elephants. They immediately reminded me of the notice in the Chinkiang club bar: "They say that a camel can go fourteen days without a drink, but who the hell wants to be a camel!"

I shouted for the boy to bring me a large bottle of beer. I never needed a drink more. Feeling a little better, I wondered why I was sweating and found that I was lying on hot bricks. It was the usual North China "bed," a raised platform of bricks with a fire underneath. This is called a "kang," and is a very ingenious and practical solution to the heating problem in a country where fuel is scarce and most of the houses are unheated even in the bitterest cold. It is hard lying on top of this brick bed, but you are kept warm and it also warms the bedroom. It was the first time I had slept on a kang and as I had not been in an excessively observant state when I went to bed, I naturally wondered where the heat came from.

The next five days were more or less a repetition of the first. I had, however, mentioned the matter of a pass to Mr. Li, and he kindly invited the Commissioner for Foreign Affairs to the last feast. By the time the party was well under way, the Commissioner would have given me the freedom of all the cities in North China. I got a pass and signed the usual declaration that I went at my own risk and I and my dependants waived all claims against the Government if I was killed or captured by bandits.

Late the same evening Paul Pi and I boarded a westward-bound military train. Mr. Chun had offered to get me a first-class compartment, and was as good as his word. A crowd of more or less sober feast companions came to see me off, and as the train pulled out I heard a rather raucous chorus of: "I loh ping an!" (May your road be peaceful!)

V

I HAD not noticed, when boarding the train, that all the windows but one in the compartment were broken. By broken I mean completely out of the frame. The one exception had been only partly broken, and the lower half sported one big lonely triangle of glass a couple of feet high. There was nothing I could do about it anyway.

Mr. Chun, who knew more about the state of the carriages than I, had, with commendable forethought, given us a hurricane lamp, and by its light I now inspected our new quarters. Once upon a time, before soldiers had used it, it had been a first-class compartment; now it was the most complete wreck I had ever seen.

Everything movable had been taken, including all the light fittings and wires. The seat-coverings had vanished, and most of the stuffing was on the floor. Two seats had, apparently, been broken up for fire-wood, for there were bits of charred wood in a corner where a camp-fire had been made. The toilet and wash basin had, of course, been taken away, and the faucets and piping were wrenched off. The floor was covered in excrement. It was bitterly cold and sleeting outside, and an icy blast came whistling through the apertures of the windows.

The military-train guard of five men under a sergeant was quartered with us and squatted in a recess between our coach and the next. Their quarters were comparatively draught-free, and the men hospitably invited us to join them. I had brought with me a small spirit-stove and kettle and the soldiers had water in a bucket, so I got Paul to make tea. I shall always remember that little impromptu tea-party as we squatted on the floor, warming our frozen hands on the cups and drinking the hot steaming tea to thaw out our insides.

Then I passed the cigarettes round and we chatted. The soldiers were all farm labourers from Hei Lung Kiang Province, putting in the slack season in Chang Tso Lin's army and hoping to make enough money to get back in the spring. In the army they received eight dollars a month and food, whereas in Manchuria they made no money at all in the winter months and had to live on their scanty savings. Every spring they were broke and half-starved.

The train was crawling up a long steep ascent towards the Pingdichuen pass, the highest point on the railway, some five thousand feet up; snow came tearing through the windows with the rising wind and settled on the litter on the floor. Through the cracks in the flooring where the lino had been ripped off came a steady draught, and that jagged piece of glass made weird singing noises in the strong wind. In spite of my thick sheepskin coat my teeth chattered with cold, but the soldiers seemed quite comfortable. They were used to the Siberian cold of the Amur country and this was nothing to them. I got up and, much to their amusement, danced a sailor's hornpipe to get circulation back, while Paul Pi suffered in stolid silence and immobility. After an eternity the train came to a jerky stop at Pingdichuen station right on top of the pass. I went out to stretch my legs but was met with such an icy blast and shower of snow that I sought shelter again at once. We waited and waited for the train to proceed down the other slope and away from the arctic regions, but it never budged. Finally the sergeant went out to inquire and came back with the news that the military commander had taken our locomotive to move troops from the next station.

There had been a mutiny among the Shansi troops at Fengchen which, incidentally, was my destination before proceeding to Kweihuacheng. We had a branch office under Kalgan at Fengchen and a big stock of wool I wanted to see. The manager had been warned by telegram of my arrival.

The hours crawled by and I was nearly frozen to death. We broke up one of the seats and made a camp-fire in the corner. The work of smashing the seat warmed me up a bit, and I felt better after the fire was lit and my feet and hands thawed out. The glass triangle made such a fiendish noise in the gale that I kicked it out; then we squatted round the fire till dawn. The sergeant again went out for news and came back to say that there were about four hundred men in open cattle trucks, a good many of whom had frozen to death. The dead were now being carried out on to the platform.

He shrugged and said with a grin: "Me yu fah tzu, wei tau lunn de hrann." (Can't be helped, it is very cold in the open.) That typical Chinese expression, Me yu fah tzu, always infuriates foreigners because it is a stock phrase for covering up shocking happenings which *could* be avoided. It pretends to mean an Act of God when it is obviously an Act of Man, but it would never do to blame the man responsible and make him lose face. Better by far that a thousand or more should die than one man lose face by exposing the rottenness at the root of things.

I said angrily: "How can they send men out in open trucks in the winter? It is murder."

He shrugged again and replied: "Only a few died, twenty or so, and they will get good coffins, much finer ones than they could afford themselves. But many more are frostbitten and will get maimed: that is worse, for they are thrown out to starve."

While we were talking we heard the locomotive whistling, then felt it hit us with a bang and we were off. We passed a long row of dead on the platform. A thin layer of snow covered their uniforms, but their faces were showing and looked very peaceful.

We arrived at Fengchen during the forenoon. Mr. Yu, the manager, met us. He looked very anxious. "Come with me, quickly," he whispered, "there is a short cut here."

There was a small door in the picket fence backing the station and he led the way to a waiting Peking-cart. He invited me to enter, and as I did so I could see soldiers heaving dead bodies out of the cattle trucks. Rigor mortis must have set in long ago for they were as stiff as logs. I had only a glimpse, for the next moment Mr. Yu lowered the front curtain and the cart started with a jerk. Paul Pi and Mr. Yu were walking.

It was a horribly bumpy trip, but fortunately not a very long one. When the cart stopped and Yu opened the front curtain I found myself in an enclosed courtyard, and as he helped me out he apologised for the unceremonious departure from the station.

"It is far from safe for you here," he explained. "The soldiers are in a very ugly mood and we may have trouble at any moment. They are shooting their general today."

He told me about the revolt and subsequent looting of the shopping district. Many of the people had been bayoneted. Fortunately the looting and murdering had been confined to the shopping and residential districts, and our compound, being in the outskirts, had escaped, but if they started again we might not be so lucky.

At present the military quarters were surrounded, and machine-guns were posted at the end of every street until the execution of the general was over. "The shooting will be done near here," Yu said excitedly, "and we may be able to see it from an upstairs window in the warehouse at the back."

I was famished and more interested in food than in executions; in any case I cannot bear the idea of seeing people killed when they are helpless and tied up, as is a man facing a firing-squad. Most Chinese love it. I asked Yu what was in the idea of shooting the general and not the looters. He said it was a very good idea, for the ringleaders were going to shoot him and then they would lose plenty of face. Besides, it was so much more practical and cheap to shoot one man than to shoot all the looters. There were such a lot of them and ammunition was very expensive up here, for the bandits were paying one dollar for each cartridge.

The food arrived and interrupted this rather interesting discourse on the economic aspects of executions on the Mongolian border and the Chinese way of making the punishment fit the crime.

We had barely finished eating when a man ran in and said that the execution party was coming. Then I heard the drums in the distance and all the Chinese rushed out towards the warehouses. Yu urged me to come, but I told him I had seen so many executions that they bored me. If I had told him that I loathed them he would have thought me strange. Soon afterwards I heard a volley and the muffled sound of drums. Then I went to my rooms and lay down on the warm kang to get some much needed sleep.

The next few days were rather anxious. The tension was such that I could almost feel it in the air. I was more or less a prisoner in the house, for my presence in the streets might have been the match to start the fireworks.

The whole place had been placarded by Feng Yu Hsiang with

pictures of the students who had been shot in Shanghai on May 30th that year while leading the mob in an attack on the police station. The pictures of the huddled bodies on the ground had been reproduced in large quantities, and Feng, in his retreat, had postered every town with them and added such appropriate slogans as "Kill every Foreigner on sight!" "Behold what the Foreign devils have done to our patriots!" "Kill the red-haired barbarians before they kill you!" This was one reason why all foreigners had been evacuated to the coast.

Never had agitators in China been presented with more precious propaganda for the purpose of stirring up hate than those photographs of executed students. I had looked at them in Kalgan, and thought of the millions who died every year, unsung and unhonoured, the heaps of mutilated bodies I had walked over at Meng Cheng, the two thousand Manchus massacred in Nanking, and the long row of women suicides laid out on the banks of the moat at Nanking. They had no propaganda value, poor souls, and found unknown graves.

And when I thought of the frozen bodies I had seen thrown out on the platform like carcases, I was seized by a cold fury that such things could exist side by side in the same country. But cold fury does not get you very far in China where four hundred million people had suppressed their grievances for centuries and hysteria is never far from the surface, however poker-faced that surface may appear.

In Kalgan Chang controlled with an iron hand, and Chang would have no anti-foreign nonsense: but at Fengchen it was different, and as I had little liking for playing the principal role at a funeral I remained indoors, watching the scowling faces in the street outside through a slit in the shutters.

Eventually the air cleared and I could get some work done. I felt a bit tired after the tension, for restful sleep is out of the question when travelling in the interior under such conditions. From previous experiences I had developed an extra sense which warned me when anyone approached my door, even when I was asleep. Chinese always walk without a sound on their felt slippers, so it was not sound that would wake me but a curious sudden awareness that someone was near. I would be wide awake in a moment and call out sharply: "Get out—or I shoot!" tear the door open and see a shadowy figure disappear like a wraith. It never failed, and always there had been someone there.

Other travellers I had met had the same faculty, which was particularly active when sleeping in strange native inns, which often harbour thieves and cut-throats. The only drawback is that one never feels quite refreshed by such sleep, but of course it is more important to be alive than refreshed, so I did not grumble too much.

I stayed in Fengchen a couple of weeks as there was a good deal to do. Rail transportation of goods from there to Kalgan had come to a stop a month or so before I arrived and we were using camels. This sounds simple, but nothing is simple in China that can possibly be made complicated. Bandits had never been more active than they were since this great armed force had moved in, for the coalition of Chang Tso Lin and Yen Hsi Shan against Feng Yu Hsiang had brought nearly half a million men into the field.

I had heard of these difficulties before, but now I was in a district where I could see the results of the general lawlessness which ruled the country outside the narrow strip, the railway zone, controlled by the military. Caravans had to be protected by armed escorts or toll paid to the bandits, and the latter proved to be the cheaper method of insurance. There was a regular tariff of so much per bale which was paid in advance to the bandit chief's agent in Fengchen. Then the caravan leader received a spear with a red tassel, which he carried conspicuously when riding at the head of the caravan. This was a symbol that the caravan was protected and saved the bandits the bother of tracking and ambush, for they could see from afar that the caravan had paid toll.

The only check then necessary was the final one at the border of the bandits' territory where the receipt for the toll was produced and the bales counted. It was simple enough when we had only to deal with one bandit chief, but now the business had become so lucrative that rival gangs had started to cut in and chaos would result if I did not find a solution. This was one of the chief reasons why I had come up-country.

Hitherto we had done business with the local bandit chief, who went under the name of Hsu Lao Ho (Tiger Hsu), but another bandit, Sun Mo Ling, had made a big name for himself in the Kalgan district during the last few years. He was rapidly extending his "sphere of influence" by mopping up the smaller fry and was at the moment challenging the Tiger. I had long talks with Mr. Yu, when we discussed ways and means of overcoming bandit interference with our caravans, and the hold-ups and further overheads occasioned by the extra tolls which were demanded.

A Bandit Suppression Commissioner had been appointed a few years previously. He was a former bandit chief named Dammuran Serang, a Mongol, who had done good work. The Chinese Government knew from experience that it was useless to employ the military in this kind of job, for the soldiers had to sell ammunition to live, and could not be expected to fight their main source of income. It was therefore common practice to appoint the most powerful bandit chief to a high official position to fight and suppress the other bandits. It was setting a thief to catch a thief, and the bandits proved more loyal, efficient and honest than the Regular Chinese Army officers of even the highest rank. This Dammuran Serang had cleaned up the minor bands around the border with his own gang, leaving only Tiger Hsu and his followers in circulation. It would not do for him to clear them *all* out, for then there would be no need for a Bandit Suppression Commissioner. He had made a gentleman's agreement with Tiger Hsu that he would not interfere with him as long as he carried on only with his legitimate protection racket.

The coming of a great army and thus a new source of plentiful ammunition available for private sale to the bandits had complicated matters considerably. There were also hundreds of deserters who had joined the bandits, taking their weapons with them. It looked as if the caravans would soon meet with the greatest difficulties: it was not only the Fengchen–Kalgan route which was imperilled, but the whole remaining inland supply route which I had hoped to link up with it. All rail traffic, insofar as the four hundred miles between Kalgan and Paotow were concerned, must be left out of my calculations for an indefinite period. At the moment Feng was retreating to prepared positions at Paotow. Chang Tso Lin and Yen Hsi Shan were allies, but no two war-lords ever remained allies for a moment longer than suited them. The fight for supremacy between the two generals would come sooner or later and chaos on the railway was inevitable.

Camels and a comparatively safe route would be the only answer to my problem. It would be a costly business, but costs would play a secondary role provided that I got the cargo through. The cost of transport could be calculated if we used camels, but we could not possibly estimate the cost by rail, even if it were possible to use the railway. At that time the cost of being put on the waiting list for a thirty-ton truck was two hundred and fifty dollars, and to that must be added freight rates which increased weekly. The great unknown factor was, of course, *when* rail transport would be resumed again.

Few business men had ever been faced with so many strange problems. An extra hazard with rail traffic was that two generals were in control of the rolling stock: one looking after supplies, the other after troop movements. The latter could only get his share of the receipts by taking locomotives away from the goods trains and sometimes commandeering a whole train. Then the cargo would be pitched out on the platform and would remain there until an appropriate sum of money was forthcoming.

We had two thousand bales of camels' wool lying at various stations between Fengchen and Kweihuacheng, and, in all, we had eight thousand bales to move to Tientsin if I could find ways and means to get them through this maze of difficulties. There was only one hope—Dammuran Serang, the strong man of the border, and if I could secure his aid and a couple of hundred of his tough ex-bandits as escort, I could send the caravan through Sun Mo Ling's territory without undue risk.

Dammuran had his headquarters at a place called Harnut, where he lived in baronial style. And so I went to Harnut.

VI

THE drive was a very long and bumpy one in a Peking-cart, and was bitterly cold, until I came down to the two thousand five hundred-foot level, where the Mongolian plateau, rising almost sheer to the north, gave some shelter from the freezing wind. Both Paul and Yu came with me to make my visit more imposing.

Dammuran's headquarters looked very substantial and were well guarded. Long before we came within sight, mounted scouts intercepted us and asked my business. They were a tough-looking crowd of Mongols who sat their horses well enough to remind me of centaurs.

I gave one of them my big red Chinese card and said I came on important business. He streaked off at full tilt and, as we came nearer Harnut, he returned with a small troop of men as a guard of honour.

"That is a good sign," Yu said, as we saw them coming, and my own hopes went higher.

It is a curious thing in China that the names of the principal foreign firms are known throughout the country and a perfectly unknown representative is accepted as if he were the principal of the firm. Our hong name, as it is called out there, An Lee Yang Hong, appeared in bold characters on my card, and proved a sufficient guarantee of my bona fides and the importance of my visit, but the guard of honour was an extra and propitious gesture that gave me bigger face than I had hoped for.

We had no sooner entered the main hall than servants came in with tea and cakes, and soon afterwards Dammuran himself appeared. He was a short, powerfully built man, bow-legged like all Mongols, and with the most arresting kind of beard I had ever seen. It came sticking out from under his chin, plaited like a pigtail, and was about six inches long. He had bold black eyes in a network of wrinkles, like most open-air men, and a swarthy weatherbeaten complexion.

He had "Big Chief" written all over him, and we had not been long in conversation before I knew that he was just as direct as a Chinese official would be tortuous. He was, in fact, a typical, decisive man of action.

And so I put all my cards on the table and asked if he could help. He made no secret of the fact that Sun Mo Ling had become a thorn in his flesh and that sooner or later there must be a show-down. Then he added: "It may as well be over your caravan as over anything else, and I will help you." He sent for one of his officers and had a short talk with him in Mongolian, which I could not understand.

Our talk was followed by a big feast, with great quantities of wine. Harnut, in that remote corner of the borderland, was the last place where I had expected to be served with such a splendid repast, but it was the "capital" of that prince of bandits and it had a reputation to keep up. I had heard about Dammuran previously from "Duke" Larson; now I had a chance of knowing this remarkable man, the "Vicar of Bray" of Mongolia.

Governments came and governments went, but Dammuran remained the undisputed master of the border. Since he had started to serve the Government, law and order had returned to districts where previously chaos had reigned and no man's life had been safe. There was no one who could fill his place, and no one dared try to oust him. His men were loyal, well paid and well cared for and could not be bought over. They had small farms which they cultivated for Dammuran on a crop-sharing basis and which they had a chance of owning.

It was clearly the reason for his strength that he shared his riches with his men, and he was reputed to be very rich. To me it was remarkable that an ex-bandit with a price on his head should become a pattern of what an official should be, and the only honest official the border had ever produced.

My respect and admiration grew as I spoke to him and got to know him. I remember asking him why the military had never been able to put down banditry. He laughed heartily and gave me the reply I had before. "Because they are Chinese and they argue like this: 'Why should I fire a cartridge at a bandit when I can sell it to him for one dollar?'"

When the feast was over we started to plan. He said an escort of three hundred men would be necessary, all mounted, of course. He paid his men six dollars a month when on ordinary service and ten on active service. I would have to pay active service rates and perhaps a bonus to each man when the job was successfully done. I would need two thousand camels to proceed in two convoys fourteen days apart.

After escorting the first caravan to Kalgan his men would return to the border of Tiger Hsu's territory and meet the second convoy there. He would arrange with Tiger Hsu to place a reserve of a couple of hundred men at his disposal in case of any serious opposition by Sun Mo Ling.

This cooperation was beyond my wildest dreams. All I had to do now was a mere bagatelle when compared with what had been accomplished. I had to find two thousand camels, pick up four thousand bales of wool scattered over four hundred miles of war-torn country and romp back to Tientsin. I can laugh when I think back on it, the whole thing sounds so utterly impossible, this friendly alliance with the ex-robber baron assisted by the notorious Tiger Hsu. And I really thought the rest a trifling matter, for once a safe route for the caravans was assured the main problem was solved. Dammuran told me that there would be little difficulty in finding the camels as the whole caravan trade across the Gobi was held up, and even though the military commandeered camels right and left, there would be plenty to spare.

Feng Yu Hsiang was now at Paotow, but Dammuran had heard that a big force would be sent against him and predicted that within a month Feng would be in full retreat into Kansu Province, for Paotow had no natural defences and scanty food reserves.

We celebrated our agreement with a two days' feast. Dammuran had few visitors and was not at all averse to making the most of this opportunity. There was an orgy of eating, drinking, belching, playing forfeits and listening to weird and mournful Mongol airs played and sung by the minstrels in attendance.

The aftermath was very painful. That long, bumpy drive back

to Fengchen was a nightmare. My head was very, very sore and aching and my stomach queasy and sensitive, and every time the wheels hit a rock I could have screamed. A diet of beer and aspirin, however, put me right in a couple of days, and even the *misère* of this record hangover could not dim my elation over the results of my visit.

When I got back I put in long hours with Mr. Yu on a good deal of organising work to ensure that everything would go forward smoothly, and it was only then that I found out from a chance remark of his that Fengchen had been Feng Yu Hsiang's great ammunition depot prior to his retreat. The Russians had been sending their long convoys of lorries laden with ammunition along the sparsely populated route from Urga to dump their loads at Fengchen, right off the beaten track. No wonder, when we speculated in Tientsin about the source of Feng's war supplies, we never hit on this spot.

VII

FENGCHEN lies in a bare windy spot about four thousand feet up, and the trip to Kweihuacheng was downhill all the way. I was glad to get out of the bitter cold up there, for no Chinese house, apart from the kang, is heated in the winter. It was also lucky that the journey was downhill, as the locomotive, like most of the rolling stock, was in a shocking state through want of even elementary attention.

Kweihuacheng was a big, sprawling place facing the high jagged peaks of the Mongolian escarpment. There were two cities: the very old walled city, and the new, which filled the gap between the old city and the railway. Mr. Ma, our agent there, met us at the station with a very handsome Peking-cart, but I preferred to walk, as I was still stiff and sore after my Harnut journey.

This was a real caravan city with hoary traditions, and the only wares displayed in the shops and stalls were articles of use to the camel-drivers, horsemen and carters: saddles and bridles, harness and stirrups, riding-boots and saddle-cloths. Many handsome prayer rugs were also on show, as from here westwards Mohammedans predominate.

We were soon at our offices, a collection of very roomy buildings in a huge enclosed yard, itself a regular caravanserai. There were many guest-rooms, some of them occupied by visitors with whom we had business connections. I had two nice light rooms placed at my disposal.

Mr. Ma was thin and pale—an opium smoker, perhaps—but he had a very clever face and kind, live eyes, that made me think he had probably had a couple of pipes to brace himself up before meeting me. The inevitable feast was prepared to welcome me. I certainly had to pay a heavy price in wear and tear on my digestion and alcoholic capacity for being the only foreign representative of the firm to visit the various offices. Custom demanded that a big firm like Arnhold's must provide feasts of the most expensive and elaborate kind for the sake of face. Custom also demanded that I should partake of everything in the way of food and drink placed before me, that I drink with the best of them, belch with the loudest, play forfeits and shout with the noisiest.

We were about fifteen at table and the noise became deafening as the feast proceeded and the wine and spirits thawed us out. I heard to my chagrin that Owen Lattimore had already been there and had slipped off on his long desert journey only two days before my arrival. I would have given anything to have seen him off on his hazardous adventure and it was maddening not to have known. But I also heard that George Soderbom was in the town with his brother, John: they had had some trouble with the soldiers and had barricaded themselves in a house they shared with Tony Oberg, who was then away. It was too late then to look them up, but Ma promised to send a man to show me the way the next day.

I was very much looking forward to meeting George again, and the following morning I went along with a guide, whom I certainly needed in the maze of alleyways we went through. I thought it strange that suddenly the people in the streets seemed to have vanished and I met only scowling soldiers. My guide pointed to a semi-foreign-looking house and said: "That is his house"—and vanished.

There was a high wall round the house and the gate was shut. I went over and banged at it, waited but got no reply. I hammered away once more, and then a small trap-door opened cautiously and a villainous-looking Chinese, with one eye and an ugly red socket where the other had been, glared at me suspiciously. I told him sharply to open the gate as I wanted to see George, but he only shut the trap-door and went away.

I banged furiously again and eventually heard heavy footsteps coming towards me. The trap-door opened and I was looking at George, who gaped at me. Then came a broad grin of recognition and a surprised: "Ras, what the hell are you doing here?

Come in, quick! We are expecting an attack at any moment. Can you use a rifle?"

He unbarred the door as he was talking and I slipped in. The door was slammed to and bolted, and George almost crushed my hand in his huge paw. Then he led the way into the house, where I met his brother John, very pale and emaciated and a startling contrast to George. On a dining-table lay a small arsenal of rifles and a couple of revolvers, with cartridges in clips ready to use.

I said: "What the devil is this?"

George laughed. "Only a little trouble with the soldiers. They attacked my boy yesterday because he's a foreigner's servant, and strung him up by his thumbs. I heard of it and I am afraid I went a bit berserk before I cut him down—laid out cold half a dozen or so, and they have threatened to come and massacre us all. *I'll* massacre the bastards!"

He grabbed one of the rifles. "Can you use a Springfield? It works like this." He showed me the simple action. He was apparently in his element and chatted away. His brother John was quieter but appeared quite unaffected. He looked sick though, and coughed incessantly.

George suddenly turned to me: "But what the hell are you doing up here, away from the fleshpots of Tientsin?" I told him that I had followed his advice and just slipped off.

"And I thought I had scared you off by telling you about the murders of Knowles and Martinson. Have a gin to celebrate, and welcome to Kweihuacheng!"

The one-eyed beauty came when he roared, "Boy! Bring pink gin! I take it that you'll stay until the party is over?"

"Yes, I'll stay, of course."

As we drank, he told me about Lattimore's departure. It had to be effected in secret to avoid hostile troops and was no easy job. The reason for the unrest was those dead students again and the placards Feng had on display everywhere. Time went on, but nothing happened until we heard a loud banging at the gate. George went out and found a Chinese officer who had come to inquire about the trouble.

George invited him in and then called for the boy. He showed his thumbs, which were badly lacerated, and told the officer what

.ATE 13
'op: Staff at Fengchen
ottom: Wool piling up at Paotow

PLATE 14

Top: The Bandit Suppression Commissioner Dammurra Serang's wife and little son (*left*) with two wome servants

Bottom: The author and the mysterious Mr. Bien

had happened. Then George broke in and told him what he had seen and done. When the officer left he assured George that there would be no more trouble. I stayed with them for tiffin, but left before tea, as another feast was awaiting me. When I left them there were no soldiers in the streets.

That evening a new man arrived at our offices. He was a Mr. Bien, a merchant from Shansi. He was powerfully built and had an air of authority about him unusual in a Chinese merchant. He was very good company though, a wonderful trencherman, and could he drink!

The feast was followed by a party which went on till the small hours. There were three mahjong tables going for those who liked a gamble, and, what with the slamming down of the mahjong bricks, the excited shouts of the gamblers and the even louder shouts of those playing forfeits for drinks, it was like bedlam. Few people have the tremendous capacity of the Chinese for enjoying a party, probably because few people have the same need for relaxation: they also have the rare distinction of never being quarrelsome in their cups. They belch and spit, but remain perfect gentlemen to the last tottering footstep.

And so it was here. Bien and I had become very friendly, not because of the enormous quantity of wine and Kaoliang (Chinese gin) we had drunk, but because we were mutually attracted. Coming from Shansi, which is famous for wild boar, I asked him about the shooting there and heard to my surprise that he was very keen on wild boar-shooting. That confirmed my suspicions that he was not a merchant, for no Chinese merchant would be interested in field sports, but I said nothing. When the party broke up it took a considerable time to get to our rooms, because the display of excessive politeness made it difficult to decide who should go through the door first.

A whole week was devoted to feasting, and the mornings only were available for business. I had told Mr. Ma about my arrangements with Dammuran, and he, in turn, told me about the position in Kweihuacheng and Paotow. There were four thousand bales of camels' wool at Paotow, but Ma said that it was certain death for me to go there as all foreigners were proscribed in Feng's territory and I would be shot on sight. It was Feng's men who had murdered Knowles and Martinson.

As bad luck would have it those four thousand bales were the most important, for they were of the highest quality and I had ear-marked them for the first convoy. I had in all eight thousand bales to get through, so that the camels must make two journeys to Kalgan. The two thousand bales of camels' wool at wayside stations could wait and a further two thousand bales of Tibetan sheep's wool could also wait, but not the four thousand bales lying at Paotow. It was useless to send Chinese down to Paotow to arrange for transportation for all Chinese were regarded as spies and would be shot by Feng or detained by the Shansi people for fear that they were carrying messages.

This was indeed a blow. Dammuran had predicted that Feng would be thrown out of Paotow within a month, but this was not certain and I could not wait a month. I visited George that day and asked his advice, and he said emphatically: "Don't go, you'll only be scuppered."

That should have been sufficient warning, but there is a little voice within me which begins to whisper when there is an adventure round the corner. After all, the little cherub up aloft who had always looked after me and had got me out of so many scrapes before could be depended upon to get me out of this too. I had been lucky in the past, so why not back my luck again? That night I discussed the matter with Ma and the others, but all were against me, Bien most of all: in fact, I got quite annoyed with him and went to bed in a huff.

In the middle of the night I woke up suddenly, sensing that someone was outside my door. I grabbed my small Browning, turned up the lamp and called out: "Get out—or I shoot!" To my surprise the door opened slowly and I saw Mr. Bien, finger to lip. I put down the automatic and got up. He came over to me on soundless feet and sat down on the kang. From the next room came loud snores, and it was clear that my voice had not wakened my neighbours.

Bien whispered: "Here is something to help you on your journey." He handed me a tiny card with some minute characters, so small that I could not decipher them.

"When you get to Paotow, demand to see Colonel Yuan and give him this. On no account let any of the Shansi military find it, or you'll be shot. Hide it well. At Saratsi you will meet

Feng's outposts. If you are stopped there, say you have an important message for Colonel Yuan in Paotow. Don't tell a soul here that I have been to see you."

Then he whispered, "I loh ping an!" (May your road be peaceful!) and tiptoed out again.

I sat for a while looking at the tiny card, with my mind in a whirl. All this had happened suddenly and unexpectedly, and I was trying to sort it out. The solution to the riddle of who this man Bien might be was forming in my mind. Was he, I wondered, one of Feng's secret agents. It was no use wasting time on speculation; the main thing was that I had the card which Bien had assured me would see me safely through.

How to get to Paotow presented no difficulty. For there was an empty train going there every day. In China, negotiations are just as important as fighting and, therefore, a train invariably went back and forth between the opposing forces, as a token that the parties were open to parley. I knew that this train left for Paotow daily at about noon, but I had no idea about the control of passengers. I lay awake for some time, pondering until I was too tired to think, and then fell asleep.

The next morning I went down to the station to see the controllers at work, but I soon found that there were no passengers and no control. To make quite sure that I would not be stopped by officious military transport officers I went with Mr. Ma to call on the local general, to whom I explained that the fighting had placed our firm in a difficult position regarding the big stock of cargo in Paotow and I simply must get there to see what could be done. He knew Mr. Ma well and placed no difficulties in my way, but warned me of the danger. That meant that I would not be searched, and that my temporary hiding-place for the card inside the lining of my fur cap would be safe enough.

VIII

I LEFT the next day, taking a very frightened Paul Pi with me as my personal assistant, for I had to keep up the appearance of going there purely on the firm's business. That card had made it clear to me that Bien's business was being carried out at the same time, but I had no idea of what that business was.

The main thing was that it would, I hoped, be instrumental in keeping me alive and make it possible for me to carry out my plan. Nevertheless I was under a great deal of tension as the train pulled out, while Mr. Ma, the whole of his staff and Mr. Bien waved and called out: "I loh ping an!"

Paul Pi had been searched, but I was only asked if I carried any documents, to which I untruthfully replied, "No." My conscience had of necessity become a very ephemeral affair during the years I had spent in China and I told the lie without the slightest qualm. In this case it was done in the best of causes—namely, to keep myself alive a little longer.

The train moved at a very slow speed and the engine appeared to be in distress, for after an hour or so it stopped with a grunt. The track followed the base of the Mongolian escarpment which towered over us to the north. Southward the country was flat and featureless—sandy, thirsty soil on the edge of the Ordos desert—and it was difficult to see where the farmlands ended and the desert began.

Close by were the burrows of marmots, a whole colony of them, and they kept bobbing out of their holes, gazing at us for a moment and then disappearing again. They were almost as big as beavers and looked very much like them—round, fat and sleek.

I sent Paul to inquire the reason for the stopping of the train, and he returned to tell me that the condenser tubes were leaking like sieves and they could not get up enough steam. This was not cheerful news, for at this rate we should get to Paotow late and the city gates would be closed after dark. This was the only railway to be Chinese-built and maintained, and the story of Omsk and Tomsk had repeated itself. When the Siberian railway was built, the people of Omsk and Tomsk refused to pay the large sum demanded of them to get the railway through their cities: the engineers then retaliated by laying the rails well outside to by-pass them. Exactly the same thing had happened at Paotow.

The Kinsui railway terminates three miles away from Paotow city, because the squeeze demanded was not paid. The station building stands in lonely state in the howling desert, and Paotow city squats three miles distant among the sand dunes. That stretch of desert between the station and the city has had an evil reputation for years as a haunt for bandits who swoop down from the near-by hills and carry away passengers passing to and from the city. Recently the son of the compradore of Liddell Bros. & Co., a prominent Tientsin firm, had been captured there and released only after a high ransom was paid. He had returned just before we left, and told the usual stories of how some of the prisoners had had their fingers cut off and sent to relatives to accelerate payment of ransom.

It was these stories which had made Paul Pi so scared, and which I now recalled when there was a chance of being marooned all night at Paotow station. However, the train started again and crept along for about an hour, and then stopped. Between Kweihuacheng and Saratsi we stopped four times, and I thought the journey would never end.

Coming in to Saratsi station I stood by the window to attract the attention of the guard. I did more than was my intention, for an officer caught sight of me, drew his revolver and fired. There was a plop in the window close to my head, where a neat hole was drilled. Then I heard loud shouting and some soldiers came running towards the train, led by the officer.

If I did not take quick and drastic action, I would be shot or bayoneted before I had time to explain anything. I was mad, too, at being potted at like that, and I dashed down the corridor to meet them, nearly colliding with the officer as he came in through the door. I grabbed the wrist of his revolver hand and yelled in his face: "Rok ni di ma ma dih tsou fi—ni yu shommo dantze—fan tung—wamba dan!"

He was so taken aback at this string of abuse that he just stood and gaped at me. The soldiers had stopped and were looking sheepish. I wrenched the revolver out of his hand and threw it out of the door, then said to him: "I carry messages for Colonel Yuan, and if you don't get out quick I'll report you!"

He slunk out, looking dumbfounded, picked up his revolver and went into the station building, together with his men. When I came back to Paul I found him pale with fright and shock. He had hardly ever been away from home before and had never been exposed to danger. I had had a fright, too, but I was also mad at that bloodthirsty fool, and it took some time before I simmered down and could look at things more calmly. There had been something extremely funny in the situation, too. The pained surprise on the captain's face at the sudden abuse and my filthy language, and the way he and his villains had slunk off, made me chuckle.

I am not going to translate my opening gambit: it would have made the most capable adept of invective green with envy. "Fan tung" and "wamba dan" mean "rice bag" and "turtle's egg," both quite inoffensive to European ears, but to call a Chinaman a "turtle's egg" is a deadly offence and a "rice bag" means an empty-headed fool. Paul was more or less in a frightened stupor and not much of a companion on the rest of that long halting journey to Paotow.

It was pitch dark when we arrived. A few soldiers carrying paper lanterns gave a dim light here and there on the platform. A bitter wind swept the station as I got out and asked one of the soldiers where I could find Colonel Yuan. He pointed to one of the buildings where a big official lantern stood on a tripod outside the door.

I had taken the card out of its hiding-place as I went in. Inside a tall man rose and looked at me with considerable surprise. I gave him the card and said "From Mr. Bien."

He grabbed it eagerly and went over to his desk, where he picked up a magnifying glass and started to study it. He was clearly very excited, and he made a few notes, which he put in an envelope and gave to his orderly: "To Marshal Feng—quickly!" he ordered.

Then he turned to me. "I have been ordered by Bien Tah Rin to do everything in my power for you. The message you brought is of vital importance. He has tried twice before to get it through, but the other two messengers were captured and killed."

I concealed my surprise and said as calmly as I could: "I only ask one favour—that you get me and my companion safely into Paotow City tonight. The road is none too safe, and the city gates are closed."

He said: "That is easy. Are you sure there is nothing more I can do?"

"'No, nothing more," I replied, with a sigh of relief, feeling rather limp after the long tension.

He shouted for one of his officers in the adjoining room and gave him a string of orders as soon as he came in. "My best cart, mule and horse. Twelve mounted men and my official lantern. You will be in command and will be responsible for seeing Bien Tah Rin's friend into Paotow quickly and safely."

In less than half an hour we moved off and disappeared into the desert in a cloud of dust. The mule in the shafts and a very mettlesome horse in the traces went at a rattling pace. Five men were riding on either side of the cart as a protective screen, and the only sound was the muffled rhythmic hoof-beats. A rising moon shed a ghostly light over the desolate scene of sand, dust and tamarisk bushes swaying in the wind. To the right loomed the last mountain of the westerly spur of the Mongolian escarpment: to the left and ahead there was nothing but howling desert.

It was a weird journey and I was almost overcome by this sudden turn of fortune. Nervous tension is always great when travelling on the Mongolian border, where feasts and deadly peril ring the changes so quickly. Fear is always lurking in the background, a fear that must be suppressed at all costs so that your head may be clear and cool in a crisis; otherwise you are unlikely to live very long.

That fear creeps up on you when you are alone at night and makes you aware of soundless feet in the dark passages of an inn or the dark, mysterious alleyways of the cities. There were nights when I said to myself, "I can't stand this uncertainty and strain any longer. I am going back tomorrow." Tomorrow came—and it was just this uncertainty that lured me on through the uncertainties ahead. For here *anything* may happen—and success, failure, life and death is on the lap of the gods. Life is never more intense and worth living than when death lurks round the corner.

The little cherub up aloft had looked after me again, bless him, and I had discovered part of the Bien riddle. Colonel Yuan had called him Bien Tah Rin: His Excellency Bien. I was getting warmer.

As I sat musing and watching our escort, the walls of Paotow city loomed up in the moonlight. We were at the gate soon afterwards. The soldiers banged on the heavy iron-studded doors with their rifle butts and yelled: "Kai men, Bien Tah Rin di peng yu lai!" (Open the gate—His Excellency Bien's friend is coming!) A slit was opened and we were scrutinised by a soldier on guard inside. A short parley followed and then the gates creaked open on ancient rusty hinges.

I asked one of the guard to direct me to the offices of An Lee Yang Hang, and he jumped upon the shafts and showed us the way through dark, mean streets, flanked by low, dirty houses which even the moonlight could not beautify. We took the manager and staff completely by surprise, but they rose nobly to the occasion. Servants hurried and scurried, tea was brought in quickly and inside an hour a good substantial meal was served. I wanted the escort to have a hot meal as they had to return that evening and they were soon wallowing in food. The officer had his supper with us. I was tired and did not linger after the meal was over, but flung myself down on the warm kang and slept like a log.

I was busy on the following days making contact with people who had camels hidden away out in the desert. The snag was that they did not dare to bring them in while Feng remained in Paotow. He had commandeered camels right and left, and it was clear that he was collecting transport animals for a withdrawal.

On the third day I called on Colonel Yuan to thank him for his assistance and found him very busy. The place was swarming with soldiers, and it was clear that something was afoot. A runway had been prepared and Feng's private plane, a very small machine around which a Russian pilot was fussing, stood ready to depart. I did not want to take up Colonel Yuan's time and said good-bye as soon as I had thanked him.

He looked very tired and rather grim as he said: "The Shansi attack is timed for tomorrow night, but they will not find us here thanks to Bien Tah Rin and you."

I pondered over this as I left him. I was not particularly proud of being the unwitting cause of saving Feng's skin by bringing the warning of the attack. That afternoon we heard the roar of a plane and later on I saw it flying westwards towards Ninghsia. In it was Feng, the so-called Christian general, arch-traitor and plotter, Communist and anything else that he thought would serve his purpose, on his way out of Chinese politics forever. To me it was a momentous occasion, because that night Feng's army vanished into the desert and I could get busy.

We met the camel-owners that same night, and during the following days the camels were collected from the desert and brought in. The Shansi advance came as expected, the day after Feng retreated, with a prodigious artillery fire from the mountains which soon stopped when it was found that the bird had flown. However, it was impossible to get together more than a thousand camels in Paotow, so I had to modify my plans and send off only half the total required from there and the rest from Kweihuacheng.

After the agreements had been entered into with the camel-owners we feasted, and I had a chance to relax, if Chinese feasts can be regarded as relaxation. Here I tasted for the first time that vicious drink Pei garr—a kind of liquid dynamite, far far more potent than any other drink I know. It also gives you a fearful head the day after. I don't know what it is made of, but one of the guests upset a cup of it on the dark, varnished table and a big white circle appeared immediately, the varnish being dissolved down to the wood. I should not think a lot of it would do one's inside much good, but there was no other spirit available for the forfeit games and forfeits as played by the Chinese require quantities of drink.

I also had a chance to look around this unique desert city, for here there was no new city as at Kweihuacheng. Everything was ancient and bore the stamp of the desert and the caravan life, the tempo of the daily life was the same as the slow even tempo of the caravan trail and no innovations were visible. In such a place I should not have been the least surprised to see Marco Polo riding through the main street at the head of his caravan. Nothing seemed to happen inside these ancient walls for years on end except the changing of the garrisons as the war-lords came and went: even the uniforms of the changing guards were the same, only the armbands were different.

Just outside the city walls were the famous springs where Kien Lung, the fighting Emperor, had watered his horses and camels over three hundred years before. The Yellow River lay about five miles to the south and there the bank was covered with mountains of wool from the rafts bringing the Tibetan produce.

And yet something *had* really happened there a few weeks before that had set all tongues wagging in the tea-houses and streets and wherever people forgathered to gossip. It was a strange story of a bandit who had been executed after giving himself up.

My agent was, like most Chinese, a wonderful story-teller and mimic, and he related the story to me one evening when we were alone. I am telling it as near the way it was told me as I can remember.

IX

"A WEEK or so before Feng reached Paotow an old man rode in from the desert. He had one stiff leg from an old wound and walked with difficulty. He was poor, too, and went to one of the cheapest inns. He had just been thrown out of a bandit gang after a big row with the Chief over a job he had bungled because he was not quick enough on his feet. The Chief had abused him in front of the others and had called him a brainless idiot, a turtle's egg, and many other bad things.

"The old bandit's name was Chang and he was both angry and sorry. Angry because he had lost face, and sorry because he was being sent away to starve. He was too old to join another gang and too old to do coolie work. Worst of all, he had gambled away all the money he had saved for his funeral and had only a few dollars left, which, with his horse and saddle, was all he possessed, and from now on he must eat bitterness and starve until he died. Then, worst thought of all, he would have a pauper's coffin and no ghost furniture or ghost money to make him comfortable in the Spirit World.

"You no doubt know the Chinese saying: 'the best thing in life is to be assured of a fine funeral'; and you know that this means not only a good coffin, but plenty of ghost furniture, all those nice things made of paper that you see in the funeral processions—servants, carriages, chests-of-drawers, silver dollars and silver ingots—that we burn at the funerals so that they accompany us into the Spirit World. Those things are not made up there, you see, so we must bring them with us.

"Chang was thinking of all this with bitterness as he rode off alone into the desert, and when he eventually reached Paotow he went to the cheapest inn, where he tied up his horse in the compound and went in to get some food. Some coolies were sitting there, talking very excitedly about the new Bandit Suppression Commissioner appointed by the Military Governor in Kweihuacheng.

"I must explain that the nephew of the Military Governor had been kidnapped by bandits some time ago and they demanded fifteen thousand dollars ransom. The Governor is very mean and sent a message back that he would only pay five thousand. The bandit chief cut one ear off the nephew and sent it to his uncle, who became very cross because the ransom had been raised to twenty thousand. This he paid, but he was so furious that he sent a Magistrate here with some special troops to fight bandits and he had special powers as Bandit Suppression Commissioner.

"He did not have any success at all, as Chinese soldiers are no match for the bandits. Then he thought that if he offered a reward he might have better luck, so he offered a reward of one hundred dollars for each bandit, dead or alive. It was common knowledge that the Military Governor was getting more and more impatient and the Magistrate more and more worried, and this reward was his last hope.

"It was this that the coolies were discussing as Chang sat there tired and bitter, thinking about his own troubles and the Chief's insults, calling him a useless, brainless idiot, when even a dead bandit was worth one hundred dollars.

"One hundred dollars. What would he not do for one hundred dollars? This kept on ringing in his head as he went to bed. He slept badly, for that maddening one hundred dollars kept ringing in his head. Then, suddenly, he had an idea and jumped off the kang with excitement. He thought out a plan, and went back to sleep."

The agent, I have forgotten his name, paused. I had noticed that his eyes had become duller and that the pace of the story had slackened. "Please excuse me," he said, "I must have another smoke."

He lay down on the hard opium couch, dipped the long silver pin into the opium jar to pick up some of the treacly-looking stuff on the point and held it a few moments over the naked flame of the small lamp until the opium bubbled and grew to a big lump which he smoothed expertly with his finger-tip as he twisted the pin. He repeated this a few times until the opium was cooked to his satisfaction. Then he inserted the needle into the hole in the nipple of the onion-shaped bowl, pressed the small lump of opium firmly on to the nipple, and withdrew the pin.

His thin, sallow face caught the faint glow from the lamp as he put his head down on the hard low pillow and moved the pipe over to the naked flame. The pipe gurgled as he smoked it eagerly; five, six long drags, deeply inhaled, and then he lay quiet for a while, savouring the drug.

He smoked another pipe and was a different man when he rejoined me. "Where was I?" he asked, and, when I told him, "Yes, of course, the plan," he said, and continued chuckling:

"Chang was up very early the next morning and went down to the Tah gieh (main street) to look for a coffin shop. We have a very good coffin shop here belonging to a Mr. Liu, a fat, happy man and a great story-teller, who is very popular in the tea-houses on account of his funny stories.

"Chang found Liu's shop and went around pricing the coffins. There was one he liked very much but it cost seventy-five dollars, and he did not know if there would be enough left for ghost furniture. The man in the shop was rather rude, because Chang was so poorly clad. He was just on the point of looking for another shop when Mr. Liu came in from the back, and his broad smiling face and big belly gave Chang confidence. He asked if he could see Liu privately, and the two went into a back room.

"There Chang told Liu about his plan. It was this: if Liu would sell him a coffin and ghost furniture for one hundred dollars, he would take him along to the Magistrate and give himself up on condition that Liu got the reward. Chang was lucky in meeting a man like Liu, for someone else might have raised the alarm and claimed the reward. Not so Liu.

"He slapped his fat legs with joy and laughed so that his big belly shook like a jelly, and the tears rolled down his fat face. This was something after his own heart. What a story for the tea-houses!

"Chang could see nothing funny in it and thought Liu was making fun of his proposal. But Liu soon reassured him and asked him what he wanted. Chang said that first of all he wanted that coffin he had looked at if there would be enough money left for ghost furniture. They made a list. The most important, said Chang, was to get a fine horse and groom, and then he suddenly remembered that he had his own horse and saddle to raise extra money on. Liu bought them for fifty dollars.

"Then Chang said he wanted plenty of silver dollars and silver ingots, a pavilion and a couple of servants. After that there was quite a lot of money to spare and Chang, who had lived most of his life in the saddle, could think of nothing more.

"Liu added a few items and suddenly said: 'Would you like a motor-car, a big red one?'

"Chang had never seen a motor-car, but had heard that they were wonderful things, and so it was agreed that there should be a motor-car to end the list.

"Then they went together to the Magistrate and were admitted at once when they stated that they had come to see him about the reward. The great man was sitting at his desk in the big reception-room in the Yamen. He had two secretaries, and of course a lot of underlings were listening at the half-closed doors.

"Chang went up to the desk and said: 'My unworthy name is Chang and I came to ask about the reward. Is it quite true that one hundred dollars will be paid for a bandit brought in dead or alive?'

"'Yes,' replied the Magistrate.

"'Cash, and at once?' asked Chang.

"'Yes.'

"'I claim the reward,' said Chang, 'but I owe the money to Mr. Liu here and he wants to make sure he gets it so he has come with me. Is it possible to have the reward paid to him?'

"'Yes,' said the Magistrate. 'But where is the bandit?'

"'I am the bandit,' Chang replied, to the Magistrate's surprise and consternation, but he recovered his composure.

"'How do I know that?' he asked, sternly.

"Chang was quite taken aback, but replied, after a short pause: 'I can tell you the names of the people we hold for ransom and I know the date we cut off the ear of the Military Governor's nephew. It was the fifth day of the twelfth moon. It was the left ear. I was there, and saw it.'

"'But why do you give yourself up?' asked the Magistrate. 'You'll be shot.'

"'I know that,' said Chang, 'but I had a quarrel with my Chief and he cast me away. There are many other reasons, but it is a long story and I do not want to waste any more of the Great Man's time. Before I am taken away I would like to see the money paid to Mr. Liu.'

"Soldiers had run in to grab him, but before he was led away the money was paid over to Mr. Liu.

"That evening the story went round the tea-houses like wildfire, and Mr. Liu had a very busy time telling it. Chang became the hero of the whole town, and the next day, when he was paraded round the streets bearing the placard inscribed with the crimes he had committed, the whole town turned out to cheer and admire him. It must have been Chang's happiest day. All his life he had been a poor, hunted nobody and now, suddenly, he was not only famous but was also assured of a splendid funeral. He went along grinning and bowing, and everybody could see that he was very pleased.

"The execution took place the next day. The market-place was so packed with people that the soldiers found it difficult to march him through. Everyone who was important had found good places near the wall where he was going to be shot. Liu had brought the coffin and all the ghost furniture, and Chang was allowed to inspect it and make sure it was all there. He stood for a while and gazed at the red motor-car in wonder. Then he was taken over to the wall and people called out to him to speak.

"It is customary here that people make a speech before they are executed. Chang was quite ready to speak and said:

"'I have only very little to say. My Chief called me a brainless idiot. Now, look at my coffin and the ghost furniture here. Do you think I am brainless?'

"The crowd roared back: 'No!'

"'And do you think my Chief will get a red motor-car when he is buried, like mine over there?'

"'No!' yelled the crowd. Everybody was laughing; Chang too.

"Then he turned to the soldiers and said: 'I have no more to say. You can shoot now.'

"Liu and I looked at him after he fell. He was still smiling at his own joke. He was quite as sure as we were, that the spies of his

Chief would tell him the story and make him very angry, so the old fox got his revenge as well."

The agent chuckled as he went over to the opium couch for a final smoke, leaving me in a brown study. Here was another twist in the maze of the Chinese mind which was new to me: to the Chinese this was a story with a perfect ending.

Chang was satisfied, so was Liu. The Magistrate was overjoyed, and the townspeople were delighted. The only one to lose face was the bandit chief, the villain in the piece, and that is how it ought to be.

But if I know my Chinese, the Magistrate reported to the Military Governor that he had caught and executed the very bandit who had cut off his nephew's ear. If he had not done so, he would have lost a wonderful opportunity of gaining big face.

X

THE Shansi forces had taken over control in Paotow so quietly and with so little fuss that I had hardly been aware of it. Feng's men had just vanished like ghosts into the desert and Shansi soldiers took their place, both at the station and within the walled city. Only the effect of the rail stoppage was being felt and this attained alarming proportions as more and more caravans arrived.

Within the city the warehouses were packed to the roof, and every available open space was piled with bales of wool in mountainous heaps, thirty feet and more high. Down by the banks of the Yellow River the landscape had been completely altered by these hills of wool awaiting transportation. I could do nothing about it and it was high time that I returned to Tientsin and broke the spell of the desert and the western horizon, which kept on calling me whenever I heard the deep booming notes of the camel-bells from the outward-bound caravans. Paotow, to most people on the coast, was the ultimate in remoteness, but whenever I looked westward I realised that I was only on the fringe of that vast hinterland and that a four months' journey still separated me from Central Asia. However, I had work to do in Tientsin, and I needed a bath and some insect powder as the kang was hatching bugs quicker than they could be killed.

I had only to make certain arrangements in Kweihuacheng and Fengchen regarding the two caravans, before setting out for home. I should have loved to have gone with the first caravan, but could not spare the time: besides, I felt that I could trust the agents to look after things effectively. I also felt confident that Dammuran's escort would see the caravans safely through.

There was a final feast to survive at Paotow and another one at Kweihuacheng. On arrival there I found a letter awaiting me from Mr. Bien, who had left without giving his destination. I could understand the letter only in parts and got Mr. Ma to translate it for me. I can remember the main points, and it ran something like this:

"My felicitations on your getting safely through to Paotow and my everlasting gratitude for your service to me and my master. I must apologise for the rudeness of one of our officers in Saratsi: it was reported to Colonel Yuan who had him shot. The only thing I can now do in return for your service is to warn you that this year will be one of great danger to foreigners. Leave the country, if you can, until this trouble is over. It is doubtful that our paths will cross again. Farewell!"

It was a strange letter. The danger, to which he referred, had been apparent ever since Sun Yat Sen had started to stir up the South by his lectures and his book *The Three Principles of the People* (San Min Tso Ih), which was called his political testament. But in the North Chang Tso Lin ruled with an iron hand, and as long as this was the case the danger was still distant. Communists were proscribed wherever he ruled and he, rightly at that time, regarded Sun's creed—*The Three Principles of the People*—as Communism wrapped up in pale-pink paper.

We had so many other problems in the present that future ones were laid aside; so that even as I read Bien's warning I gave it only a passing thought. The news about the shooting of the captain at Saratsi was more interesting: I could have shot him gladly myself at the time and it would have given me a great deal of satisfaction, but, however indifferent to the value of human life I became in China, I always hated executions, whether by sword or bullet.

However, I had little time for reverie or speculations now. There was work to do and when that was done a farewell feast to attend, one that promised to break all existing records. The rest of the camels having been procured, all the camel-dealers were present, together with local merchants and two of Dammuran's officers, whose men feasted in the servants' quarters. Tiger Hsu had also sent a representative to arrange for the escort of the caravans.

We were all there happily playing together the forfeit game

beloved by the Chinese, throwing our hands out and yelling numbers, and draining our cups when we had guessed wrong. There were respectable merchants, bandits and ex-bandits and myself, of pirate stock if I went far enough back. It was refreshing meeting those tough-looking bandits—active, virile, open-air men, so different from the average ease-loving Chinese merchant, to whom any kind of sport or manly activity was anathema. The following day, a more or less sober multitude saw me off when I boarded the military train.

I found another passenger in my compartment, a Belgian priest from a small town in the far West, near Ninghsia. He told me a fascinating story of how the Catholic Mission carried out their work in his district. There were villages and even towns where all the inhabitants were Catholics, which had their own defences and militia and had kept both soldiers and bandits at bay. Intensive cultivation had been introduced by the fathers, grape vines and fruit trees imported and cultivated and irrigation ditches dug, so that they could survive droughts. They were entirely self-supporting and prosperous in a land where they were surrounded by want and poverty, those two hand-maidens of Chinese soldiers and bandits.

He also told me some interesting stories of Feng Yu Hsiang, who, in order to get revenue, had decreed that large tracts of land should be put under poppy cultivation as soon as spring came. Opium-growing was a very lucrative business and the biggest revenue producer. "At the same time he denounced Britain for bringing opium into China," the Reverend Father said, chuckling, "a typical Chinese way of supporting home industries and dealing with competition."

He fascinated me, this powerfully built, bearded man—a strange mixture of the practical man of action, scholar and priest. A man of great courage and inflexible purpose, I felt sure, who had done great things in his lonely outpost without losing the friendly glint in his warm brown eyes or modesty in his manner of telling the story.

From his haversack he produced home-made bread, stale after his long journey but still good, raisins, dried figs, persimmons and a bottle of excellent red wine—all home-produced.

I had only two tins of sardines to add to our joint larder,

apparently the only kind of foreign food available in Kweihua-cheng, but to the Reverend Father the sardines were a great delicacy. Paul Pi had brought mantou, the native unleavened bread. He was becoming more and more cheerful as the prospect of getting home with his ears and finger-joints intact became brighter. He had worked very hard and had been invaluable to me by doing all the detailed work.

At Fengchen I said good-bye to the priest and we stayed there only one day to complete the convoy arrangements and then went on to Kalgan. I was getting more and more impatient to be back in Tientsin, now that the main job was done.

In Kalgan I called on Rustad and Mamen and received disturbing news of the state of things in Outer Mongolia. Russian Communists were clearly in complete control at Ulan Bator Khoto, which had become a great military centre; an important airport had been constructed there, and no one could enter Outer Mongolia without a pass from Moscow.

Japan had taken counter-measures in Manchuria and had applied to the Chinese government for airport facilities in Inner Mongolia. Several Japanese intelligence officers were now established in Kalgan, and it was clear that the latent tension between the two giants, Russia and Japan, was rapidly coming to a head. This would, of course, make the position more and more precarious in North China where previously it had been only threatening and uncertain. Now we were faced with fateful facts, for China had apparently surrendered Outer Mongolia to Russia, and reports from Sinkiang province (Chinese Turkestan) indicated that this important slice of China was rapidly coming under Soviet control.

This was not pleasant news to ponder over on the last lap of my journey, but I soon chased all the worrying thoughts away as I revelled in a hot bath in the B.A.T. Mess and sat down to a delicious dinner afterwards. The chief dish was my favourite beefsteak-and-kidney pudding, a perfect meal to chase away the persistent taste of stewed shark-fins and ancient eggs.

I arrived in Peking too late for the night train to Tientsin, and was just making up my mind, not very gracefully, to spend the night at the Wagon Lits, when the stationmaster told me that there was a military train going later in the evening. This brought me to Tientsin at two in the morning, when I startled my family by appearing with a beard and looking like a ruffian in my dirty sheepskin coat. The fact that I had sprinkled my hair and beard liberally with insect powder made recognition difficult, but Elizabeth piped up at once: "It's Daddy's voice, anyway!" It was the only part of me she recognised. But Jock had known me as soon as I opened the garden gate. He came bounding out from the front veranda with a joyous yelp, jumped right into my arms and slobbered all over me.

A couple of months passed, after my return, and still no news of the caravans. I was really getting worried and was preparing to go up-country again when a telegram arrived from Kalgan:

> CARAVAN ARRIVED BUT TWO CAMELS AND FOUR BALES MISSING STOP CARGO EXPECTED TO ARRIVE TIENTSIN WITHIN ONE WEEK STOP CHARGING FOUR BALES TO DAMMURANS ACCOUNT STOP LI

I took the telegram in to the Chief Manager and put it on his desk. He had been very sceptical about the caravan from the beginning and was often sarcastic during the long wait for news.

Now he jumped up from his desk, flushed with excitement. "Splendid—wonderful news! Let's celebrate!"

We did. We shut down our desks with a bang and drove to the Country Club. I am afraid the Chief got a bit tipsy as the long celebration progressed. As for me, I was too case-hardened on Mongolian raw spirits to let a few bottles of champagne make me fuddled, even though they were magnums. We drank many toasts after dinner: To the first thousand camels and the last thousand. To that jolly old bandit Tiger Hsu, to Dammuran Serang, to Li, and to the two lost camels—poor devils, meandering around in the wilds of Mongolia, with fourteen days' interval between drinks.

The Chief sent frequent requests to the Philippino band to play "The Campbells are coming," which led to worrrds with a Campbell who objected to our singing "The Camels are coming," until he was initiated into the secret. He then joined our party because he was so impressed with our toast: "They say that a camel can go fourteen days without a drink, but who the hell wants to be a camel!"

He was a good honest soul with a good honest thirst. He drank only whusky, neat—lots of it, because he was so sair worrit aboot the puir beasties who went fourrteen days withoot a drink. When the party broke up he was nearly in tears, trying to figure out a problem that had worried him: if one camel can go fourteen days without a drink, how many drinks have 1,998 camels to go without? He gave it up with a dismal sigh and shook his head: "Thank God I am a Campbell and no Camel!" With this observation he walked out with the elaborate care and dignity of the inebriate.

During the drive home the Chief waxed more and more generous. "What about a trip to New York and London, Ras? You deserve it. Nice change for you after Mongolia! Japan, with a week or so at Hakone—'Empress of Canada' to Honolulu, dinner at the Royal Hawaiian Hotel and the Hula dance on Waikiki Beach. Then C.P.R. across Canada, on to New York and London, and a nice leisurely return via Suez. Take the family along and enjoy yourself. The firm pays, of course!"

As far as I can remember it was Pieper Heidsieck he had been drinking with such wonderful results. What was even more remarkable, he remembered it all the next morning.

It was a wonderful world tour and it cost a wonderful lot of money, but that caravan had yielded record profits of about a quarter million dollars, for camels' wool had soared, and the camels did two trips that winter. No other cargo came through.

I knew, however, when I left, that the situation in China was rapidly reaching a climax. Japan had nearly a million men under arms in Manchuria, Soviet Russia was building up a considerable air force in Outer Mongolia and China's millions were being whipped into a frenzy of anti-Japanese and anti-foreign hate.

The country was riddled with Communist propaganda from Canton, where Borodin had been very much *persona grata* with the Kuomintang, the coming political party.

However, we had been living under tension and in the shadow of civil wars so long that my senses had got blunted and I gave little thought to the conditions I would meet on my return.

THE END